African Political and Economic Philosophy with Africapitalism

African Philosophy: *Critical Perspectives and Global Dialogue*

Series Editors: Uchenna B. Okeja, Nelson Mandela University; and Bruce B. Janz, University of Central Florida

The *African Philosophy: Critical Perspectives and Global Dialogue* book series aims to promote emerging critical perspectives in different branches of African philosophy. It serves as an avenue for philosophers within and between many African cultures to present new arguments, ask new questions, and begin new dialogues within both specialized communities and with the general public. By merging the critical and global dimensions of thoughts pertaining to important topics in African philosophy, this series beams the lights and rigour of philosophical analysis on topical as well as classical questions reflective of the African and African diaspora search for meaning in existence. Focused on the best of African philosophy, the series will introduce new concepts and new approaches in philosophy both to intellectual communities across Africa, as well as the rest of the world.

Recent titles in the series:

African Political and Economic Philosophy with Africapitalism: Concepts for African Leadership, edited by Ephraim-Stephen Essien and Frank Aragbonfoh Abumere

A Post-Colonial Reconstruction of Africa, by Pieter H. Coetzee

Well-Being in African Philosophy: Insights for a Global Ethics of Development, edited by Bolaji Bateye, Mahmoud Masaeli, Louise Müller, and Angela Roothaan

African Philosophical Adventures, by John Murungi

Beauty in African Thought: Critical Perspectives on the Western Idea of Development, edited by Bolaji Bateye, Mahmoud Masaeli, Louise Müller, and Angela Roothaan

Rethinking Sage Philosophy: Interdisciplinary Perspectives on and beyond H. Odera Oruka, edited by Kai Kresse and Oriare Nyarwath

Odera Oruka and the Human Minimum: An African Philosopher's Defense of Human Dignity and Environment, by Michael Kamau Mburu

Africa beyond Liberal Democracy: In Search of Context-Relevant Models of Democracy for the Twenty-First Century, edited by Reginald M.J. Oduor

Menkiti's Moral Man, by Oritsegbubemi Anthony Oyowe

Partiality and Impartiality in African Philosophy, by M. Molefe

Menkiti on Community and Becoming a Person, edited by Edwin Etieyibo and Polycarp Ikuenobe

African Philosophical and Literary Possibilities: Re-reading the Canon, edited by Aretha Phiri

African Political and Economic Philosophy with Africapitalism

Concepts for African Leadership

Edited by
Ephraim-Stephen Essien and
Frank Aragbonfoh Abumere

LEXINGTON BOOKS
Lanham • Boulder • New York • London

Published by Lexington Books
An imprint of The Rowman & Littlefield Publishing Group, Inc.
4501 Forbes Boulevard, Suite 200, Lanham, Maryland 20706
www.rowman.com

86-90 Paul Street, London EC2A 4NE

British Library Cataloguing in Publication Information Available

Library of Congress Cataloging-in-Publication Data

Names: Essien, Ephraim-Stephen, editor, author. | Abumere, Frank Aragbonfoh, editor, author.
Title: African political and economic philosophy with Africapitalism : concepts for African leadership / edited by Ephraim-Stephen Essien and Frank Aragbonfoh Abumere.
Other titles: African philosophy (Lanham, Md.)
Description: Lanham : Lexington Books, [2024] | Series: African philosophy: critical perspectives and global dialogue | Includes bibliographical references and index.
Identifiers: LCCN 2023054772 (print) | LCCN 2023054773 (ebook) | ISBN 9781666931105 (cloth) | ISBN 9781666931112 (ebook)
Subjects: LCSH: Capitalism—Africa, Sub-Saharan. | Economic development—Africa, Sub-Saharan. | Africa, Sub-Saharan—Economic conditions—21st century. | Africa, Sub-Saharan—Economic policy. | Africa, Sub-Saharan—Politics and government—21st century.
Classification: LCC HC800 .A56852 2024 (print) | LCC HC800 (ebook) | DDC 338.967—dc23/eng/20231129
LC record available at https://lccn.loc.gov/2023054772
LC ebook record available at https://lccn.loc.gov/2023054773

Contents

Introduction

Ephraim-Stephen Essien and
Frank Aragbonfoh Abumere

This book aims to create (on the one hand) and explore (on the other hand) African development philosophies suitable for black sub-Saharan African countries. As a relatively new academic discipline focused on thought informed by indigenous moral values among black peoples in the sub-Saharan region, African political philosophy involves philosophizing normatively about government by traditional black African people with a view to advancing a better African society. African political philosophy does not mean that its themes, views, concepts, and approaches are exclusively African. It does not also mean that only thinkers in Africa could hold these concepts. It does not also mean that all African thinkers hold the same views. "African" is used in African political philosophy geographically to demarcate certain perspectives that are unique and peculiar in sub-Saharan African thought and practice that tend not to be the case elsewhere. An African political and economic philosophy should address the origin and method of political power, the guarantee of human and civil liberties, and how economic goods are generated and distributed in African societies. African socialism by Nkrumah, Senghor, and Nyerere tried to do this but failed both politically and economically. Africapitalism as a new economic philosophy seems to obviate the inadequacies in Afrisocialism and offers an option for an African economic philosophy. But can a neo-Afrisocialism offer anything good for the African economy? And what political styles or models could you recommend or create for governing African countries?

The year 2020 marks 135 years since Africa became a made-in-Germany product. This political business and manufacture took place in Berlin with Otto von Bismarck as the CEO of the lucrative venture. It took Bismarck just a pencil and a piece of white paper to draw boundaries of Africa and share the portions to the powers of Europe for their economic consumption.

The orderly sharing formula initiated by Bismarck could not be obtained in Southern Africa. In Southern Africa, it was a survival of the fittest for the Euro-American powers. The white imperialists fought and killed each other, for example, in the Anglo-Boer Wars. The survivors could not take it lying low with the black population thereafter. The British had the Cape Colony; the Dutch, the Transvaal and the Orange Free States. No black could go to school nor walk near a white-skinned demigod. The consequence was always undesirable. The white knees were on the black necks.

But the white knees had been stuck on the black necks since four hundred years ago, before Bismarck's business summits in Berlin (1884–1885). Same European powers had, hitherto, committed crimes against humanity in human trafficking, buying Africans from their fellow Africans in exchange for alcohol and glittering mirrors for their African dealers to look at their faces and smile after consuming the gin to stupor. One of the results of that first business had been the making of America through Spain and Portugal. Another was the making of the capitals of Europe and their cathedrals through the sweats of African slaves in European factories. Encouraged by the gains in their first business venture during their trade in purchase of African persons, though, discouraged by the cunning abolition of slave trade by some of their paid folks, the powers of Europe devised another business strategy to enjoy Africa through colonization by dismembering, severing, and splitting African ethno-cultural ties in the partition of Africa. They, however, came with the Bible from their cathedrals, to tell Africans to forgo their gods and culture and replace them with God. During the process of evangelization, European education was introduced to Africa. At least, this would help them to learn the Bible and propagate the message, still for the white man's conquest of his culture over the blacks.

From learning Catholic catechisms in their African homeland, Nnamdi Azikiwe, Kwame Nkrumah, Leopold Senghor, and Julius Nyerere later had the luck of receiving Western training in Europe and America. There, they experienced first-class racism and racialism just like what happened to George Floyd in Minneapolis on May 25, 2020—only a few days ago. But they were more troubled by the need for African identity, which had been either lost or diminished through slavery, colonialism, and racism.

Having been schooled in European and American education, and having been influenced by Pan-African movements by Marcus Garvey and W. E. B. Du Bois, these African princes deployed their training to their indigenous cultural values to see how that might serve as the social foundation of their societies, different from Europe and America. So, the pioneer African philosophers were sociopolitical and economic philosophers. This made the documented version of African philosophy to begin with sociopolitical philosophy. The first African philosophers were motivated by a strong sense of nationalism, a search for identity, a search for freedom, a search for emancipation from servitude, and a search for cultural rebirth. These pioneer African philosophers were nationalists who fought for African freedom against colonialism, and some of them later became "philosopher-kings" in their countries. Azikiwe (1931, 1937, 1961, 1978, 1980), Nkrumah (1945, 1954, 1962, 1965, 1970), Senghor (1964, 1967), and Nyerere (1964, 1967) wrought political independence for Africa through their socioeconomic and political philosophies and political activism. All of these figures shared something in common: they modified socialism and planted it on African soil. Unfortunately, their African socialism failed economically. Politically, their regimes turned out to be repressive, such that some of them had to be ousted from power. They had no tolerance for civil liberties. All of this means that their theories failed politically and economically. Even so, they succeeded in establishing political theorizing on sub-Saharan Africa, and, by this fact, also succeeded in establishing our documented version of African philosophy on African traditional communitarian values.

African political philosophers of the second generation were not politicians like the first-generation African political philosophers. Rather, they were mostly university lecturers whose major works appeared mainly in the 1980s and 1990s. Ezekiel Ogundowole (1982), Claude Ake (1987, 1996) and Segun Gbadegesin (1991) from Nigeria; Kwasi Wiredu (1996) and Kwame Gyekye (1997) from Ghana; Ernest Wamba-dia-Wamba (1992) and Bénézet Bujo from the Congo (1997); Henry Odera Oruka from Kenya; and Mogobe Ramose (1999) from South Africa all fall into this category. Political power, civil liberties, and economic goods based on African communitarian ideals were the focus of the majority of this batch of African political philosophers. However, they romanticized too much on political ideologies and idealistic "isms," without emphasizing economic power as the substratum for any political power.

Behold! A contemporary generation of African political philosophers, Batch C, is emerging in the academy and the industrial sector, setting a slight difference in novelty from the second batch of African political philosophers who were mainly academics. Contemporary African political philosophers and political economists have expanded the field of African political philosophy, addressing a wide array of fresh issues, such as how to: conceive of the nature of freedom, distribute resources in light of familial or ethnic ties, ground non-Western models of socioeconomic development, characterize the proper role of civil society, view the proper aim of public universities, think about compensatory and transitional justice, consider the nature and proper function of law, develop an autochthonous African capitalism based on African realities (Amaeshi, Elumelu, Agbakoba) or simply Africapitalism (Amaeshi, Elumelu), emphasize productive justice as a motivation toward economic development, a concept advocated in a philosophy of African development (Agbakoba). In all these, three issues stand out for determining an African political philosophy, namely, political power, civil liberties, and economic goods. What is the best-suited model for attaining political power in Africa? What political model will guarantee civil liberties in our African societies? What model should guide generation and distribution of economic goods given our African societal peculiarities?

Our African experience, then and now, has been a repudiation of anything black or African in the eyes of Europe, America, and currently China. Trade in human persons has resurfaced. The struggle and partition of Africa by European powers in the nineteenth century has reemerged, but this time, by China and America and the dominant European nation over Africa, France. There is an ongoing struggle and partition of Africa by Sino-American powers. On June 1, President Paul Kagame had to expel 18 Chinese from Rwanda and sent them back to China for mistreating Rwandan workers and grabbing lands for farming from them, warning that Africans do not want to be slaves again (www.thevoicenews.net). While China is busy trying to occupy all of black Africa and pretending generosity in giving gargantuan loans, America is stationing military bases all over Africa and acting the big brother in defending Christians in Nigeria against fundamentalist attacks. With the emergence of the Covid-19 pandemic and its apocalypse of the emptiness of nations and peoples, Africa must rise to prove herself a strong force to reckon with. This can begin from our mental theorizing on how best we can have a legally organized public life through government. This, then, becomes the role of African political and economic philosophy. Poverty, diseases, illiteracy, and insecurity must be adequately addressed in any philosophy that must guarantee us the Africa We Want.

To address the above questions, the book is divided into 3 parts and thirteen chapters. Essien's chapter 1 recognizes the emergent Africapitalism as an indigenous economic theory within African sociopolitical philosophy. The chapter answers the following questions: What is African sociopolitical philosophy? What is Africapitalism? Is Africapitalism practicable? Is there any existing business practice in Africa to prove the applicability, relevance, and workability of Africapitalism? Yes! The Igbo apprenticeship system! Is the Igbo business apprenticeship and start-up funding a middle ground between business and philanthropy, so as to qualify for the requirements of Africapitalism? If it is, we would be able to conclude that the practice is an application of Africapitalism as an African business philosophy. We shall, therefore, put up the following logical hypothesis: if the Igbo business apprenticeship and start-up funding system in Nigeria is a middle ground between business and philanthropy, then the Igbo business apprenticeship and start-up funding is a practice of Africapitalism. As a case study, we adopt business apprenticeship and start-up funding system among Igbo people of Southern Nigeria, where apprentices get settled or established by the master or mistress after some years of training and service. The master or mistress, often referred to as "Oga," ensures that the mentee gets his or her own business firm after a prescribed period of business training. In the end, there is economic growth and social development. Africapitalism comes into this study as the latest philosophy in the history of African sociopolitical and economic philosophy.

In chapter 2, in the words of Sharomi, Africapitalism seemingly exudes a contemporary hope in the abyss of want bedeviling Africa. It seeks sustenance beyond the purview of the state and its many relations. In this chapter, I attempt a moralist interrogation of the philosophy of Africapitalism. Therein, I take the doctrine of moralism (as a sage), as espoused by C. S. Momoh, to advance the principles and method of Africapitalism. Momoh's moralism is a doctrine that puts the other before or alongside the self. It holds that honesty, service, and concern for the interest of the other ought to be the basis and the measure of all actions and policies. He anchors it on five principles. In critiquing Africapitalism, I underscore the need to ground it on footings able to withstand the myriad of challenges faced by theories or ideas (new or that have succeeded elsewhere) when introduced into the African milieu. My interrogation will equally attempt to bathe it from the murky waters of capitalism, African socialism, egoism in political authorities, potential indiscipline of individuals (specifically the entrepreneurs), and criticism of intellectuals. I will further emphasize the need for the inclusion of entrepreneurial moralism in its principles, hoping to make it sustainable. I believe that probity is always as essential as any philosophy evolved for human development. I employ the dialogic method to explore the potentialities of Africapitalism.

In chapter 3, Arodovwe avers that Africa contrasts sharply with other developed continents in terms of economic progress, technological and scientific advancement, and sociopolitical stability. Yet, 40% of the world's natural resources are domiciled in the continent. Regrettably, development programs for the continent have largely originated from the West rather than from Africa and have emphasized aid rather than trade. The Structural Adjustment Program and New Partnership for Africa Development are two ready cases in point. Are there, therefore, some hidden conspiracies, as Rodney would have us believe, to keep the continent perpetually underdeveloped? Ogundowole and Elumelu use their theories of self-reliancism and Africapitalism, respectively, to interrogate the situation. For Ogundowole, sustainable development is realizable only when a people depend largely on themselves for their needs through maximum utilization of their human and natural resource endowments, and through creative, purposive management of their environmental assets. Self-reliancism, he says, is the natural consequence of the dialectical clash of capitalism and socialism; it is a product of the synthesis of the beneficial aspects of capitalism and socialism. For Elumelu, capitalism must be adapted in such a way that it factors in the common good, social well-being, and development of the communities of the areas implicated in its operation. This would effectively rebrand the ideology as practiced in the West into a new form he refers to as Africapitalism. I consider Ogundowole and Elumelu's arguments as complementary and convincing, with the potential of filling the ideological vacuum for an African economic philosophy. I argue that the ideology of self-reliancism and Africapitalism can be amalgamated into an adequate development ideology for Africa in the twenty-first century.

While Amoateng's chapter 4 discusses how different forms of power relations and layers of interests, rules, norms, laws, organizations, and habits of states, world markets, international organizations, multinational corporations, and local firms have shaped the international political economy of Africapitalism. Specifically, the chapter analyzes the idea of Africapitalism from ancient to modern Africa. The principal arguments are as follows: first, the idea of Africapitalism originates in the ancient African chiefless states; second, political institutions and public decision-making largely account for poverty and underdevelopment in modern African states; and finally, the concept of Afrocapitalism provides a better avenue for global Africa—Africans both at home and abroad—to craft productive institutions capable of enhancing human and economic development. The analysis is in sharp contrast to the prevalent economic-based views such as the resource curse, resource scarcity, and foreign aid and loans that have frequently been discussed as major drivers of poverty and underdevelopment in modern African states. The policy implications are that African states must focus on tackling political determinants of poverty far more than other socioeconomic impediments of development, and the private sector is best placed to achieve social wealth in modern African societies.

Then in chapter 5, Abumere thinks Africapitalism (as seen in its principles) is simultaneously predicated on the fact that there is a failure of governments to perform their moral responsibility for economic development and a reflection of what it means to rectify the consequences of such abnegation of responsibility. Therefore, in this chapter, he does not rehash the debate on what it means to have an original or authentic African social, economic, and political philosophy or whether Africapitalism is an authentic African economic philosophy (after all, the most important and relevant aspects of such debate have been dealt with by some of the previous chapters). Rather, he shows how the failure of governments to perform their moral responsibility for economic development leads to a morally, socially, economically, and politically undesirable condition in Africa and what moral implications this has for the private sector in view of the tenets of Africapitalism. As he already alluded to, it is such failure of government Africapitalism seeks to rectify and it is such morally, socially, economically, and politically undesirable condition that Africapitalism seeks to ameliorate through its principles. To contextualize this discussion, he focuses on Nigeria and its infamous resource curse.

Chapters 1–5 constitute "On Africapitalism," which is the first part of the book. "On Development" (chapters 6–9) and "On Leadership" (chapters 10–13) are the second and third parts of the book, respectively. While the first part is a special focus on Africapitalism, the second and third parts deal with various topics and issues in development and leadership, respectively. The chapters on Africapitalism include Ephraim-Stephen Essien's African Political and Economic Philosophy with Africapitalism (chapter 1); Abayomi Sharomi's A Moralist Interrogation of Africapitalism as an African Economic Philosophy (chapter 2); Emmanuel Ogheneochuko Arodovwe's E. K. Ogundowole's Self-reliancism and Tony Elumelu's Africapitalism: Complementary Economic Ideologies for Sustainable Development in Africa (chapter 3); Nana Kwasi Amoateng's International Political Economy of Africapitalism (chapter 4); and Frank Aragbonfoh Abumere's Africapitalism and the Moral Implications of African Governments' Abnegation of Responsibilities. The chapters on development include Emerson Abraham Jackson's Import Substitution Industrialization (ISI) as an Economic Philosophy Model for Africa (chapter 6); Anthony Raphael Etuk's Constitutionalism and the Crisis of Development in Africa (chapter 7); Thaddeus Metz's Replacing Development: An Afro-communal Approach to Distributive Justice (chapter 8); and Philip Osarobu Isanbor and George Uzoma Ukagba's Black Consciousness Philosophy as Politics of Responsibility for Sustainable African Development (chapter 9). The chapters on leadership include Alex J. Wilson's Akan Sociopolitical and Economic Thoughts as a Leadership Model for Ghana and Africa (chapter 10); Godwin Michael Adahada's Ubuntu as a Social Leadership Model in Africa: Focus on Nigeria (chapter 11); Frank Aragbonfoh Abumere's Managing Diversity and Protecting Racial and Ethnic Minorities in Africa: The Limitations of the Quota System (chapter 12); and Frank Aragbonfoh Abumere's Power in African Politics: What It Is and How It Ought to Be Used (chapter 13).

Part I

ON AFRICAPITALISM

Chapter 1

African Political and Economic Philosophy with Africapitalism

Ephraim-Stephen Essien

INTRODUCTION

In this chapter, we shall observe that Africapitalism is an emergent indigenous economic theory within African sociopolitical philosophy. We shall answer the following questions: What is African sociopolitical philosophy? What is Africapitalism? Is Africapitalism practicable? Is there any existing business practice in Africa to prove the applicability, relevance, and workability of Africapitalism? Yes! The Igbo apprenticeship system! Is the Igbo business apprenticeship and start-up funding a middle ground between business and philanthropy, so to qualify for the requirements of Africapitalism? If it is,we would be able to conclude that the practice is an application of Africapitalism as an African business philosophy. We shall, therefore, put up the following logical hypothesis: if the Igbo business apprenticeship and start-up funding system in Nigeria is a middle ground between business and philanthropy, then the Igbo business apprenticeship and start-up funding is a practice of Africapitalism. As a case study, we adopt business apprenticeship and start-up funding system among Igbo people of Southern Nigeria where apprentices get settled or established by the master or mistress after some years of training and service. The master or mistress, often referred to as "Oga," ensures that the mentee get his or her own business firm after a prescribed period of business training. This will lead to economic growth and social development. Africapitalism finds place in this study as the latest development in the history of African sociopolitical and economic philosophy.

WHAT IS AFRICAPITALISM?

Africapitalism is a new economic model within modern African sociopolitical philosophy which upholds the thesis that the African private sector has the power to transform the continent through long-term investments, creating both economic prosperity and social wealth. It involves the developmental impact of the entrepreneur on his immediate society. Africapitalism is the middle ground between business and philanthropy (Elumelu 2014). It is an economic philosophy that embodies the private sector's commitment to the economic transformation of Africa through investments that generate both economic prosperity and social wealth (Amaeshi and Idemudia 2015). The basic features of Africapitalism include:

- Transforming private investment into social wealth (Elumelu 2014)
- Promoting entrepreneurship
- Inducting elements of social enterprise
- Emphasizing local value creation—this involves an explicit effort on the part of businesses and African policymakers to facilitate more value addition within African economies to ensure more of the benefits of the continent's natural resources remain in Africa.

BACKGROUND

African political philosophy concerns African leadership models for determining political power, civil liberties, and economic goods in African states. It aims to develop sociopolitical leadership models suitable for and peculiar to governing black sub-Saharan African countries. As a relatively new academic discipline focused on thought informed by indigenous values among black peoples in the sub-Saharan region, African sociopolitical philosophy involves philosophizing normatively about government and leadership by traditional black African people with a view to advancing a better African society (Metz 2015). African sociopolitical philosophy does not mean that the themes, views, concepts, and approaches are exclusively African. It does not also mean that only thinkers in Africa could hold these concepts. It does not also mean that all African thinkers hold the same views. "African" is used in African sociopolitical philosophy geographically to demarcate certain perspectives that are unique and peculiar in sub-Saharan African thought and practice that tend not to be the case elsewhere. African sociopolitical philosophy addresses the origin and method of political power, the guarantee of human and civil liberties, and how economic goods are generated and distributed in African societies. How economic goods are generated or distributed is a concern of Africapitalism as an economic model.

HISTORY OF AFRICAN POLITICAL PHILOSOPHY

Any documented version of African philosophy begins with sociopolitical philosophy. Nnamdi Azikiwe, Kwame Nkrumah, Leopold Senghor, and Julius Nyerere had the luck of receiving Western training in Europe and America. There, they experienced first-class racism and racialism, just like what happened to George Floyd in Minneapolis on May 25, 2020. But they were more troubled by the need for African identity, which had been either lost or diminished through slavery, colonialism, and racism. Having received training in Europe and America, and having been positively influenced by Pan-African movements by Marcus Garvey and W. E. B. Du Bois, these African princes deployed their training to their indigenous cultural values to see how that could serve as the social foundation of their societies, as different from Europe and America.

The first African philosophers were motivated by a strong sense of nationalism, a search for identity, a search for freedom, a search for emancipation from servitude, a search for decolonization, a search for cultural rebirth. These pioneer African philosophers were nationalists who fought for African freedom against colonialism, and some of them later became "philosopher-kings" in their countries. Azikiwe (1931, 1937, 1961, 1968, 1978, 1980), Nkrumah (1945, 1954, 1962, 1965, 1970), Senghor (1964, 1967), and Nyerere (1964, 1967) wrought political independence for Africa through their socioeconomic and political philosophies and political activism. All of these figures shared something in common: they modified socialism and planted it on African soil. Unfortunately, their African socialism failed economically. Politically, their regimes turned out to be repressive, such that some of them had to be ousted from power. This means that their theories failed politically and economically. Even so, they succeeded in establishing political theorizing on sub-Saharan Africa, and, by this fact, also succeeded in establishing our documented version of African philosophy based on African traditional communitarian values.

The second generation of African sociopolitical philosophers were not politicians like the first-generation African sociopolitical philosophers (Metz 2015). Rather, they were mostly university lecturers whose major works appeared mainly in the 1980s and 1990s. Some of them include Ezekiel Ogundowole (1982), Claude Ake (1987, 1996) and Segun Gbadegesin (1991) from Nigeria; Kwasi Wiredu (1996) and Kwame Gyekye (1997) from Ghana; Ernest Wamba-dia-Wamba (1992) and Bénézet Bujo from the Congo (1997); Henry Odera Oruka from Kenya (1997); and Mogobe Ramose from South Africa (1999). Political power, civil liberties, and economic goods based on African communitarian ideals were the focus of the majority of this batch of African sociopolitical philosophers.

A contemporary generation of African sociopolitical philosophers has emerged in the academy and the industrial sector, setting a slight difference in novelty from the second batch of African sociopolitical philosophers who were mainly academics. Contemporary African sociopolitical philosophers and political economists have expanded the field of African sociopolitical philosophy, addressing a wide array of fresh issues, such as how to conceive of the nature of freedom, distribute resources in light of familial or ethnic ties, ground non-Western models of socioeconomic development, characterize the proper role of civil society, view the proper aim of public universities, think about compensatory and transitional justice, consider the nature and proper function of law (Metz 2015), ground Western capitalism on African realities (Amaeshi, Elumelu, Agbakoba) or simply Africapitalism (Amaeshi, Elumelu), emphasize productive justice as a motivation toward economic development, a concept advocated in a philosophy of African development by Agbakoba. Ezekiel Ogundowole (2011), Thaddeus Metz (2012, 2015, 2021), Tony Elimelu (2014), Bernard Matolino (2012), Kenneth Amaeshi and Uwafiokun Idemudia (2015, 2019), and Joseph C. A. Agbakoba (2019) all fall within the present generation of African political and economic philosophers. The present volume, *African Political and Economic Philosophy with Africapitalism: Concepts for African Leadership*, and our forthcoming *History of African Political Philosophy* are expected to add to the literature in African political thought, and, specifically, to its historical evolution.

In all these, three issues stand out for determining an African sociopolitical philosophy: political power, civil liberties, and economic goods.

Tony Elumelu's Africapitalism focuses on economic goods. It is primarily an economic philosophy. It nonetheless requires some political push in the form of governmental policies and legislations to make it a state economy. Tony Elumelu, the originator of Africapitalism, upholds that Africapitalism is the middle ground between business and philanthropy (Elumelu 2014).

IGBO BUSINESS PHILOSOPHY

Typically, the Igbo business philosophy, that is, the apprenticeship and start-up funding system, involves a specified period of training, learning, teaching, and mentorship of a youth under the tutelage of a master or mistress, requiring diligence, loyalty, prudence, and honesty from the apprentice, wherein the mentor sets up a new enterprise for the apprentice with start-up funding upon successful completion of the training. Among the Igbo people of Southeastern Nigeria, apprentices get settled or established by their masters or mistresses after some years of training and service. The master or mistress, often referred to as "Oga" or "Boss," ensures that the mentee get his or her own business firm after a prescribed period of business training. Igbo business philosophy is the Igbo apprenticeship system, which involves business tutelage, service, training, and "settlement." In the end, human capital development is involved for job and wealth creation, leading to economic growth and social development in the community.

Tony Elumelu and Obinna Iyiegbu (Obi Cubana) practice business with philanthropy as their special type of Igbo business philosophy. They practice what is called philanthropreneurship, which is contained in Africapitalism insofar as the latter involves charity in business. This is the middle ground between business and philanthropy. So, we conclude that the practice of Igbo business apprenticeship system is an application of Africapitalism as an African business philosophy. Africapitalism is, therefore, a practicable and realizable economic philosophy.

REFERENCES

Agbakoba, Joseph. (2019). *Development and Modernity in Africa*. Cologne: Rudiger Koppe Verlag.

Ake, Claude. (1987). "The African Context of Human Rights," *Africa Today*, vol. 34, pp. 5–12.

Ake, Claude. (1996). *Development and Democracy in Africa*. Washington, DC: The Brookings Institution.

Amaeshi, Kenneth. (October 2, 2013). "Africapitalism: Unleashing the Power of Emotions for Africa's Development?" *African Arguments*. www.africanarguments.org. Accessed 7 October, 2021.

Amaeshi, Kenneth, and Uwafiokun Idemudia. (2015). "Africapitalism: A Management Idea for Business in Africa?" *Africa Journal of Management*, vol. 1, no. 2, pp. 210–223. https://doi.org/10.1080/23322373.2015.1026229.

Amaeshi, Kenneth, and Uwafiokun Idemudia, eds. (2019). *Africapitalism: Sustainable Business and Development in Africa*. London: Routledge.

Anna Leach. (December 16, 2014) "14 Ways African Governments Can Extract More from Their Natural Riches | Global Development Professionals Network," *The Guardian*. amp.theguardian.com. Accessed 7 October, 2021.

Azikiwe, Nnamdi. (1968). *Renascent Africa*. London: Routledge.

Bujo, Bénézet. (1997). *The Ethical Dimension of Community: The African Model and the Dialogue Between North and South*, trans. C. N. Nganda. Nairobi: Paulines Publications Africa.

Court, Alex. (December 5, 2014). "Nigerian Billionaire Pledges $100 Million to Help Grow 10,000 African Startups," *CNN*.

Doane, Deborah. (February 25, 2014). "Social Enterprise: Can It Succeed Where Traditional Development Has Failed?" *The Guardian*.

Edwards, Ruby. (July 12, 2013). "Can Africapitalism Save the Continent?" *The Guardian*.

Elumelu, Tony O. (May 9, 2012). "Entrepreneurs Should Be Watching Africa," *Financial Times*.

Elumelu, Tony O. (April 22, 2013). "The 3 Ingredients for Sustaining Africa's Growth," *Financial Times*.

Elumelu, Tony O. (November 20, 2014). "The Rise of Africapitalism," *The Economist*.

Gbadegesin, Segun. (1991). *African Philosophy: Traditional Yoruba Philosophy and Contemporary African Realities*. New York: Peter Lang.

Gyekye, Kwame. (1997). *Tradition and Modernity: Philosophical Reflections on the African Experience*. New York: Oxford University Press.

Hart, Stuart, and C. K. Prahalad. (January 10, 2002). "The Fortune at the Bottom of the Pyramid," *Strategy+Business*.

Jacks, Mzwandile. (July 8, 2013). "Obama the Africapitalist: Creating a Private Sector Development," *Ventures-Africa.com*.

Masolo, D. A. (2004). "Western and African Communitarianism," in Kwasi Wiredu (ed.), *A Companion to African Philosophy*. Oxford: Blackwell, pp. 483–498.

Matolino, Bernard. (2012). "Democracy, Consensus, and Africa," *Philosophia Africana*, vol. 14, pp. 105–124.

Metz, Thaddeus. (2012). "Developing African Political Philosophy: Moral-Theoretic Strategies," *Philosophia Africana*, vol. 14, pp. 61–83.

Metz, Thaddeus. (2015). "African Political Philosophy," in *International Encyclopedia of Ethics*. Edited by Hugh LaFollette. Wiley, pp. 1–9.

Nkrumah, Kwame. (1970). *Consciencism: Philosophy and Ideology for De-Colonization*, rev. ed. New York: Monthly Review.

Nurse, Earl, and Jill Dougherty. (November 12, 2013). "Tony Elumelu: The 'Africapitalist' Who Wants to Power Africa," *CNN*.

Nyerere, Julius. (1968). *Ujamaa: Essays on Socialism*. New York: Oxford University Press.

Ogundowole, E. K. (2011). *Self-Reliancism: Philosophy of a New World Oder*. Lagos: Correct Counsels Ltd.

Oruka, Henry Odera. (1997). *Practical Philosophy*. Nairobi: East African Educational Publishers.

Preston, Caroline. (June 5, 2012). "Nigerian Banker Urges Business Approach to Poverty in Africa," *The Chronicle of Philanthropy*. www.csmonitor.com. Accessed 7 October, 2021.

Ramose, Mogobe. (1999). *African Philosophy Through Ubuntu*. Harare: Mond Books.

Rosenkranz, Rolf. (January 6, 2014). *Tony Elumelu's New Africapitalism*. Devex.

Senghor, Léopold Sédar. (1964). *On African Socialism*, trans. Mercer Cook. London: Pall Mall.

Stern, Gabriella. (May 8, 2014). "'Africapitalist' Says It's Time for Private Sector to Step Up," *The Wall Street Journal Frontiers*. www.wsj.com. Accessed 7 October, 2021.

Wamba-dia-Wamba, Ernest. (1992). "Beyond Elite Politics of Democracy in Africa," *Quest: An African Journal of Philosophy*, vol. 6, pp. 28–42.

Wiredu, Kwasi. (1996). *Cultural Universals and Particulars: An African Perspective*. Bloomington: Indiana University Press.

Young, Holly. (June 13, 2014). "Social Enterprise to Africapitalism: Do the Alternatives to Capitalism Work?" *The Guardian*.

Chapter 2

A Moralist Interrogation of Africapitalism as an African Economic Philosophy

Abayomi Sharomi

Africa is a part of the multifarious global system. Unfortunately, Africa has no true valuable impact in this ever-evolving configuration. More sadly, most African leaders do not govern well enough to provide the basic minimum of human existentialities needed for human flourishing. Thus, there is a void to the self and the other. Africapitalism seemingly exudes a contemporaneous hope in this abyss. It seeks sustenance beyond the purview of the state and its relations. It challenges the private sector to look beyond their profit seeking for shareholders and incorporate stakeholders (or perhaps their community of operation) into the bigger picture of economic prosperity and social wealth. Africapitalism is a nascent philosophy that aims to contextualize the ideals of a market-driven economy in Africa by not forgetting the belief of the "care for the other." Although the notion "caring for the other" is arguable in the African context, we cannot deny the fact that such care is more beneficial for humanity and specifically for Africa.

This chapter uses the dialogic method to midwife the need for a greater sense of moralism from Africapitalists, who are the proposed champions of Africapitalism. The beauty of an idea is not in its conception or articulation, but in its practical effect on individuals and the society at large. The discussion ensues between a retired professor (named The Sage) and his young tenant (named Africapitalist). Africapitalist is one of the recently selected entrepreneurs by the Tony Elumelu Foundation to champion the philosophy of Africapitalism and the future of Africa. His recently gingered enthusiasm cannot escape notice, and the usual curiosity of The Sage has led him to inquire about the new drive of the youngster, Africapitalist. Their conversation educates both parties on the potentialities and challenges of Africapitalism.

AFRICAPITALISM AND THE SAGE

Africapitalist: Our dear Sage, good evening, trust you had an interesting day and as usual you are watching the setting of the sun with interest, any thoughts for the day?

The Sage: Well my growing friend I am always awed by the setting of the sun because if one is opportune to grow in age but decline in strength and abilities like me you will understand and appreciate that the setting of sun is a reminder of your setting days. . . . Welcome back from the day's work, I hope it was a fruitful one.

Africapitalist: Hmm, growing in age but declining in strength and abilities, well you are not showing such signs of decline and your thoughts are always inspiring. And thank you, my day was productive.

The Sage: Yes you are right, there is a stage at an old age for some persons where you return to being as though you are a baby, when all energies are lost. That said, I cannot but notice a new energy that you are exhibiting lately. It seems you are driven by something new.

Africapitalist: Yes dear Sage, the future is promising and young Africans are on the verge of taking Africa to a desirous level of economic sustenance, a place where our proclivities are transformed into realities on the economic front. My motivation, dear Sage, is the philosophy of Africapitalism. I am one of those described as the future of Africa. We are young entrepreneurs with a different idea of business success which incorporates financial and social wealth; we do not seek wealth at the expense of the society but with the interest of the society at heart. We are taking a private sector approach to the business of development in Africa. As entrepreneurs, we stretch our arms wide in our business dealings in our environment not deep into the environment.

The Sage: Hmm, very interesting, the philosophy of Africapitalism. Is this a concept from the combination of Africa and capitalism? Or is it an African form of capitalism? You know, much as we like to praise the communal nature of Africa, we cannot deny the fact that pre-colonial and contemporary Africa has its share of oppressions at economic, political and social levels. Nonetheless, your brief insight into Africapitalism is thirsty and I believe this will be a long discussion. I suggest you freshen up and come grab a chair next to me so you can enlighten me on this new philosophy.

Africapitalist: Okay dear Sage, I'll be back shortly.

After a short while, Africapitalist returns to join The Sage in what turns out to be a long evening of discourse on Africapitalism.

The Sage: Welcome, the night is ours to relish in thought, though the day is far spent, the night is still young. Africapitalism, tell me about it. Make it brief but don't miss out anything.

Africapitalist: In his reasoning, Tony Elumelu opined that it is better to support people in a more sustainable way by increasing their access to economic opportunities rather than simply investing in amenities like basic health, education, and access to food that do not make them self-sufficient (Elumelu, 2016). The former way makes us (young entrepreneurs like me) less dependent and able to lift ourselves out of the doldrums of poverty. This approach, he says, fosters the spirit of enterprise and decent work, and will preserve dignity and reinforce self-reliance. It also enhances social stability because minds are constructively engaged (Elumelu, 2016). This is the life-force of Africapitalism.

The Sage: Hmm, a good spirit I must say. But does this differ from prevalent empowerment schemes instituted by governments, local, regional or international organizations, individuals, groups etc.? These schemes have interesting beginnings but later wither only for its remnants to be re-modeled under different appellations or similar new schemes set up with little or no effect.

Africapitalist: The difference is found in the letters of Africapitalism.

The Sage: Interesting! What says the letters of Africapitalism?

Africapitalist: Africapitalism is an economic philosophy that embodies the private sector's commitment to the economic transformation of Africa through investments that generate both economic prosperity and social wealth (Amaeshi & Idemudia, 2018, p. 19). This Elumelu argues will engender the meeting point for business and political action needed for the rebirth of Africa. Furthermore, as an economic idea, it (Africapitalism) will require efficient economic coordination by diverse actors, such as the state, civil society and markets. In order to do so, it will need to tap into the moral psychology of the actors (moral agents) and hypothesise human behaviors and needs (Amaeshi & Idemudia, 2018, p. 22).

The Sage: Haa, I love this fact that moral agents are central to the being of Africapitalism.

Africapitalist: Yes dear Sage, the separation of the moral content of capitalism is one of the banes of capitalism and Africapitalism does not want to face the same fate. That is why Amaeshi and Idemudia (2018, p. 28) rightly point out that Africapitalism is an attempt to re-imagine entrepreneurship and reunite capitalism with its moral roots in Africa. In this voyage of re-imagination, Africapitalism considers four values of foundation necessary to its commitments. These are: sense of progress, sense of parity, sense of peace and sense of place.

The Sage: What do these senses entail?

Africapitalist: The sense of progress is predicated on the creation of social wealth in addition to the pursuit of financial profitability. This sense goes beyond just material accumulation to also include psycho-social human well-being (Amaeshi & Idemudia, 2018, p. 29). With the aim of bridging the gap of wealth inequality, Africapitalism envisages a sense of parity. Africapitalism is driven by a counter-current of progressivism, which recognizes that growth needs to be inclusive. . . . it promotes a form of entrepreneurship that strives to create financial and social wealth for all stakeholders and not just for shareholders (Ibid., p. 30). Capitalism thrives on contests and conquests to the unequal benefits of entrepreneurs and shareholders which lead to socio-environmental imbalances to the detriment of humanity. The sense of peace and harmony is one which ensures balance between economic prosperity for the entrepreneur and shareholders and social wealth all stakeholders. Finally, the fundamental of Africapitalism is the sense of place and belonging. It is a direct response to globalized capitalism, which often takes place for granted and prioritizes cost instead (Ibid., p. 31). Against the detrimental denigration of place by globalization, Africapitalism is underpinned by the value of sense of place and rootedness. It strives to restore in managerial decision making the link between place and economics on the one hand, and between place and self-identity on the other hand (Ibid., p.32). Patriotism, being a linguistic project and emotional economic sentiments are other provisos of the sense of place and belonging.

The Sage: Quite interesting and impressive I must admit. Your depiction of the philosophy of Africapitalism has motivated me to seek further understanding of it. I suggest we call it a night and meet in a few days within which I would have consulted literatures and we will have a more robust discussion on the concept.

Africapitalist: That is fine by me dear Sage. I trust your critique will birth further issues that can entrench our Africapitalism.

The Sage: A quick one, how do we differentiate Africapitalism from African socialism? Don't forget that African Socialism was at its root a search for an indigenous model of economic development that would be revolutionary both in time and scale (Akyeampong, 2018, p. 2). This was an attempt to move as far away from capitalism which was the basis slavery, racism and colonialism that mostly debased Africa and Africans. But a lot of things turned out wrong along the way. Kebede (2017, p. 448) for instance writes that the defense of African unanimity does no more than support the vices of social conservatism, including dictatorship, the one party system, and the idea of president for life, so characteristic of postcolonial Africa and often paraded as African socialism. This perhaps is why Yacouba and Wologueme (2018, p. 28) opined of African Socialism that: even though the first trial failed, socialism is still the main door needed by African people to step into the true independence. The neo-socialism should be the political battle for African leaders to move forward. The new generation, the scholars advice, should use the lessons from the failure of socialism to empower the new-socialism. So, to ask my question differently, is Africapitalism not neo-socialism that tries to avoid the word "socialism" because it is value-laden?

Africapitalist: Well, Africapitalism should not be compared with African socialism or seen in its light, neither is it neo-socialism. Africapitalism is a private sector driven initiative to use businesses to drive development. It seeks to tap into the energy and vision of young entrepreneurs to seek beyond profits and add value to profiting. The accruable wealth is better distributed beyond shareholders to stakeholders. Amaeshi and Idemudia (2018, p. 28) point out that in this kind of voluntary wealth distributivism, one's economic and social power is measured by his or her economic empowerment of others. It is a thinking of the self and the other and acting for both parties. Idemudia et al. (2018, p. 7) clearly point out that there is a need to rethink the nature of the business-society relationship in Africa from business and society to business in society, partly as a way to restore the connectivity between business and society, and to reaffirm business's social obligations to societies in view of both the particularities of the African context and the unique competences businesses bring to Africa in pursuit of their private interests. It is these notions of connectivity, social obligations and business competences that can be leveraged to serve societal good that informs the concept of Africapitalism. This has no inclination toward socialism. Africapitalism does not seek political leadership to propagate its practicable idea of African development through entrepreneurial enablement. On leadership, Okupe and Amaeshi (2018, p. 131) aver that a responsible leader is one with a values-based and principles-driven relationship between the private-sector leaders and stakeholders who are connected through a shared meaning and purpose through which they seek to rise to higher levels of motivation and commitment for achieving long-lasting value creation and actualizing responsible change in their organisation and their society.

The Sage: Good. So let me get a better understanding then we will talk more.

During the intervening period, The Sage gets hold of *Africapitalism: Rethinking the Role of Business in Africa* and a few other articles on the subject matter. Their next meeting turns out to be an interesting critique of the ideas of Africapitalism as understood.

The Sage: I must admit that the propositions of Africapitalism are emancipatory. It can put Africa on the path to development if judiciously executed by all necessary collaborating parties including the state, the society, business leaders, investors, entrepreneurs, civil society etc. I equally agree with Elumelu's assertion that the private sector has a crucial role to play in the development of Africa. Entrepreneurs as representatives of the private sector are essential to the development of any society. Entrepreneurship, cites Tamaa et al. (2014, p. 437), is widely recognized by government officials throughout the world not only as a key mechanism for enhancing economic development, . . . but also as a good solution because it provides a relatively non-controversial way to increase the proverbial pie, creating jobs and enhancing per capita income growth. What is essential for this important role of the private sector are strong businesses based on strong principles and guided by strong institutional frameworks, this combination will strengthen economies across the African continent thereby fostering human flourishing. It is also worthy to note that the private sector is the largest sector in any state hence there is the potential of more effective development of the state when the private sector is enabled to thrive. There are more citizens than the make-up of government, hence at various levels of engagement (micro, small, medium or large), private businesses drive the economy of a country.

Africapitalist: You are quite right dear Sage, Africapitalism emphasizes the importance of the private sector in the business of development and here the entrepreneur is fundamental.

The Sage: Before I delve into that aspect of the entrepreneur (which by the way is my primary interest) I need your clarification on the uniqueness of Africapitalism. Have Africans not been practicing capitalism albeit on a smaller level? What makes the concept of Africapitalism different from what we've always done? Perhaps it is a way of just following the trend of buzz wording.

Africapitalist: The recent experience of capitalism in Africa is exploitative and African entrepreneurs have adapted such practices thinking that is the way to go. A lot of businesses are out there just for the profits and this reasoning is what Africapitalism seeks to change in the emerging young entrepreneurs . . .

The Sage: [cuts in] We can equally argue that the progenitor of Africapitalism started out like that, so where along the line did his ship change course? Ferns et al. (2014, p. 51) rightly note that Elumelu (one of the four elites they analysed) is an economic elite. Citing Davis as justification, they point out that these elites have, either by themselves, or through family lineage, acquired a disproportionate amount of wealth relative to occupying a small proportion of the population. . . . So we may be curious to ask at what point he thought of Africapitalism. Why is he now calling for a new way of doing business that will be unique to Africa different from how he has been doing business for decades?

Africapitalist: A curious reflection on the current social, economic and political state of African states points to the need to change the course of things for the better. Reflecting on his (Elumelu) beginnings and the current state of African economic development must have made him agree that there is the need for more contextual approach to lingering state of economic development. This provoked the need for a philosophical approach grounded in our peculiarities and needs. The existence of a few big businesses (like Elumelus') or multinational corporations, despite being private sector driven, has proven incapable of breaking the cycle of insufficiency in African states. Through the economic philosophy of Africapitalism a new perspective to private sector involvement in African economic development is envisaged. The principles include, among others, to unlock the creative potentials in individuals, strategically invest in worthy development sectors and make more people share in the purpose of these investments toward a purposeful future of their communities.

The Sage: How is Africapitalism different from empowerment schemes for youths which public officials (and politicians) take pride in providing for their communities?

Africapitalist: I can say the difference is in the basis. Empowerment schemes are set up out of political interests and presented as doing the populace a favor to get them out of poverty. This aims at satisfying the mostly egotist tendency of public authorities who are more interested in showing that they are doing something to alleviate the insufficiency of the populace rather than doing so. This is not what Africapitalism stands for. Africapitalism is an economic development philosophy that sees the entrepreneur at the heart of societal development. They are essential to the development of the economy and their understanding of success in business is hinged on economic prosperity and social wealth. Thus, the Africapitalist sees himself or herself as a driving force in human and material success of the society, that's an understanding of the sense of belongingness. I belong to the society and the society belongs to me. I succeed in the society and the society succeeds in and with me. This is the kind of moral reasoning that is missing in western capitalism or in the words of Amaeshi and Idemudia (2018, p. 28) "to realise its goals, Africapitalism must bring its moral intuitions and principled commitments into alignment with modern economic practices." It implies the restoration of African-ness in capitalism, reflecting the economic and social practices implicit in African culture and tradition (Ibid., p. 28), believing that there is arguably a higher sense of caring beyond the self in African culture and traditions.

The Sage: You have touched on my area of interest morality and the entrepreneur. We need to ask the fundamental question: If the separation between the institutions of capitalism and its morality is the bane of capitalism, how do we ensure Africapitalism does not face the same fate in the near or distant future?

Africapitalist: I have noted how Amaeshi and Idemudia (2019, p. 20) identify the duality if Africapitalism to be an imaginative management idea and a creative moral-linguistic artefact that embodies a new space for appropriating and re-moralizing capitalism in Africa.

The Sage: To achieve its aims Africapitalism is said to need to tap into the moral psychology of actors but this moral basis is not factored into its principles. What exactly are the moral intuitions of Africapitalism? Africapitalism according to Ferns et al. (2018, p. 64) draws so prolifically from non-indigenous ideas and sources that it occasionally seems to reproduce certain Western ideas about capitalism. For example, the very organizations criticized for hampering the development of a uniquely African variety of capitalism—e.g., the World Bank and IMF—are relied upon to support the bulk of claims made in the Africapitalism manifesto. This rather shows that Elumelu's mindset is as noted stuck in the Western mindset. If he wants to build his philosophy on morality of the entrepreneur which should be transferred to his/her business outlook and practice then he can look for moral theories from African scholars with African mindset. For instance Momoh's theory of moralism has the propensity to add to the values of Africapitalism.

Africapitalist: What does Momoh's moralism entail and how can it apply to Africapitalism?

The Sage: Moralism as espoused by C.S. Momoh (1991, p. 125) is an ideology based on morality. To understand this it is necessary to point out the difference between morality and ethics. Morality is more concerned with actions unlike ethics which gives consideration to ethical speculation and formalism (Momoh, 1991, p. 126). Thus our actions are moral or immoral but the theoretical prism within which actions are adjudged right or wrong are the province of ethics. Omoregbe (1993, p. 5) succinctly puts it that ethics presupposes that we already have a sense of morality, and it is the systematic study of the fundamental principles underlying our morality. Hence morality is the basis of ethics; the latter is the explicit reflection on, and the systematic study of the former. Moralism according to Momoh (1991, p. 127) is a doctrine that puts the other before or alongside the self. It holds that honesty, service and concern for the other ought to be the basis and measure of all actions. There are parties to any relationship, for instance, the state and its citizens; the members of a family or community; an organization, its shareholders, employees, customers, stakeholders (including host society) etc. In all relationships it is essential to rightly think of the other before and when acting.

Africapitalist: Then moralism is simply saying that we should act morally with the golden rule principle of doing unto others what you want to be done unto you, or perhaps care for the other.

The Sage: It is not just caring for the other neither is it similar to the golden rule principle. The latter has the tendency to condone immorality because you could choose to keep quiet in the face of a wrong since you will want the same silence when caught in a similar circumstance. Care ethics seeks to maintain relationships by contextualizing and promoting the well-being of care-givers and care-receivers in a network of social relations (Sander-Staudt, 2020). Care in this wise involves maintaining the world of, and meeting the needs of, ourself and others (Ibid.). What moralism enjoins is that: “in any action within relationships, the other must be thought of first or alongside the self.” Momoh (1991, p. 129) emphasizes that what moralism is saying is that everyone and every unit in the society has a duty to perform with no corresponding right to assert and the guideline for performing that duty is that satisfaction of the legitimate, legal and moral needs and wants of the other.

Africapitalist: Okay, I see.

The Sage: Moralism is based on five interconnected principles namely: think of the other before or alongside yourself; help; think of the interest of the weak before or alongside that of the strong; help the weak before the strong; the interest and help of the whole is paramount and supreme (Ibid., pp. 127–129). You will observe that the other four principles seem to be derivatives of the first which is the core of the moralism, hence my relation of this doctrine to Africapitalism will focus on the first principle.

Africapitalist: How would you relate moralism to Africapitalism?

The Sage: Moralism is a systemic and comprehensive ideology which allows it to relate with Africapitalism. In his conceptualization of moralism, Momoh point out the systemic nature of capitalism and socialism and this limits it operability to economic spheres of state systems. Both theories do not extend to person-to-person relations which Africapitalism aims to maintain within economic transactions. This, for instance, is exemplified in the preference of including stakeholders in the spread and not just shareholders. Remember you noted earlier that one of the banes of capitalism was the loss of its moral compass and Africapitalism seeks to correct this. The systemic and comprehensive nature of moralism allows the correction. Moralism according to Momoh (1991, p. 126) is systemic in the sense that it will oil the system and keep it going but comprehensive in the sense that it is applicable to non-official and person-to-person relationship. This gives room for stakeholders and allows the private sector to take the lead in African economic development especially through entrepreneurs.

Africapitalist: Quite interesting I must say dear Sage. How can moralism fill the moral gap and suit the African context?

The Sage: Now you have just hit the nail on the right spot. The four principles of Africapitalism are prospective but incomplete in my view. If the outcome of Africapitalism depends on the attitude of the moral agents then there is the need for a fifth principle that focuses on the moral agents and unifies the four principles. I call this the sense of moral temperance as demonstrated in entrepreneurial moralism.

Africapitalist: Hmm, entrepreneurial moralism, please tell me more dear Sage . . .

The Sage: The sense of moral temperance binds the other four senses (values) into the entrepreneur and his/her business demenor. We should not easily forget that a mention of "moral" brings individuals to the center of the topic of discourse. It takes a high sense of morality to truly think of others (in the right way) while thinking of the self. This is what I call entrepreneurial moralism. A sense of moral temperance will allow the Africapitalist understand that he/she is not doing the community a favor when thinking about and acting for the wellbeing of the community alongside profits derivable from operating in the community. Rather, this should be understood as another operation or mechanism of the organisation. The entrepreneur (i.e. the Africapitalist) is central to the success of Africapitalism. Describing who an Africapitalist is, Okupe and Amaeshi (2018, p. 179) propose that the philosophy requires leadership that is responsible, transformational and geared toward societal change. To become such an individual requires a sense of moral temperance. Such transformational leadership talks about moving beyond harmonizing interests toward organizational goals to pursuing sustainable development is essential.

Africapitalist: But businesses show responsibility, for instance in CSR activities, this can be seen as being moral and responsible.

The Sage: Responsibility is hinged on a sense of morality. The attempt to neutralize morality is not suitable for the philosophy of Africapitalism if it is to rise above self-interest or organizational interest. I agree with Okupe and Amaeshi's (2018, p. 181) citation of Gini that leadership has a moral dimension, but I argue further that the basis of good leadership is a sense of moral temperance. The moral element of leadership goes beyond exercise of social, economic or political powers, rather it is an emotive disposition that is brought toward exercising such powers, a disposition of thinking of the "other" before or alongside the "self." Rather than seeing "moral" in a subjective sense, moral should be seen as proceeding from a subjective sense to an objective reality of organisational leadership that thinks of the stakeholders. This sense is described by Okupe and Amaeshi (2018, p. 183) when they say: an effective leader is one who has a holistic and germane view of the wider effects of leadership decisions of organisations on society, and takes concerted action toward decisions that will benefit the society.

Africapitalist: So to what extent can the entrepreneur seek profit in his/her business?

The Sage: Mind you, this sense is not saying that interests of the entrepreneur is not important; who wants to invest and not profit? Moralism is proposing that crony capitalism, exploitation and excessive self-interest (even if masked with some goodwill and CSR) should not be the goal in business. The principle of moralism aligns with Holt and Littlewood's contention (2018, p. 203) that if we really want the best and brightest entrepreneurs to come up with the most innovative solutions to the myriad of social, economic and environmental problems facing Africa, then we have to realize that their altruism has to be balanced alongside a need to generate an income. That is, there needs to exist a concurrence between their interests and those of the community.

Africapitalist: You noted that this sense of moral temperance binds all other four senses together in the entrepreneur; could you shed more light on this?

The Sage: As clearly stated by Amaeshi and Idemudia (2018, p. 28) "Africapitalism is an attempt to re-imagine entrepreneurship and reunite capitalism with its moral roots in Africa." Who is expected to do this? The entrepreneur or better still, the Africapitalist. He or she plays an important role in the provision of positive human conditions needed for progress and prosperity. The young entrepreneurs who are envisioned as the future of Africa ought to shun corruption and crony capitalism and embrace the sense of parity. Africapitalists should not think that the success they should immediately aim for is like that of Tony Elumelu, Mark Zuckerber, or even Andrew Rugasira. The balance, harmony and peace needed for economic prosperity and social wealth should be understood by the Africapitalist just as the need for emplacement, self-identity and patriotism which positions Africapitalism as a "powerful emotional economic tool for Africa's sustainable development" (Amaeshi and Idemudia, 2018, p. 34). The sense of moral temperance allows the Africapitalist bring these senses into perspective in doing business.

Africapitalist: These issues are thought provoking dear Sage and I thank you for bringing them to the fore. But the conversation does not end here . . .

The Sage: [cuts in] . . . of course it does not end here, this is just the beginning and there are more perspectives to this understanding. Moralism suits the core of Africapitalism and opens vistas of opportunities for Africa. Thus, as we provoke the spirit of entrepreneurship in Africa let us do so with a spirit of moralism. Entrepreneurial moralism entails the incorporation of moral conditions and requirements in individual entrepreneurs

REFERENCES

Akyeampong, E. (2018). African socialism; or, the search for an indigenous model of economic development? *Economic History of Developing Regions*, 1–19. https://doi.org/10.1080/20780389.2018.1434411.

Amaeshi, K. (2018). Africapitalism: Why Africa needs a tailored economic principle. Available at https://www.africanliberty.org/2018/11/21/africapitalism-why-africa-need-a-tailored-economic-principle/. Accessed 14/10/2020.

Amaeshi, K., & Idemudia, U. (2018). Africapitalism: A management idea for business in Africa. In K. Amaeshi, A. Okupe, & U. Idemudia (Eds.), *Africapitalism: Rethinking the role of business in Africa*, pp. 19–41. Cambridge University Press.

Elumelu, T. (2016). Africapitalism: Empowering people works much better than giving them aid. *The Guardian*, 19 May.

Ferns, G., Okupe, A., & Amaeshi, K. (2018). Business elites to the rescue! Reframing capitalism and constructing an expert identity. In K. Amaeshi, A. Okupe, & U. Idemudia (Eds.), *Africapitalism: Rethinking the role of business in Africa*, pp. 42–70. Cambridge University Press.

Holt, D., & Littlewood, D. (2018). Social entrepreneurship and Africapitalism: Exploring the connections. In K. Amaeshi, A. Okupe, & U. Idemudia (Eds.), *Africapitalism: Rethinking the role of business in Africa*, pp. 195–214. Cambridge University Press.

Idemudia, U., Amaeshi, K., & Okupe, A. (2018). Introduction. In K. Amaeshi, A. Okupe, & U. Idemudia (Eds.), *Africapitalism: Rethinking the role of business in Africa*, pp. 1–18. Cambridge University Press.

Kebede, M. (2017). Re-imagining the philosophy of decolonization. In A. Afolayan & T. Falola (Eds.), *The Palgrave handbook of African philosophy*, pp. 447–459. Palgrave.

Momoh, C. S. (1991). *Philosophy of a new past and an old future*. African Philosophy Project Publication.

Okupe, A., & Amaeshi, K. (2018). Who is an Africapitalist? Reimagining private-sector leadership in Africa. In K. Amaeshi, A. Okupe, & U. Idemudia (Eds.), *Africapitalism: Rethinking the role of business in Africa*, pp 167–194. Cambridge University Press.

Omoregbe, J. (1993). *Ethics: A systematic and historical study*. Joja Educational Research and Publishers Limited.

Sander-Staudt, M. (2020). Care ethics. In *Internet Encyclopedia of Philosophy*. Available at https://iep.utm.edu/care-eth/. Accessed 9/12/2020.

Tomaa, S., Grigorea, A., & Marinescu, P. (2014). Economic development and entrepreneurship. *Procedia Economics and Finance*, 8, 436–443.

Yacouba, C., & Wologueme, B. (2018). From the failure of African socialism: How to set a new trend for a new generation. *Open Journal of Social Sciences*, 6, 27–36.

Chapter 3

E. K. Ogundowole's Self-reliancism and Tony Elumelu's Africapitalism

Complementary Economic Ideologies for Sustainable Development in Africa

Emmanuel Ogheneochuko Arodovwe

One of the challenges that emerged at the twilight of colonialism in Africa in the 1960s was that of reorganizing the continent's political, economic, and social systems to suit the societal goals and aspirations of the indigenous peoples. This was thought necessary in light of the ugly experiences of racism, slavery, imperialism, and colonialism which the continent had undergone in quick succession within a period lasting over four hundred years. The result of this experience, on the psychological front, was a significant alteration to the peoples' sense of worth, identity, and worldview; while on the economic front, a disadvantageous economic practice wherein the continent was limited to the extraction and exportation of raw materials in exchange for the finished products of the European colonizers. As a reaction to this negative colonial legacy, early African intellectuals and independence heroes advanced ideologies to salvage the situation and position the newly independent states on a defined ideological path that should ensure progress and sustainable development.

Franz Fanon's *The Wretched of the Earth* provided the early ideological ingredient with which the mental chains of colonialism were shattered and yokes of racial inferiority broken in preparation for effective anticolonial resistance and self-retrieval. Aime Cesaire and Leopold Sedar Senghor produced important literary masterpieces designed to reestablish the beauty of blackness, and the pride in the distinct cultural ways and worldviews of black Africa. The Negritude Movement they founded became an ideological rallying point for prosecuting the historic task of decolonization in the latter half of the twentieth century.

To provide the ideological direction on the economic and social front, African thinkers of the time promoted the idea of "African Socialism." It was thought to be neither capitalist nor Marxist-socialist but a rather unique model of socialism. Julius Nyerere's *Ujaama* (familyhood) was the most practical experimentation of this ideology in Africa in his country of Tanzania. Other proponents included Mamadou Dia of Senegal, Kwame Nkrumah of Ghana, Tom Mboya of Kenya, and Leopold Sedar Senghor of Senegal.

Over half a century after these patriotic and concerted efforts toward the redemption of Africa, very little appears to have been achieved. If anything, the continent has sunk deeper into the cesspool of underdevelopment and backwardness. Africa's unenviable tag as being Third World peoples now looks irredeemable. The number of migrant deaths as they seek escape routes from the continent to some European "paradise" has now become a matter of course with constantly rising figures. Very little production is going on in Africa with its contribution to global trade put at a paltry 2%. Poverty, despair, social ills, and diverse kinds of challenges have brought the continent to its knees, cap-in-hand for aid and support from wealthier societies, who are not only largely responsible for the African despicable situation but also have ulterior motives of their own to satisfy.

It is in the light of the foregoing that the recommended philosophies for development by Ogundowole and Elumelu are worth considering. Ogundowole is an African philosopher who has done extensive work in the past four decades on matters of African liberation and development. He propounds the ideology of self-reliance as the panacea to Africa's social, economic, and political challenges. He argues that the ideology is superior to both capitalism and socialism and is the natural successor to both. Tony Elumelu is a Nigerian economist and philanthropist. The Tony Elumelu Foundation he heads is the leading champion of entrepreneurship in Africa, with the objective of catalyzing economic growth, eradicating poverty, and creating jobs in the African continent. He argues for capitalism with a human face; one driven by the private sector but which takes very seriously its social responsibility of wealth redistribution and reinvestment, inclusive growth, and development of communities. I share Ogundowole and Elumelu's optimism regarding the potentials for redemption of Africa through the self-reliance and Africapitalism ideologies they have respectively propounded. The chapter provides an exposition and critique of Ogundowole's self-reliance and Elumelu's Africapitalism as the recommended ideological antidotes to Africa and the world's economic challenges in the twenty-first century.

CONCEPTUALIZING SELF-RELIANCISM

There are several approaches to conceptualizing the ideology of self-reliancism. Let us begin with the position that it is derived from the term self-reliance. Self-reliance, according to Ogundowole, is the tendency to do everything by oneself using one's available resources and skills. As a national principle, self-reliancism is the resolve and demand of a people to organize their entire activities into a definite set of preferences and priorities that hold the greatest promise for progress-enhancing development. It is the conscious, purposive activity of a people to direct their political, economic, educational, social, and cultural goals and practices along lines that guarantee sustainable development for the people therein. This implies a purposive attempt to concentrate in what Elumelu calls "strategic sectors," while also deliberately leaving such areas that are not so strategic to societal development at that particular point in time (Idemudia and Amaeshi, 2019).

A second way to define self-reliancism is to take the position that it is the successor ideology to both capitalism and socialism. A major implication of the age of modernity was its insistence on liberalism, individualism, and free action. The consequence when applied to the political sphere was liberal democracy, and cosmopolitanism in the social sphere. Capitalism was the consequence of the modernist ideology in the economic sphere. It was thought that a capitalist economic system where all men sought their self-interest and where the state stayed away from all economic activities, allowing citizens to "sort themselves out" in a self-seeking market arena, was the natural economic principle consistent with an age that emphasized reason and liberty.

Capitalism, therefore, as presented and defended by the theorists of the eighteenth century, seemed a very optimistic ideology with huge hopes and glorious expectations for society. Yet, there were scholars who at the time showed great reservations about the prospects of capitalism. Among them were Edmund Burke and G. W. F. Hegel. Their point was that freedom could not be granted unlimitedly since men were naturally egoistic and their wants insatiable. Therefore, such unchecked economic freedom could easily result in the strong, intelligent, and smart class in society taking advantage of the weak toward their impoverishment. An alternative ideology to capitalism was therefore sought. It was Karl Marx (1818–1883) and Frederick Engels (1820–1895) who provided the alternative in socialism. To underscore their impact, the world, beginning from the early decades of the twentieth century up to the last, was polarized into two diametrically opposed ideological camps—the capitalist West and the socialist East, as led by the United States of America and the Union of Soviet Socialist Republics (USSR), respectively.

No other event depicts the tension which existed between the two camps than the Cold War, which lasted from 1945 up to 1989. It turned out that the USSR caved in and disintegrated, signaling the end of the war. The general interpretation given to this event by scholars sympathetic to the capitalist

West was that it proved beyond doubt that capitalism was a superior ideology to its socialist counterpart. Indeed, Francis Fukuyama's *The End of History and the Last Man* is paradigmatic in this regard. The tendency then was to rally the world and whip everyone into line toward the acceptance and adoption of capitalism with its twin sister, liberal democracy as the paradigm for sustainable development in the post-Cold War era.

This is where self-reliancism, and indeed Africapitalism, emerges as a challenge to this position. It holds that it is erroneous to think that only two alternatives exist when the question of ideologies for running societies is posed. Ogundowole propounds self-reliancism as an ideology appropriate to serve as the panacea for Africa's, and indeed global, advancement in the twenty-first century. The ideology is built on a few fundamental principles: First, it accepts the dialectical theory as the most accurate explanatory model for the development of nature and society. Consequently, it holds that the dialectical opposition between capitalist individualism and socialist collectivism provides the basis for the emergence of self-reliancism. Second, unlike capitalism and socialism, it holds the cultural and linguistic component as germane to societal development, a point that is now being reinforced with a new understanding of the self and identity in postmodern philosophical thought (Taylor, 1989). Third, self-reliancism believes development is self-reliance. It involves maximizing the environmental, natural, and human resources of a people toward meeting the needs of the immediate society.

THE THEORETICAL FOUNDATION OF SELF-RELIANCE

The theoretical framework of self-reliancism is *dialectical realism*. It differs from Hegel's dialectical idealism and Marx's dialectical materialism. What is common to all three is the concept of dialectics. Dialectics, says Ogundowole, is the most general and comprehensive law of development. "Dialectics is a body of propositions concerning laws of development that are applicable to all spheres of objective reality—nature, society and human thinking, which if properly applied can enable one to arrive at correspondingly correct viewpoint of this reality" (Ogundowole, 2011:27). The notion of the dialectics as introduced by Hegel suggests the idea of progress through motion, hence its historical orientation to thought. It is to Hegel's credit that the study of nature and phenomena assumed a historical character, Ogundowole says. Yet Hegel's dialectics was essentially idealistic. Marx's dialectical materialism was aimed at filling the gaps in Hegel's idealistically oriented notion of the dialectic. It focused attention on "concrete historical man and concrete human society with the particular material condition of its existence" (ibid. p. 21).

This focus guided Marx into studying man's concrete material condition through the prism of socioeconomic formation which he used to comprehend various stages of human societal and economic development—beginning from a nonexploitative communalistic formation to the oppressive and exploitative capitalist formation of Marx's time. But Ogundowole reasons that "the development of every historic epoch is complex, many-sided and contradictory" (ibid., p. 26).

It is exactly at this point that he considers both Hegel's dialectical idealism and Marx's dialectical materialism inadequate to provide a satisfactory interpretation to contemporary events. Hegel's methodology was not only unidirectional, it also came with a heavy dose of mysticism and otherworldliness. Marx's methodology also imposed a particular direction—an economic direction—at the expense of all others. But Ogundowole argues that the dialectical method is universal and versatile. As a result, it can assume any direction at any point in time—idealistic, materialistic, cultural, political, and so on. It becomes imperative, therefore, that a multidirectional orientation to dialectics as a theory of advancement and progress is required, hence *dialectical realism*.

Dialectical realism demands that "everything is examined in the process of its development and change." However, this preoccupation with analysis does not hinder the equally imperative need of synthesis in the task of the study of society. This implies that in seeking to understand various aspects of the dialectical process, the analytic function is complemented by the synthetic one of "singling out that aspect that constitutes the basis, the root source of the phenomenon, of the entity, the essence of the object" (ibid. p. 28).

Since dialectics is characterized by contradictions in the form of cataclysmic clashes between opposites, Ogundowole inquires about the various aspects and diversities that the contradictions in contemporary society seem to include. He identifies them as follows:

> The contradictions between the world socialist system and the world capitalist system, the contradiction between the two political cum military blocs and the non-aligned movement, the contradictions between countries within each of the two blocs, on one hand, and between countries within the non-aligned movement itself, on the other; the contradictions between the industrially advanced neocolonialist subjugationist capital state and the economically subjugated and so backward new state of the world; the contradictions between different countries and groups of countries inside the capitalist camp and as well as inside the socialist bloc; the contradictions in relations between the bourgeoisie and the peasantry, and between the peasantry and working class, the working class and the unemployed; between the youth and the old stratum of contemporary societies; the contradictions between the national liberation movement and

> imperialism, the contradictions within the national liberation movement itself; the contradiction between the nationalization policy and practice of the transnational corporations—an exploitative policy and practice of the transnational corporations— an essential arm of neo-colonialism and the springboard of subjugationism; the contradictions within the new state between the forces of radical transformation of the society along the line of total and complete emancipation, at national self-determination and recovery and the forces of reaction, conservatism and traditionalism—another dangerous arm of neo-colonialism, etc. (Ibid., p. 29)

All these contradictions, Ogundowole says, are interwoven, creating an extremely complex picture of reality. As a result, only a dialectical realist methodology which attempts to comprehend changes in society from such a panoramic standpoint can understand the pathologies of the world's challenges and administer the right prescriptions for its recovery.

Ogundowole then seeks to identify which, out of the diverse contradictory clashes of our age, is the most fundamental on the basis of which all others can be comprehended. He answers that "the breakdown of the colonial system and the rise of scores of new independent sovereign states with their problems of social, economic, and cultural development" are the most fundamental (ibid., p. 30). This, he believes, is the substructure giving impetus to all the other observed contradictory processes. There are three major justifications for this position. First, it was this breakdown of the colonial system and the rise of numerous independent states that necessitated the global policy of the New International Economic Order and which has become the dominant theme at special sessions and at the General Assembly of the United Nations since the past decade of the twentieth century. Second, a major dialectical tension which appears to be at its zenith in our age is that between "the national nature of the ownership of raw materials and the foreign nature of their exploration, exploitation and appropriation." These, Ogundowole holds, are reducible to the fundamental contradiction identified above. Third, this contradiction seems to exert a decisive influence on all the others. It indeed has a direct bearing and cataclysmic impact on the diverse observable dialectical processes in contemporary times. Looked at closely, Ogundowole writes that "the fundamental contradiction is indeed, the one between the forces of self-reliancism and national recovery, and the forces of imperialism, neo-colonialism and subjugation" (ibid., p. 32). It is this contradiction, he says, that expresses the main direction of development, and dictates a new path of societal motion in the present epoch, the one of the breakdown of colonialism and the rise of new independent states striving for total and complete emancipation in all spheres of human activity, for national self-realization, through self-reliance.

ON AFRICAPITALISM

Africapitalism is an economic ideology whose purpose is to redefine and organize the operation of capitalism in Africa along humanistic and egalitarian lines. It is an ideology that seeks to blend the best of African values with Western economic theories as a basis of sustainable development in Africa. It rejects the wholesale replication of the individualist and exploitative character of Western capitalism, urging for an adapted brand that is in tandem with African communalistic values of brotherhood and solidarity.

Capitalism was the social consciousness in Europe which instigated the Scramble for Africa, as well as imperialism and colonialism (Lenin, 1963). It is an ideology that measures success by property ownership and celebrates individual acquisitiveness, even if at the expense of the common good. Capitalism encourages competition for political, economic, and social advantages over others. Unfortunately, these competitive tendencies often extend beyond the individual level to social groups such as communities, ethnic groups, and nation states. Such adversarial relations generate tensions, crises, and in extreme cases, wars. Operating largely on the Machiavellian principle of "the end justifying the means," these competitions breed injustice, oppression, subjugation, and exploitation. These temperaments were passed with formal education to Africans during the contact with the Europeans and have remained largely so till date. It is this borrowed temperament that now partly explains the preponderance of wars in postcolonial and postindependence Africa, just as much as in the international system. Whether they go by the terms civil wars, world wars, cold wars, or trade wars, they are all underpinned by a sense of capitalist competition (most times unjust and even illegitimate) for some desired advantage over others.

These capitalist values are antithetical to those in Africa, which has been proven to be communalistic and humanist in its pristine precolonial social consciousness (Nyerere, 1968; Nkrumah, 1967; Senghor, 1964; Rodney, 1972). African value systems stand in diametric opposition to the capitalist materialism and reductionism that characterize Western thought. While admitting, as Nkrumah (1967) notes, that communalism in Africa did not prevent the existence of social classes in society, for example, rich and poor; relations among peoples were largely underpinned by a humanist temperament that meant each individual saw his well-being in the welfare of the group. The unique feature of Africa's social organization of the past, in Nkrumah's view, is "crystallized in its humanism and its reconciliation of individual advancement with group welfare." Rodney corroborates the point made by Nkrumah when he held that

> African communal societies had differences such as age-grades and differences between ordinary members and religious leaders such as rain makers. However, those were not exploitative or antagonistic relations. (Rodney 2009: 440)

This social disposition is entrenched in metaphysical thoughts of the African cosmoculture. Among the Bantu, for instance, the concept of *ubuntu/botho* encapsulates the virtues of compassion, generosity, honesty, magnanimity, empathy, understanding, forgiveness, and the ability to share (en.unesco.org). These characteristics define "personhood," that is, what it means to be a person in the Bantu worldview. The Bantu express this temperament in such sayings as: "*motho ke motho ka batho babang, umuntu ngumuntu ngabantu*" (a person is a person through other people). J. S. Mbiti's classic phrase "I am, because we are, and since we are, therefore I am" encapsulates the spirit of this communalistic disposition of the African. The Urhobo express the same spirit in different ways, for instance, through the name "*Aguariavwodo,*" meaning "Our strength derives from our solidarity," and in the song poem "*Ona orho*" (This is Greatness)

Ona orho, Ona orho
ohwo ohwo vwo ma te ohwo
ona orho

(translation)
This is greatness, this is greatness
Each of us joining with the other,
Therein lies our greatness.

In contradistinction to the Cartesian *Cogito* (I think, therefore I am), Senghor characterizes the African's essential disposition to her object of knowledge as that of "feeling." "I feel, therefore I am" is how the African subject studies her object of knowledge, he says. "Feeling" as used in this dictum shares synonymy with the meaning of *ubuntu/botho* enumerated earlier.

Elumelu uses Africapitalism to urge for a synthesis of these core values of African metaphysical thought and the essentials in Western capitalism. Like Ogundowole, he does not apply the either/or approach, but calls for a blend that incorporates the positive aspects of both philosophies. Africapitalism's core values, according to Elumelu, include entrepreneurship, long-term investments, focus on strategic sectors, inclusive development dividend, and value-added growth (Idemudia and Amaeshi, 2019).

PREVIOUS ECONOMIC PHILOSOPHIES IN AFRICA

Self-reliancism and Africapitalism have had ideological predecessors that attempted to understand and provide possible solutions to Africa's socio-political and economic challenges. A variant of socialism termed "African socialism" was the economic ideology widely adopted by African thinkers in the early periods of post-colonialism. The immediate inclination for the outright rejection of capitalism was understandable. Capitalism had proven to be individualistic, exploitative, and, in its logical prolongation, imperialist, with colonialism as its ultimate result. The African thinkers, fresh from emancipation from suffocating European imperial rule, had to reject capitalism in its entirety for its counterpart socialism. Yet, African socialism was differentiated from Marxist (scientific) socialism in at least two respects. First, unlike Marxist socialism, it was not preceded by fierce antagonistic class struggles—as in the West. Second, it was believed to be rooted in traditional African folkways of communal living, universal access to the means of livelihood, and a strong moral commitment to the good of the community appropriately reinforced with religious sanctions. In this sense, it was seen as a modern form of the communalistic mode of production without having to go through the intermediaries defined by adversarial class relations of the Western societies. African socialism, therefore, became the major ideological predecessor to self-reliancism and Africapitalism on the African continent.

But as Ogundowole asserts, these interventions have been largely ineffective. He classifies these efforts into two broad groups: First is the group that believes that proper understanding of foreign (European) ideologies and adequate reaction against them is the solution to the African predicament. The second group thinks that generating local indigenous philosophies as alternatives to the colonially inherited ones is the panacea to Africa's development. The first group has Senghor's *Negritude* as the most celebrated instance. Their attempted cultural philosophical autarky, however, Ogundowole considers practically unrealistic.

The second camp has Kwame Nkrumah, Frantz Fanon, and Julius Nyerere as promoters. Their urge for a creative approach in studying Euro philosophical heritage as a prerequisite to developing a workable indigenous alternative ideology for development is commendable, says Ogundowole. Yet, the ideologues themselves were limited by the fact that they sought these new directions while confined to the polarity which the capitalist-socialist divide had imposed on their thoughts. They could not imagine that there could be a third ideological alternative.

Nkrumah, for instance, believed that African problems were as a result of colonialism, imperialism, and neocolonialism, resulting in the importation of ideologies alien to the African native environment of communalism and solidarity. For him, the conscience of the African society was plagued with three strands of incompatible and competing ideologies. He said in this regard:

> African society has one segment which comprise our traditional way of life; it has a second segment which is filled by the presence of Islamic tradition in Africa; it has a final segment which represents the infiltration of the Christian tradition and culture of Western Europe into Africa, using colonialism and neocolonialism as its primary vehicles. (Nkrumah, 1964:68)

To resolve the situation and set the continent on the path of progressive development, there is a need for a harmony among these ideologies in such a way as to preserve the original underlying humanistic principles of the African society. Rejecting capitalism for its celebrated exploitative and inhumane character, Nkrumah reasoned that a socialist system is the one in most agreement with the communalism, humanism, and egalitarianism which had characterized traditional African society from inception. Nkrumah reasoned further that all supposed abstract metaphysical constructs and ideologies were "products of their social milieu," and that the content of the education and values taught to the young ones in Africa was faulty as it bore little relevance to their social environment. Yet, his alternative ideology, "*philosophical consciencism,*" failed to create the advancement and progress he had envisaged.

Nyerere's *Ujaama* (familyhood) was viewed as an African variant of socialism that was natural to the people and didn't have to emerge through a historical process mediated by antagonistic class struggles, as scientific socialism had thought. He conceived of development as self-liberation which leads to self-reliance. He rejected capitalism because of its exploitative tendencies, which he said was alien to the African mental disposition. Ogundowole writes of the theory:

> It is such that it eschew exploitation of the abilities, enterprises, intelligence and hard work of others, deplore acquisitiveness for the purpose of gaining or consolidating power, and reject personal wealth accumulated or concentrated in such order as to be tantamount to, or effect a vote of "no confidence" in the social system. On the other hand, this mental disposition affirms a willingness to work, to earn a living and by that denies the parasitism of living off the benefits of hospitality of the labour of others. "mgeni siku mbili; siku ya tatu mpe, jembe" (treat your guest as a guest for two days; on the third day, give him a hoe). (Ogundowole, op. cit., p. 51)

Ogundowole also identifies a second generation attempt at the interrogation of Africa's underdevelopment in the works of thinkers such as Samir Amir, Claude Ake, Eskor Toyo, Wamba de Wande in the 1970s and 1980s, but like the generation before them, he says, they remained within the confines of the Marxist interpretive categories of *modes* and *relations* of production, regardless of whether these categories neatly applied to the African unique situation or not.

His stricture with this perspective is that the consumerist nature of the African society makes such Marxist-oriented categories of analysis unsuited for the continent. He holds that strict class divisions, which were the templates for Marx's analysis of European societies, cannot be so easily applied to African ones because Africa is not, strictly speaking, an industrial continent, and so there are no production relations, as in the West. The means to acquisition of wealth in Africa is largely through seeking political offices and diverting public funds to private accounts, which Marx describes as "primitive accumulation." And so, unlike the Western capitalists who became rich through appropriating wealth created by the working class in the process of material productive activities, the African wealthy class produces nothing, and can therefore not be appropriately described as "bourgeoisies."

Frantz Fanon agrees with Ogundowole in this regard. In discussing the "The Pitfalls of National Consciousness," he holds that the national bourgeoisie suffer from intellectual laziness in seeing themselves as perfect replicas of the departing colonizers. He faults this manner of thinking, holding that the national middle class has neither the industrial capacity nor productive orientation of the foreign bourgeoisie:

> Neither financiers nor industrial magnates are to be found within this national middle class. The national bourgeoisie of underdeveloped countries is not engaged in production, nor in invention, nor building, nor labor, it is completely canalised into activities of the intermediary type. (Fanon, 1967:149)

To comprehend Africa's unique situation, therefore, Ogundowole suggests that we must extend our enquiry to the foundations of African states. In doing so, it is discovered that, unlike the classical states of Europe whose foundations developed from commonly held cultural values, such as language, African states stood on very porous foundations, bordering on arbitrariness. Boundaries were drawn in Africa to suit the colonizers' whim of effective domination and maximum exploitation. Given this, the patriotic attachments which serve as the latent force driving citizens to amazing accomplishments for their societies are conspicuously absent in Africa. The second generation ideologues, Ogundowole says, appeared indifferent to these African peculiarities, and this greatly undermined their genuine efforts. In his analysis of the structures of African societies, he says:

> Modern states in Africa are the creation of foreign intruders who without consideration of the interest of the indigenous peoples, their needs, history and cultures, broke up, mutilated ethnic integers, split and re-grouped the pieces

> together with incompatible other groups resulting in the fact that there exist in Africa today multi-national, amalgam states, mistaken as nations. Whereas in truth, the African state embodies many nations or nationalities in itself being an amalgam. The amalgam nature of the African state makes the state to be its own real problem. (Ogundowole, 2004:149)

In retrospect, Ogundowole thinks that the first conference of Africa's new leaders at the dawn of independence in Addis Ababa, Ethiopia, in 1963 would have been the glorious opportunity to outlaw the arbitrarily drawn boundaries, restructure the continent, and set it on the path of progress-enhancing development. Instead, the leaders in that conference gave tacit approval to the colonial boundaries, apparently because they were desperate for the offices the colonialists had left behind, and the prospect of overseeing such large political structures beclouded their sense of sound judgment.

As a corrective, Ogundowole holds that an indispensable requirement of a self-reliancist ideology for Africa would mean a significant alteration, both in content and form, to the present nature of most African states to reflect cultural, social, and historical affinities. This logically leads to Ogundowole's demand for restructuring as a nonnegotiable requirement for the adoption of the self-reliancist ideology in Africa. This is discussed in detail later. The next section discusses the conception of development in self-reliancism.

SELF-RELIANCISM AND AFRICAPITALISM AS ECONOMIC IDEOLOGIES OF DEVELOPMENT

Self-reliancism and Africapitalism are both anchored on the theory of dialectics. Ogundowole sees dialectics as bearing both ontological and epistemological perspectives, and it regards thought and cognition as equally being in a state of coming into being and development, hence the historical nature of its conception of development. Crucial also to the dialectical principle is that it emphasizes qualitative change. As Ogundowole puts it: "from a dialectic-ontological perspective, development is not any change in the structure of an object but only such a change that is qualitative in nature and character" (ibid. p. 174).

Besides, it sees development as intrinsic or immanent, realizable through a series of historical changes of the object. As an immanent process, "the transition from the lower to the higher is contained in the lower in a concealed form, and the higher is but the developed lower." More importantly, for Ogundowole, development can assume three possible trajectories with only the third representing progress. Development which is "back and forth" is self-canceling. It is oscillatory motion. It depicts motion without movement. Applied to society, it represents an economy's continual oscillation between boom and recession. A second form of development is backward directed. This bears the feature of downward thrust motion. This is regress. Only the third kind of development is desired. It is unidirectional and usually along the optimal trajectory. It alone represents progress. Hence, progress-enhancing development is that which translates to social, economic, and cultural advancement of a people.

Walter Rodney seems to share this self-reliancist conception of development. Rodney holds that development is a many-sided process. At the level of the individual, it implies increased skill and capacity, greater freedom, creativity, self-discipline, responsibility, and material well-being. Economic development, which is at the level of the society, is said to take place, according to Rodney, as its members increase jointly their capacity for dealing with the environment. This capacity for dealing with the environment is dependent on the extent to which they understand the laws of nature (science), the extent to which they put that understanding into practice by devising tools (technology), and on the manner in which work is organized (Rodney, 1972:2).

One of the errors in rightly assessing development by African leaders and economic policy formulators, says Ogundowole, is to compare the present, superficially, with the past by assuming that since the streets and cities appear more "modern" than they used to be, and more technological products are now owned by citizens, then that represents progress. He faults such a manner of thinking as amateurish and unusually simplistic. He says to judge development appropriately, we must ask, for instance, if the value of the currency has strengthened or at least maintained its worth over a definite period of time. He provides a typical explanation:

> A lecturer II in a university service could procure for himself in mid-seventies a new Peugeot 504 car with an amount which is equivalent of his one-year salary. Presently, the price of the lowest of the 504 Series is about #2.5 million. Therefore a lecturer II now needs about ten years' salary to purchase one . . . this is a proof of the drastic (reduction) fall in the purchasing power of the average citizen. (Ogundowole, 2004:176)

A central thesis running like a red thread through the self-reliancist ideology is the place of indigenous production in the satisfaction of the daily needs of a people. A society which depends on the other for the satisfaction of its needs would only be registering the backward form of development. Ogundowole expresses it most succinctly in the following way:

> Development is borne out of the activities of the humans. These activities are directed towards the constant satisfaction of human needs and wants. Satisfaction of human needs can be met foremost through material production. Production of the material needs of the society then is at the root of progress-enhancing

> development. This is so because the attempt to produce and meet the material needs of the society and so to sustain the lives of the humans in a society unavoidably brings together man, his cosmic environment and his intellectual powers. This is why there exist production of material life of the society. Taken away from the people, genuine development cannot take root in a society. In other words, for development to take place in a society, the mass of the people must be involved in the process of material production, distribution and exchange making use of all the possibilities within their immediate environment first and foremost. (Ibid. p. 179)

Furthermore, self-reliancism holds that in starting up production activities, "efforts at domestic capital formation" must be upheld, in the sense of sourcing the capital from among the people rather than externally generated. This is because, as Nkrumah notes, foreign capitals which are injected into local economies to galvanize production do exploit rather than advance the local people. Ogundowole recommends that the sourcing of capital for a self-reliancist development program must involve contribution from all segments of the society: "local agricultural raw material producers, individual entrepreneurs, institutions capable of fabricating machine tools, local and state governments . . . ", and so on. As he says, "only internally-based development possess the capacity for sustainable development." Besides, "democratisation of the development process enhances solidarity among the people and is a veritable means of de-entrapping Africa from the internal subjugationist spider's web." My understanding of this democratically enriched economic system is that it would be in the form of the public-private partnership which has become dominant among developed societies in contemporary times.

A further point Ogundowole makes is that between self-sufficiency and self-reliance. This distinction is crucial since it could be erroneously thought that self-reliance tends toward economic autarky, which is not practicable. Ogundowole's point is that it is self-sufficiency rather than self-reliancism that tends toward materiality and therefore autarky. Hence he explains that national self-reliance does not insist that a nation must provide all its people's needs, taking cognizance of the fact that nations are not equally endowed. It thus recognizes the interplay of activities and needs among nations, but only to the extent that such interplay does not breed exploitation and economic injustice. Hence, self-reliancism he says, does not breed isolationism; instead, it encourages cooperation on mutually agreeable and beneficial terms.

Indeed, Nkrumah, in discussing the threats of neocolonialism in Africa, had also warned of the sinister motives of the West to keep Africa tied to her apron strings through lopsided economic policies that benefitted them. He encouraged international economic interactions and exchanges, but only to the extent that it did not lead to exploitation:

> The result of neo-colonialism is that foreign capital is used for the exploitation rather than the development of the less developed parts of the world. Investment under neo-colonialism increases rather than decreases the gap between the rich and the poor countries of the world. The struggle against neo-colonialism is not aimed at excluding the capital of the developed world from operating in the less developed countries. It is aimed at preventing the financial powers of the developed countries being used in such a way as to impoverish the less developed. (Nkrumah, 1965:ix)

CONCLUSION

This chapter has provided an exposition of E. K. Ogundowole and Tony Elumelu's ideological programs for the development of African states. It has been shown that both ideologies adopt the theoretical framework of dialectic theory of development for their arguments, in which a superior ideology emerges as a synthesis from the positive aspects of two earlier existing theories. It has been demonstrated that self-reliancism and Africapitalism have implications that cut across the economic, social, and cultural sectors of society. It is in this area that both ideologies stand superior to their predecessors such as Nyerere's *Ujaama*, Nkrumah's *philosophical consciencism*, and Senghor's *Negritude*. On the whole, self-reliancism and Africapitalism seem to be in agreement on an economic system that is public-private in character. In light of deteriorating and worsening conditions of living in all ramifications in the African continent, it is imperative that policy drivers and leadership in Africa take Ogundowole and Elumelu seriously as a response to the present challenges in the continent.

BIBLIOGRAPHY

Falaiye, Muyiwa (2012) *A Philosopher Interrogates African Polis: How Can We Get It Right?* University of Lagos, Nigeria, Inaugural Lecture Series, Lagos: Unilag Press.

Fanon, Frantz (1966) *The Wretched of the Earth*, trans. Constance Farrington, New York: Grove Press.

Hatch, John (1970) *A History of Nigeria*, London: Martin Secker and Warburg Ltd.

Herder, J.G. (2002) "Treatise on the Origin of Language", in Forster, N. ed., *Herder Philosophical Writings*, trans. Michael Forster, New York: Cambridge University Press, pp. 65–164.

Lenin, V.I. (1937) *Imperialism: The Highest State of Capitalism*, London: Lawrence & Wishart.

Nkrumah, Kwame (1965) *Neo-Colonialism*, London: Panaf Books.

Nkrumah, Kwame (1967) *African Socialism Revisited*, Prague: Peace and Socialism Publishers.

Ogundowole, E.K. (2004) *Philosophy and Society*, Lagos: Correct Counsels Ltd.

Ogundowole, E.K. (2011) *Self-Reliancism: Philosophy of a New World Oder*, Lagos: Correct Counsels Ltd.

Rodney, W. (1972) *How Europe Underdeveloped Africa*, Lagos: Panaf Publishing.

Senghor, S.L. (1964) *African Socialism*, London: Oxford University Press.

Taylor Charles (1989) *Sources of the Self: The Making of the Modern Identity*, Cambridge: Harvard University Press.

Uwafiokun Idemudia and Kenneth Amaeshi (eds.) (2019) *Africapitalism: Sustainable Business and Development in Africa*, London: Routledge.

Chapter 4

International Political Economy of Africapitalism

Nana Kwasi Amoateng

Capitalism has been widely discussed within the context of different academic disciplines, including economics, politics, political economy, and philosophy. Like the other disciplines, the philosophical understanding of capitalism has largely been investigated from a Western viewpoint to understand power dynamics and socioeconomic relations between different state and nonstate entities. For instance, Bjerg (2014) has highlighted *the philosophy of crisis capitalism* in which a Marxist ideology is used to understand the functioning of financial markets. Other popular authors such as Michalis Skomvoulis, Kohei Saito, Ardis B. Collins, Nicholas Mowad, Michael J. Thompson, Richard Dien Winfield, Lisa Herzog, Nathan Ross, Tony Smith, and Louis Carre have also examined Hegelian capitalism through the lens of poverty, consumption, mechanized labor, market imperatives, human subjectivity, religion, and modernity, among other things (see Buchwalter 2015). Furthermore, the philosophy of capitalism has been studied from an Heideggerian standpoint, focusing on an ontic investigation—study of beings (*Seiende*)—of what capitalism does (cf. Bjerg 2014, 20). To advance the metaphysical understanding of capitalism, Bjerg (2014) has also pursued an ontological study of the essence or "to be" (*Sein*) of money. In turn, some authors have sought to understand the philosophy of capitalism by comparing and contrasting socioeconomic realities between European and non-European states. For example, Nuyen (2008) has demonstrated how European capitalism is compatible with some elements of Chinese philosophy.

The idea of capitalism is also central to both the popular and unpopular African philosophical traditions such as logic, ontology, ethics, epistemology, political thought, philosophy of science and mathematics, philosophy of education, Afrocentrism, Pan-Africanism, Afropolitanism, nationalism, decolonization, neocolonialism, Africana philosophy, Afro-Caribbean philosophy, and Ubuntu (cf. Mba 2019). Many of the discussions involving African philosophy of capitalism have been drawn on European political and socio-economic realities, including studies that have underlined the impact of European capitalism on African societies. For example, African philosophers such as Adeshina Afolayan, Toyin Falola, and Sanya Osha have discussed the challenges confronting Africa in the age of Western idea of neoliberal capitalism. The latter entails a "massive increase in social and economic inequality, a marked increase in severe deprivation for the poorest nations and peoples of the world, . . . an unstable global economy and an unprecedented bonanza for the wealthy" (McChesney 1999, 8).

One major gap in existing (philosophical) discussion of Africa and capitalism is the failure to adequately account for pre-European ideas of capitalism on the continent. This partly stems from the fact that a few influential scholarly outlets have sidelined the study of African economics. For example, Breckenridge (2021) has discussed the journal of *Economy and Society*'s "consistent disinterest in African economics that runs through all the schools of comparative political economy" published over the past three decades. This chapter, therefore, helps to fill a major gap in the literature by moving away from the predominant Western-influenced discussion of capitalism to an international political economy (IPE) of Africapitalism as elaborated below.

The field of IPE has contributed significantly to the understanding of international relations (IR) given the emphasis on interaction between economics and politics. As Philips (2020) has remarked, "it is impossible to understand the evolution of world affairs without understanding how the political and the economic are intertwined" (257). In this vein, IPE scholars have covered a wide range of issues involving human and economic development, international trade, international financial flows, wealth creation, inequality, public and private forms of power, migration, and formal and informal institutions, among other things. Such studies have used different theoretical lenses such as (neo-)realism, (neo-)liberalism, Marxism, postcolonial theory, constructivism, poststructuralism, and feminism. Following the traditional IR discipline, IPE debates primarily focus on "questions about power, asking what forms power takes in the global political economy, who or what exercises power, and with what political and economic, and social consequences" (Philips 2020, 256). As opposed to the predominant philosophical discussions in the other chapters, this chapter analyzes Africapitalism within the context of IPE. It pays particular attention to how different forms of power relations and layers of interests, rules, norms, laws, organizations, and habits of state and nonstate entities have shaped IPE of Africapitalism.

Capitalist forms of economic transactions have existed and evolved in Africa since antiquity (see next section). Amaeshi (2015) has highlighted how "the type of capitalism introduced by colonialists has not always been aligned with the needs of Africans. It remains overly informed and driven by agendas set outside the continent." Against this backdrop, the term Africapitalism has been coined by Tony Elumelu—a Nigerian banker and entrepreneur—to help address the long-standing drivers of Africa's perceived and actual poverty or underdevelopment, and thus the poor performance of modern African economies in the global political economy. The latter entails "all international economic transactions that occur across national borders: trade; financial flows; and foreign direct investment (commonly known as FDI)" (Hobden 2011, 71). Several factors, including neocolonialism (Nkrumah 1965), modernization (Gurr 1968), aid and loan politics (Moyo 2009), resource curse (Ross 2012; Rosser 2006), corruption (Le Van 2015; Awojobi 2014), conflict (Rodrik 1999; Kim and Conceição 2009), inefficient trade negotiations by leaders (Ohiorhenuan and Keeler 2008), and weak institutions (Acemoglu and Robinson 2008), have been invoked to explain widespread poverty and other ills in modern Africa. Currently, many African countries, including Ghana and Zambia, are using Covid-19 and the ongoing Russia-Ukraine war as part of excuses to access problematic loans from the International Monetary Fund, which mostly worsen living conditions on the continent.

In turn, the economic philosophy of Africapitalism involves understanding the central role of the private sector "to the economic transformation of Africa through investments that generate both economic prosperity and social wealth" (Amaeshi 2015). Or as Elumelu has argued, "Africapitalism describes the process of transforming private investment into social wealth" (Amaeshi 2017). Despite the heavy emphasis on the private sector, the critical role of the state, and thus politics, has been included in the analysis of Africapitalism. For example, Elumelu has underlined how "Africa's renaissance lies in the confluence of the right business and political action" (ibid.). This chapter contributes to the discussion of Africapitalism by grounding the concept's roots in ancient African chiefless states and highlighting the limitations of political and socioeconomic institutional arrangements in modern Africa. Africapitalism has a Pan-African orientation in which there is recognition of the links between the political and socioeconomic challenges facing both Africans on the continent and in the diaspora (cf. Shepperson and Drake 2008; Mazrui 1977, 68–84).

The principal argument is twofold: That the idea of Africapitalism originates in the ancient African chiefless states in which the ancient African constitution and other local institutions, including lineage and age-grade systems, engineered social wealth. The chapter further argues that inadequate generation of social wealth (widespread poverty) in neocolonial Africa largely stems from problematic political arrangements that lean toward elitism, individualism, and patronage systems involving political elites and their local and foreign clients. The analysis is in sharp contrast to the prevalent economic-based narratives on the drivers of underdevelopment in Africa, such as resource curse, resource scarcity, and foreign aid and loans, that have been discussed without reference to Africapitalism. The chapter begins by situating Africapitalism in the context of African chiefless states before examining the political and socioeconomic determinants of underdevelopment in modern Africa. The analysis then shows how universalization of Africapitalism can help to resolve development-related challenges facing the African continent and African societies across the world.

CHIEFLESS AFRICAN STATES AND AFRICAPITALISM

Different forms of states existed in precolonial Africa such as chiefless states, city-states, empire-states, and conquest states (see Chiriyankandath 2011; Williams 1987). Of these, the most advanced manifestation of Africapitalism originates in ancient African chiefless states in which democracy first manifested and attained its highest development (cf. Williams 1987). The chiefless African states consist of societies or political units without chiefs or kings—"where the people actually governed themselves without chiefs, where self-government was a way of life, and 'law and order' were taken for granted" (163). Thus, as opposed to modern (African) states in which power is concentrated in the hands of a few political elites who mostly craft personalized institutions to regulate public affairs, thereby fueling violent conflicts and other problems (cf. North et al. 2009; Albert 2005; Le Van 2015; Adeosun et al. 2016; Aderonke and Awosika 2013), the masses were responsible for wealth creation and equitable distribution of public resources in the African chiefless states. The latter entailed mutually constituted public and private sectors that ensured impersonal/fair application of laws/principles in all matters, and thus placing a great deal of emphasis on equality of households or citizens and social wealth. Africapitalism was fully actualized in the chiefless African states given that the economic philosophy of these states was centered only on equal or impersonal access to public resources. This opposes Western-based capitalism, which developed alongside liberalism by placing more emphasis on individualism and thus creating disharmony between the state or political elites and the private sector. As Mazrui (1977) has argued: "The liberal distrust of government resulted in the growth of private industry and the insistence that political authority should not interfere with the profit motive of individuals" (22).

Contrary to views that have misinterpreted the "primitiveness" of African chiefless states along the lines of "backwardness," Williams (1987) has underlined how these states are primitive in the sense of being the "first" or "beginners" in democratic practice. In this vein, Williams (1987) draws on the ancient African Constitution—"a body of fundamental theories, principles and practices drawn from the customary laws that governed Black African societies from the earliest times" (161)—to explain the form of democracy in the chiefless states. The African Constitution was generally based on egalitarian ideals; it governed most of ancient Africa; and it contained principles and practices such as the following:

> VIII. The land belongs to no one. It is God's gift to mankind for use and as a sacred heritage, transmitted by our forefathers as a bond between the living and the dead, to be held in trust by each generation for the unborn who will follow, and thus to the last generation.
>
> IX. Each family, therefore, has a right to land, free of charge, sufficient in acreage for its economic well-being; for the right to the opportunity and means to make a living is the right to live.
>
> (a) The land, accordingly, cannot be sold or given away.
> (b) The land may be held for life . . .
>
> XIV. The trouble of one is the trouble of all. No one may go in want while others have anything to give. (Williams 1987, 171–172)

In contrast to present-day Africa in which lands are being sold indiscriminately by states and traditional leaders to individuals and groups including multinational companies for mineral exploitation, households were entitled to free lands in the chiefless states. Private ownership of land in modern Africa is a colonial legacy that stems from the concept of private property, underlining the fact that colonialism's impact has been transformative rather than transitory in modern Africa (cf. Chiriyankandath 2011, 38). As Mazrui (1977) has highlighted: "The principle of freehold ownership of land, capable of being sold at any time by the owner, regardless of any offence that might be caused to ancestors buried in that area, and regardless of obligations to kinsmen, was quite alien" in Africa (23). In modern Ghana, some members of the ruling class have been accused of privatizing strategic state lands including the famous Achimota forest (Ghanaweb 2022). In contrast, households' access to free lands in the chiefless states ensured that the masses generated social wealth through farming and other activities, thereby enhancing egalitarianism—aiding households to have the same opportunities to create wealth from the lands.

It is important to add that the ancient African Constitution was grounded in two key institutions: lineage and age-grade or age-set systems. Lineage refers to "a network of kinsmen, and alleged kinsmen, all of whom descended from the same ancestor or related ancestors" (Williams 1987, 163). It helped to unify households in both African chiefless states and later kingdoms, particularly with respect to trade and warfare, among other things. Households with common lineage ties generally cooperated or worked together on different political and socioeconomic issues, including governing the chiefless states without needing an individual ruler, chief, or king. In modern African states, lineage institutions are widely discussed in terms of ethnic identities, which "are constructed when some people self-consciously distinguish themselves from others on the basis of perceived common descent (perhaps mythical), shared culture (including values, norms, goals, beliefs, and language), or—most commonly—both" (Scarritt 2011, 128). As opposed to the chiefless states in which lineage institutions consolidated the bonds between people, ethnicity has been extensively discussed as a major driver of conflict in modern Africa (Horowitz 1998; Le Van 2015; Lynch 2011; Esteban et al. 2012; Esteban and Ray 2011).

In turn, the age-grade system was mostly used to organize the internal structure of the chiefless states. Against this backdrop, Williams (1987) has highlighted how classification of the local population "was determined by the period in which one was born. All persons born in the same year, belonged in the same age-grade. Each grade covered a block of years" (165). This means that people who fell within the age bracket of 15–20 years or 20–30 years, for example, had to embark on specific roles or tasks, including education and entrepreneurship in the society. The underlying philosophy upon which the age-grade system was based is as follows: "*All other things being equal*, those who were living in the world and experiencing life before others were born should know more than these others" (Williams 1987, 168). Thus, age and intelligence were the key determinants of eldership, respect, and thus the capacity to promote egalitarian principles such as equitable distribution of public resources in the chiefless states. This also means that there was recognition of seniority within each grade, given that lazy, troublemaking, and/or foolish older persons who could not promote communal living and other social virtues were less respected in the society. In contrast, the degree to which individuals, including young people and the aged, can privatize wealth (accumulate money) determines the respect that they receive in modern African societies (cf. van der Geest 1997; BBC 2019). It is important to note that persons regarded as seniors or elders within the age-set and in the larger society only played advisory roles on all matters, including land distribution for households in the chiefless states. This means that their views on public matters could be ignored, even though this rarely happened (Williams 1987, 168).

To summarize, Africapitalism was fully achieved in ancient African chiefless states in which lineage and age-grade institutional arrangements ensured that political and socioeconomic power rested theoretically and practically in the people. The rights of the community were more important than individual freedom in these African states. And as Williams (1987) has argued:

> These self-governing people did not have a Utopian society in any idealistic sense. Theirs was a practical society in every way. The laws were natural laws, and order and justice prevailed because the society could not otherwise survive. Theirs was, in fact, a government of the people; theirs was, in fact, not theory, but a government by the people; and it was, in fact, a government for the people. (170)

In turn, most modern African states, including democratic, democratizing, and autocratic regimes, have inherited colonial-based political and economic institutions, and thus a Western version of capitalism that places emphasis on individualism and patronage systems, as discussed in the next section.

MODERN AFRICA AND UNDERDEVELOPMENT

Development has been defined as follows:

> A process of enlarging people's freedoms and opportunities and improving their well-being, enabling them to lead long, healthy lives; to have access to knowledge; to enjoy a decent standard of living; and to participate in the decisions that affect them. (Khodabakhshi 2011, 252)

In contrast, underdevelopment refers to the restriction of people's access to political and socioeconomic rights, freedoms, and opportunities. Despite possessing the majority of the world's precious natural resources such as gold, bauxite, cobalt, platinum, and manganese, modern African states are widely regarded as underdeveloped. As Mazrui (1977) has argued:

> Africa is not the poorest of the regions of the world in resources but it is the least developed of the inhabited continents. Immense mineral wealth and agricultural potential coexist with some of the lowest standards of living in the world. (vi)

This puzzle stems from the fact that Africa's immense resource wealth has largely been used to develop Europe and other parts of the world to the detriment of Africans, beginning from the colonial period to the current neocolonial era. The different political and socioeconomic factors that have been discussed as determinants of poverty and underdevelopment on the continent, including neocolonialism, corruption, and resource curse, underline how the democratic principles that governed and created wealth, and thus Africapitalism, in the chiefless African states have been replaced with problematic institutions imposed by colonialism that encourage individualism, division, and greed. Mazrui (1977) has discussed how liberalism and Western capitalism initiated and enhanced individualism in modern Africa through Christianity's concept of personal accountability, the European principle of freehold land ownership, the monetization of economies, and colonialism, among other things. In this vein, modern African political regimes, including democracies and autocracies, have been crafted based on patronage systems that have led to wealth creation for political elites and their local and foreign clients, while the masses struggle to make ends meet.

Economic-based factors and indicators such as foreign aid and loans (Moyo 2009) and gross domestic product (GDP) (Ranis et al. 2000; Costanza et al. 2009) are commonly measured and cited as key determinants of poverty and underdevelopment in Africa and elsewhere. One major limitation of economic-based explanations of poverty in Africa is the tendency to underestimate the extent to which politics and other social realities fuel the continent's underdevelopment. Collier's (2000) reference to greed—understood as economic opportunities—as the single driver of conflict, and thus poverty, otherwise referred to as the low human-development conflict trap (see Kim and Conceição 2010), is a classic demonstration of how economic-based factors have been exaggerated in the understanding of modern Africa's development-related challenges. Against this backdrop, some scholars, including Acemoglu and Robinson (2008), have highlighted how political and economic institutions usually come together to determine the differences in wealth and poverty of states.

In turn, the chapter argues that politics—understood as "activities associated with the process and institutions of government, or the state, but in the context of wider power relations and struggles" (Burnell et al. 2011, 1)—is the most evident determinant of modern Africa's underdevelopment. This position restates the phenomenon of strategic arbitrage in which bad government is thought to create conducive grounds for good business. As Amaeshi (2017) has underlined: "In such an environment, it may be easy to exploit the weaknesses of poor regulation, cheap labour, raw materials and tax loopholes." Classic cases of strategic arbitrage are seen in several resource-rich African countries, including Nigeria and the Democratic Republic of Congo, where local populations have become victims of resource exploitation by multinational companies such as Shell and Microsoft. For instance, Niger Delta's oil exploitation by multinational oil companies has led to violent conflicts, pollution, and environmental degradation, among other problems (Newsome 2011; Ikelegbe 2011, 2010, 2006a, 2006b; Ikelegbe and Onokerhoraye 2016; Ikelegbe and Umukoro 2016; Okolie-Osemene 2015; Soremekun 2011). Furthermore, the African continent loses billions of dollars each year through illicit financial flows (IFFs) involving activities such as tax avoidance, corruption, and offshore accounts, and other criminal activities including trafficking in drugs, weapons, humans, human organs, and cultural property, crude oil theft, illegal wildlife trade, illegal fishing trade, and illegal logging and mining. UNCTAD (2020) has reported how between $30 and $52 billion of trade misinvoicing alone contributes to $88.6 billion capital flight each year on the African continent (14). Generally speaking, monies that African countries lose through IFFs far outweigh all financial flows including aid and loans to the continent as African political elites and foreign powers collude to create conducive grounds for theft.

African political elites—whose creation largely resulted from Western education in the wake of independence from colonial rule (Mazrui 1977, 13–14)—have the biggest say on the continent with respect to nation-building and public decision-making. This is because most modern African states have aligned with a world system in which public decision-making largely lies in the hands of a few political elites or "big men" who mostly craft personalized institutions using their local and international networks. Thus, many African political elites are part of the "looting machine," which entails a "global web of traders, bankers, middlemen, despots and corporate raiders that is pillaging Africa's vast natural wealth," thereby fueling poverty and underdevelopment (Burgis 2015, Cover Page). Africa is now an exploitative terrain in which private or individual interests thrive as opposed to collective or group interests that were promoted in the chiefless states. And as Ake (1996) has argued, African political elites and foreign (Western) agents have used the idea of development to satisfy their selfish financial and political gains, with very little or no regard for local realities. It follows that most of the economic-based factors, including foreign aid and greed, that are often cited as fueling poverty on the continent make sense only when they are viewed through the political lens, inasmuch as political elites largely shape economic choices that African states craft. Dependence on foreign aid and loans, for example, is a political choice that African elites and their networks make for African countries, thereby enhancing poverty on the continent. The current perverse political arrangements have put most African states in an international caste system in which it is almost impossible for them to escape the poverty trap (cf. Mazrui 1977; Collier et al. 2003).

In summary, political structures in modern Africa, which differ greatly from institutional arrangements in the chiefless states, have initiated and enhanced selfishness and poverty on the continent. It is unwise to think that the current institutions in African states, including elections and legal structures, can make any significant difference in terms of tackling the underlying causes of widespread poverty on the continent. Scholarly works such as Rodney (1972) and Nkrumah (1965) have highlighted the extent to which European and Western states and agents have generally contributed to Africa's underdevelopment through the Trans-Atlantic Slave Trade and colonization since the fifteenth century. China's perceived and actual contributions to this problem in modern times are also being widely discussed in both academic and nonacademic circles. Even though political movements that led African states to attain independence from colonial rule produced great leaders such as Kwame Nkrumah and Patrice Lumumba, political elites that have emerged on the continent, particularly from the 1970s to present, have largely aligned their selfish interests with multinational companies and other foreign powers, thereby creating the looting machine and reinforcing neocolonialism (cf. Burgis 2015; Nkrumah 1965). Thus, even though the long-standing obstacles to Africa's development, including local and international bribery and corruption, are widely known, political institutions capable of overturning underdevelopment of the continent are yet to emerge. This has led to the thought of Africapitalism, which aims to help improve living conditions in modern African states. The next section briefly discusses how the universalization of Africapitalism can help to deal with underdevelopment-related problems affecting Africans on the continent and elsewhere.

UNIVERSALIZATION OF AFRICAPITALISM AND AFRICAN DEVELOPMENT

The idea of universalizing Africapitalism is a Pan-Africanist concern regarding the discourse about including Africans, both on the continent and elsewhere, with respect to how the private and public sectors can help to improve the development prospects of black people. Africapitalism underlines the central role of the private or nonstate sector in tackling problematic power relations between domestic actors in African states and foreign influence in these states that have existed, at least, since the colonial period (1880s–1960s). Africapitalism, as an economic philosophy, is useful inasmuch as it can help to boost Africa's economic fortunes by reshaping politics or policymaking in a way that limits foreign exploitation of the continent's natural resources, dominance of foreign companies and goods in African markets, concentration of wealth in the hands of few elites and their networks, and overdependence on foreign aid and loans, among other things. In this vein, Amaeshi (2015) has underscored the values promoted in Africapitalism, including a sense of progress and prosperity, a sense of parity and inclusion, a sense of peace and harmony, and a sense of place and belongingness.

Thus far, Africapitalist scholars have not paid adequate attention to the exploitation of Africans in the diaspora. Several scholarly works such as Lovejoy (1997), Clark (1999), Pope-Hennessy (1998), Rodney (1972), Williams (1987), Nunn (2007), Nunn and Wantchekon (2011) have widely discussed how a significant number of black people who are outside Africa resulted from infamous events such as the Arab Slave Trade (AD 633–present), the Trans-Atlantic Slave Trade (1400s–1800s), and colonization. The plights of African migrants in Europe, the Americas, and Asia are also being discussed by academics and nonacademics. Thus, the destinies of Africans on the continent are intrinsically linked to the fate of Africans in the diaspora who are often confronted with racist political and socioeconomic institutions in countries such as the United States of America, Britain, China, and France. Indeed, racism has been highlighted as the key reason why Covid-19 hit black people the hardest in the United States and Britain (Gordon 2020; Wired 2020). Widespread racism and discrimination against black people are evident across different sectors, including education, law, health, sports, media, and employment (Maeso 2017; Erel 2007). This has led to emancipation movements including the civil rights movement and Black Lives Matter. The intrinsic link between the fate of Africans on the continent and those in the diaspora was seen during the movement for political independence of African states in the 1960s as people such as W. E. B. Du Bois, George Padmore, Kwame Nkrumah, and Jomo Kenyatta came together to help drive away European colonizers (Shepperson and Drake 2008).

The public sectors in neocolonial African states face serious challenges in terms of helping to improve the economic fortunes of the masses given that political elites have largely served as gatekeepers for international bodies to loot the continent (cf. Burgis 2015). It is not in the interest of the public sectors of states outside Africa, particularly those in advanced countries, to eliminate problematic institutions that exploit Africans both at home and abroad given that they have largely benefited from the existing arrangements (cf. Williams 1987; Rodney 1972). In this vein, Africapitalist scholars need to highlight the endeavors of Pan-Africanists in the private sectors on the continent and abroad who are genuinely interested in and/or have the means to boost the social wealth of Africans using available resources. Pan-Africanism in this case refers to "the attempts by the peoples of the African Diaspora and of Africa to link up their struggles for their mutual benefit" (Shepperson and Drake 2008, 2). From an Africapitalist perspective, several partnerships need to be formed among pro-African businesses from local to global scales in the areas of trade, education, entertainment, sports, art, tourism, and culture, among other things. This needs to be geared toward encouraging communal living as was the case in the ancient African chiefless states, thereby improving the living conditions of Africans on the continent and abroad.

The major threat to full realization of Africapitalism in modern African states stems from the ploys of African political elites and their local and foreign clients whose selfish interests oppose the enhancement of the social wealth of "global Africa"—Africans at home and abroad. It is clear that different strategies have been used to undermine the efforts to achieve full freedom and prosperity of Africans in the modern era. For example, the end of the Trans-Atlantic Slave Trade in the eighteenth century led to full colonization of the African continent by the nineteenth century. Similarly, the political independence of African states in the 1960s led to the current neocolonialism whose essence "is that the State which is subject to it is, in theory, independent and has all the outward trappings of international sovereignty. In reality its economic system and thus its political policy is directed from outside" (Nkrumah 1965, ix). It follows that Africapitalist scholars and business leaders need to craft robust measures to tackle the ploys of political elites and foreign powers who have undermined the progress of African people for economic gains since the fifteenth century.

CONCLUSION

This chapter has highlighted, among other things, the philosophy of capitalism and how the idea of Africapitalism originates in the African chiefless states whose creation of social wealth was largely based on the ancient African constitution, age grade, and lineage institutions. The chiefless states marked the highest development of democracy in the world as Africans governed themselves without centralized authorities such as chiefs, kings, presidents, or prime ministers (Williams 1987). The emphasis on social or communal wealth—as opposed to Western-based individualism or private property—in the chiefless states limited widespread poverty. The chapter has also shown how problematic political and socioeconomic institutional arrangements in the postcolonial era have created conducive grounds for poverty and underdevelopment in modern African states. The analysis is in sharp contrast to the prevalent economic-based views such as resource curse, resource scarcity, foreign aid and loans, and GDP that have frequently been discussed as major drivers of poverty and underdevelopment in Africa without reference to Africapitalism (cf. Moyo 2009; Ranis et al. 2000; Costanza et al. 2009; Ross 2012; Rosser 2006). The chapter has also highlighted how the universalization of Africapitalism is important for improving the living conditions of global Africa.

The policy implications include the following: African states need to situate the discussion of development within the context of Africapitalism, drawing on insights from the chiefless African states and the ancient African constitution; African states need to reform political institutions in a way that creates more room for the private sector to help boost the capacity to achieve social wealth; African states must enhance political and socioeconomic partnerships with Africans in the diaspora; and more funding is needed to advance the discussion of Africapitalism.

BIBLIOGRAPHY

Acemoglu, Daron, and James Robinson. (2008). *The Role of Institutions in Growth and Development.* Washington, DC: The World Bank.

Adeosun, A. B., Norafidah, I., and Zengeni, K. T. (2016). "Elites and conflict in Nigeria: A case study of the Niger delta insurgency." *International Journal of Political Science and Development*, 4(8), 301–314.

Aderonke, M., and Awosika, F. O. (2013). "Godfatherism and political conflicts in Nigeria: The fourth republic in perspective." *International Journal of Management and Social Sciences Research*, 2(7), 70–75.

Ake, Claude. (1996). *Democracy and Development in Africa.* Washington, DC: The Brookings Institution.

Albert, I. O. (2005). "'Explaining 'godfatherism' in Nigerian politics." *African Sociological Review*, 9(2), 79–105.

Amaeshi, Kenneth. (2015). "Why Africa needs capitalism that is aligned with its development needs." *The Conversation*, October 20, 2015. https://theconversation.com/why-africa-needs-capitalism-that-is-aligned-with-its-development-needs-48776 (Accessed May 15, 2022).

Amaeshi, Kenneth. (2017). "Africapitalism: A new way of doing business." *The Conversation*, November 9, 2017. https://www.tonyelumelufoundation.org/research-publications/africapitalism-a-new-way-of-doing-business (Accessed May 15, 2022).

Awojobi, O. N. (2014). "Corruption and underdevelopment in Africa: A discourse approach." *International Journal of Economics, Commerce and Management*, 11(10), 1–14.

BBC. (2019). "Letter from Africa: Why Nigeria's internet scammers are 'role models'". September 23, 2019. https://www.bbc.com/news/world-africa-49759392 (Accessed August 6, 2022).

Bjerg, O. (2014). *Making Money: The Philosophy of Crisis Capitalism.* London & New York: Verso.

Breckenridge, K. (2021). "What happened to the theory of African capitalism?" *Economy and Society*, 50(1), 9–35. https://doi.org/10.1080/03085147.2021.1841928.

Buchwalter, A., ed. (2015). *Hegel and Capitalism.* Albany: State University of New York Press.

Burgis, T. (2015). *The Looting Machine: Warlords, Oligarchs, Corporations, Smugglers, and the Theft of Africa's Wealth.* New York: Public Affairs.

Burnell, P., Randall, V., and Rakner, L., eds. (2011). *Politics in the Developing World*, 3rd ed. Oxford: Oxford University Press.

Chiriyankandath, J. (2011). "Colonialism and post-colonial development." In Peter Burnell, Vicky Randall, and Lise Rakner (eds.), *Politics in the Developing World*, 3rd ed. Oxford: Oxford University Press, pp. 36–52.

Clark, D. (1999). *Slaves and Slavery*. Kent: Grange Books.

Collier, P. (2000). "Doing well out of war: An economic perspective." In Mats Berdal and David Malone (eds.), *Greed and Grievance: Economic Agendas in Civil Wars*. Boulder: Lynne Rienner Publishers, pp. 91–111.

Collier, P., Elliott, V. L., Hegre, H., Hoeffler, A., Reynal-Querol, M., and Sambanis, N. (2003). *Breaking the Conflict Trap: Civil War and Development Policy*. Washington, DC: World Bank and Oxford University Press.

Erel, U. (2007). "Racism and anti-racism in Europe: A critical analysis of concepts and frameworks." *Transfer: The European Review of Labour and Research,* 13(3), 359–375.

Esteban, J., Mayoral, L., and Ray, D. (2012). "Ethnicity and conflict: An empirical study." *American Economic Review*, 102(4), 1310–1342.

Esteban, J., and Ray, D. (2011). "Linking conflict to inequality and polarization." *American Economic Review*. 101(4), 1345–1374*l*.

Ghanaweb. (2022). "Achimota forest lands: Sir John's last will exposes government?" May 23, 2022. https://www.ghanaweb.com/GhanaHomePage/NewsArchive/Achimota-Forest-lands-Sir-John-s-last-Will-exposes-government-1544123 (Accessed August 6, 2022).

Gordon, S. (2020). "Why are blacks, other minorities hardest hit by Covid-19?" *USNews*, May 6, 2020. https://www.usnews.com/news/health-news/articles/2020-05-06/why-are-blacks-other-minorities-hardest-hit-by-covid-19 (Accessed August 20, 2020).

Gurr, T. (1968). "A causal model of civil strife: A comparative analysis using new indices." *The American Political Science Review*, 62(4), 1104–1124.

Hobden, S. (2011). "The developing world in the global economy." In Peter Burnell, Vicky Randall, and Lise Rakner (eds.), *Politics in the Developing World*, 3rd ed. Oxford: Oxford University Press, pp. 71–88.

Horowitz, D. L. (1998). "Structure and strategy in ethnic conflict." *Paper Prepared for the Annual World Bank Conference on Development Economics*, Washington, DC, 20–21 April, 1998. http://web.ceu.hu/cps/bluebird/eve/statebuilding/horowitz.pdf (Accessed November 10, 2017).

Ikelegbe, A. (2006a). "Beyond the threshold of civil struggle: Youth militancy and the militia-sation of the resource conflicts in the Niger-Delta region of Nigeria." *African Study Monograph*, 27(3), 87–122.

Ikelegbe, A. (2006b). "The economy of conflict in the oil rich Niger Delta region of Nigeria." *African and Asian Studies*, 5(1), 23–56. https://brill.com/view/journals/aas/5/1/article-p23_2.xml.

Ikelegbe, A., and Onokerhoraye, A. (2016). *The Amnesty for Peace in the Niger Delta: Political Settlement, Transitional Justice and Peace-Building*. Benin City: Centre for Population and Environmental Development (CPED).

Ikelegbe, A., and Umukoro, N. (2016). *The Amnesty Programme and the Resolution of the Niger-Delta Crisis: Progress, Challenges and Prognosis*. Benin City: Centre for Population and Environmental Development (CPED).

Khodabakhshi, A. (2011). "Relationship between GDP and human development indices in India." *International Journal of Trade, Economics and Finance*, 2(3), 251–253.

Kim, N., and Conceição, P. (2010). "The economic crisis, violent conflict, and human development." *International Journal of Peace Studies*, 15(1), 29–43.

Le Van, A. C. (2015). *Dictators and Democracy in African Development: The Political Economy of Good Governance in Nigeria.* New York: Cambridge University Press.

Lovejoy, P. E. (1997). "The African diaspora: Revisionist interpretations of ethnicity, culture and religion under slavery." *Studies in the World History of Slavery, Abolition and Emancipation*, Volume II(p. 11).

Lynch, G. (2011). *I Say to You: Ethnic Politics and the Kalenjin in Kenya.* Chicago: University of Chicago Press.

Maeso, S. R. (2017). "Europe and the narrative of the 'true racist': Thinking anti-discrimination law through race." *COMBAT*, Working paper 01. https://www.ces.uc.pt/ficheiros2/files/COMBAT_Working_paper_01_October_2017.pdf (Accessed July 14, 2020).

Mazrui, A. (1977). *Africa's International Relations: The Diplomacy of Change.* London: Heinemann.

Mba, C. C. (2019). "African philosophy in the age of neoliberal capitalism." *History Compass*, 17, e12524. https://doi.org/10.1111/hic3.12524.

McChesney, R. W. (1999). "Introduction." In N. Chomsky (ed.), *Profit Over People: Neoliberalism and the Global Order.* New York, Toronto, and London: Seven Stories Press, pp. 7–18.

Moyo, D. (2009). *Dead Aid: Why Aid Is Not Working and How There Is a Better Way for Africa.* Vancouver: Douglas & Mcintyre.

Newsome, C. (2011). *Conflict in the Niger-Delta: More Than a Local Affair.* Washington, DC: United States Institute of Peace. https://www.usip.org/sites/default/files/Conflict_Niger_Delta.pdf (Accessed October 10, 2018).

Nkrumah, K. (1965). *Neo-Colonialism: The Last Stage of Imperialism.* London: PANAF.

North, D. C., Wallis, J. J., and Weingast, B. R. (2009). *Violence and Social Orders.* New York: Cambridge University Press.

Nunn, N. (2008). "The long-term effects of Africa's slave trades." *Quarterly Journal of Economics*, 123(1), 139–176.

Nunn, N., and Wantchekon, L. (2011). "The slave trade and the origins of mistrust in Africa." *American Economic Review*, 101(7), 3221–3252.

Nuyen, A. T. (2008). "Chinese philosophy and western capitalism." *Asian Philosophy*, 9(1), 71–79. https://doi.org/10.1080/09552369908575490.

Ohiorhenuan, J. F. E., and Keeler, Z. (2008). "International political economy and African economic development: A survey of issues and research agenda." *Journal of African Economies*, 17(AERC Supplement 1), i140–i239.

Okolie-Osemene, James. (2015). "Oil companies and lethal violence in Nigeria: Patterns, mapping, and evolution (2006–2014)." *IFRA-Nigeria Working Papers Series*, n°44, pp. 1–28.

Philips, N. (2020). "Global political economy." In John Baylis, Steve Smith, and Patricia Owens (eds.), *The Globalization of World Politics*, 8th ed. Oxford: Oxford University Press, p. 257

Pope-Hennessy, J. (1998). *Sins of the Fathers: A Study of the Atlantic Slave Traders 1441–1807.* Barnes & Noble Books.

Ranis, G., Stewart, F., and Ramirez, A. (2000). "Economic growth and human development." *World Development*, 28(2), 197–219.

Rodney, W. (1972). *How Europe Underdeveloped Africa.* Dar-es-Salaam: Tanzania Publishing House.

Rodrik, D. (1999). "Where did all the growth go? External shocks, social conflict, and growth collapses." *Journal of Economic Growth*, 4, 385–412. https://link.springer.com/article/10.1023/A:1009863208706 (Accessed April 20, 2019).

Ross, M. L. (2012). *The Oil Curse: How Petroleum Wealth Shapes the Development of Nations.* Princeton: Princeton University Press.

Rosser, A. (2006). *The Political Economy of the Resource Curse: A Literature Survey.* Brighton: IDS Working Paper 268. https://www.ids.ac.uk/files/WP268.pdf (Accessed December 29, 2017).

Scarritt, J. R. (2011). "Ethnopolitics and nationalism." In Peter Burnell, Vicky Randall, and Lise Rakner (eds.), *Politics in the Developing World*, 3rd ed. Oxford: Oxford University Press, pp. 127–144.

Shepperson, George, and St. Clare Drake (2008). "The fifth pan-African conference, 1945 and the all African peoples congress, 1958." *Contributions in Black Studies*, 8(5). https://scholarworks.umass.edu/cibs/vol8/iss1/5 (Accessed July 21, 2022).

Soremekun, K. (2011). "Nigeria's oil diplomacy and the management of the Niger Delta crisis." In Cyril Obi and Siri Aas Rustad (eds.), *Oil and Insurgency in the Niger-Delta: Managing the Complex Politics of Petro-Violence.* London and New York: Zed Books, pp. 99–114.

UNCTAD. (2020). *Tackling Illicit Financial Flows for Sustainable Development in Africa.* Geneva: United Nations. https://unctad.org/system/files/official-document/aldcafrica2020_en.pdf (Accessed August 3, 2022).

Van der Geest, S. (1997). "Money and respect: The changing value of old age in Rural Ghana." *Journal of the International African Institute*, 67(4), 534–559. https://www.jstor.org/stable/1161107 (Accessed August 6, 2022).

Williams, C. (1987). *The Destruction of Black Civilization: Great Issues of a Race from 4500 B.C. to 2000 A.D.* Chicago: Third World Press.

Wired. (2020). "Why coronavirus hit people from BAME communities so hard." August 22, 2020. https://www.wired.co.uk/article/bame-communities-coronavirus-uk (Accessed August 12, 2020).

Chapter 5

Africapitalism and the Moral Implications of African Governments' Abnegation of Responsibilities

Frank Aragbonfoh Abumere

Africans have been attempting (sometimes successfully and at other times unsuccessfully) to create original or authentic African social, economic, and political philosophies, theories, or doctrines. Notable successes include Kwame Nkrumah's (1970) consciencism, Julius Nyerere's (1958) *ujamaa*, Kenneth Kaunda's (1963) humanism, and Leopold Sedar Senghor's (1990) *negritude*. Following in the footsteps of those who propounded the aforementioned social, economic, and political philosophies, theories, or doctrines, is it possible to replicate their success in contemporary Africa?

There are attempts in different spheres to create contemporary original or authentic African social, economic, and political philosophies. One of such spheres is business, and one of such attempts is Africapitalism. Africapitalism is one of the most recent attempts (if not the most recent attempt) to replicate such success. Arguably, Africapitalism, although a recent African economic philosophy, seems to be gaining popularity. This is because, on the one hand, Africapitalism seems to resonate with the aforementioned social, economic, and political philosophies, theories, or doctrines, and on the other hand, in the vein of those philosophies, Africapitalism is concerned with the welfare and flourishing of the African person and her/his society.

I think Africapitalism (as seen in its principles which I shall discuss in the next section) is simultaneously predicated on the fact that there is a failure of governments to perform their moral responsibility for economic development and a reflection of what it means to rectify the consequences of such abnegation of responsibility. Therefore, in this chapter, I shall not rehash the debate on what it means to have an original or authentic African social, economic, and political philosophy or whether Africapitalism is an authentic African economic philosophy (after all, the most important and relevant aspects of such debate have been dealt with by some of the previous chapters). Rather, my aim is to show how the failure of governments to perform their moral responsibility for economic development leads to a morally, socially, economically, and politically undesirable condition in Africa and what moral implications this has for the private sector in view of the tenets of Africapitalism. As already alluded to, it is such failure of government Africapitalism seeks to rectify and it is such morally, socially, economically, and politically undesirable condition that Africapitalism seeks to ameliorate through its principles. To contextualize this discussion, I shall focus on Nigeria and its infamous resource curse—Nigeria is notoriously plagued by resource curse.

I divide the discussion into five sections: The first section is this introduction and the sixth section is the conclusion. In the second section, I briefly present Africapitalism and its principles. In the third section, I present an overview of the resource curse in Nigeria with a focus on rent-seeking behavior. In the fourth section, I explain the compound nature of Nigeria's resource curse and how the Nigerian moral economy is characterized by patron-client relations. In sum, in the third and fourth sections, I present the Nigerian condition from which the problem of whether the private sector ought to or ought not to play a leading role in the development of the country emanates. In the fifth section, which is the conclusion, I explain the moral implications the compounded Nigerian resource curse has for the private sector in view of the tenets of Africapitalism.

AFRICAPITALISM AND ITS PRINCIPLES

Africapitalism, Tony Elumelu's African economic philosophy, "is predicated on the belief that Africa's private sector can and must play a leading role in the continent's development" (The Tony Elumelu Foundation 2019, s.p.). According to The Tony Elumelu Foundation, "Africapitalism means we cannot leave the business of development up to our governments, donor countries, and philanthropic organizations alone. The private sector must be involved in the business of development" (ibid.). In other words, the economic philosophy

> is a call-to-action for businesses to make decisions that will increase economic and social wealth, and promote development in the communities and nations in which they operate. Such a decision will ultimately help businesses become more profitable as the communities they serve become well-off consumers, healthy and better-educated employees, and even entrepreneurs who go on to become suppliers and service providers. (Ibid.)

The principles of Africapitalism, as The Tony Elumelu Foundation explains, include entrepreneurship, long-term investments, strategic sectors, development dividend, value-added growth, regional connectivity, multigenerational development, and shared purpose (ibid.). The first principle, entrepreneurship, is concerned with unlocking "the power of individuals to create and grow their business ideas into successful companies" (ibid.). The second principle, long-term investments, is concerned with deploying "patient capital that creates greater and broader economic value as opposed to merely the extraction of resources" (ibid.). In the same vein, the third principle, strategic sectors, is concerned with investing "in sectors delivering a financial return as well as broader economic and social value—agriculture, power, healthcare, and finance" (ibid.). While the fourth principle, development dividend, is concerned with conducting "investments and business activity in a manner that delivers financial returns to shareholders as well as economic and social benefit to stakeholders" (ibid.).

Furthermore, the fifth principle, value-added growth, seeks to "leverage locally available human and financial capital, raw material and other inputs that create longer, more integrated, and higher value regional supply chains" (ibid.). Following suit, the sixth principle, regional connectivity, seeks to "facilitate intra-regional commerce and trade through the development of national and cross-border physical infrastructure, and the harmonization of policies and practices" (ibid.). While the seventh principle, multigenerational development, argues for a "focus on investments and economic growth strategies that build value for future generations" (ibid.). Then the eighth and final principle, shared purpose, argues for fostering "collaboration between businesses, investors, governments, academia, civil society, philanthropists, and development institutions to create conditions that will empower the African private sector to thrive" (ibid.).

AN OVERVIEW OF THE RESOURCE CURSE IN NIGERIA

As already mentioned in the penultimate section and as alluded to in the preceding section, Africapitalism is partly predicated on the fact that there is a failure of governments to perform their moral responsibility for economic development and partly predicated on a reflection of what it means to rectify the consequences of such abnegation of responsibility. Such failure and its consequences are evident in Nigeria, especially when one looks at Nigeria's infamous resource curse.

In development economics, Richard Auty (1993) famously used the term "resource curse" to explain a paradoxical condition in which some natural resource-rich countries are economically poor because they are natural resource-rich. The curse does not afflict every natural resource-rich country; Australia, Botswana, Canada, Norway, United Kingdom, and the United States, for example, are natural resource-rich but do not seem to be plagued by either underdevelopment or poor governance. However, a body of influential econometric works by some notable development economists corroborates Auty's resource curse thesis. A few examples of such works suffice to support the validity of the thesis.

Jeffery Sachs and Andrew Warner (1995) showed that from 1970 to 1989, the average growth rate of many resource-rich countries was about 1% slower than the growth rate of non-resource-rich countries. Moreover, Paolo Mauro (1995) and Carlos Leite and Jens Weidmann (1999) showed that resource-rich countries are prone to corruption. Furthermore, Leonard Wantchekon (1999) showed that "a one percent increase in resource dependence as measured by the ratio of primary exports to GDP" results in an almost 8% increment in the possibility of dictatorship (p. 2). In addition, Paul Collier and Anke Hoeffler (1998) showed that resource-rich countries, compared to non-resource-rich countries, are more prone to civil conflicts. While Michael L. Ross (2003) linked resource wealth to an exacerbation of poor governance in contexts where there is a centralization of power.

The above afflictions are caused, or at least engendered, by rent-seeking behavior. Succinctly, rent-seeking behavior refers to the acquisition of economic rent through the utilization of political means. While economic rent refers to the variation between the total costs of producing a good, service, or both and the total price of the good, service, or both. Specifically, economic rent in extractive industry refers to the "the difference between the value of production and the cost to extract it. The extraction cost consists of normal exploration, development, and operating costs as well as a share of profits for the industry" (Humphreys, Sachs, and Stiglitz 2007, 379–380).

Rent-seeking behavior abounds in resource-cursed countries because

> the value of natural resources usually far outweighs the cost of their extraction, therefore anyone who is able to secure the license to exploit the resources is automatically in a lucrative business. For this reason, there is usually a scramble for exploration of natural resources, which often leads to negative political and economic consequences in resource-rich countries. In other words, a gap known as economic *rent* exists between the value of that resource and the cost of extracting it. In such cases, individuals, private sectors or politicians, have incentives to use political mechanisms to capture these rents. (Abumere 2021, 41) (emphasis in original)

Moreover, Tornell and Lane (1999) have shown the susceptibility of resource-rich countries to rent-seeking behavior. While Ricky Lam and Leonard Wantchekon (1999) have highlighted how "a one percent increase in the size of the natural resource sector generates a decrease by half a percentage point in the probability of survival of democratic regimes," and this is the case due to "elite discretion over the process of rent distribution" (35–36). Rent-seeking behavior is especially prominent in Nigeria because unbridled avenues exploited by political elites and multinational corporations make complex and exacerbate the negative political and economic consequences of natural resource endowment (Humphreys et al. 2007, 4).

In the case of Nigeria, the problem of resource curse is multifaceted and complex. As Ross (2003) succinctly puts it, "there are five ways that mineral wealth can hurt the poor: by causing economic volatility; by crowding out the manufacturing and agriculture sectors; by heightening inequality; by inducing violent conflict; and by undermining democracy. . . . Since Nigeria is remarkably dependent on oil, it has been highly susceptible to these tribulations" (4). These "tribulations" become even more alarming when we realize that Nigeria "has annually received over half of its revenues—sometimes as much as 85 percent—directly from the oil sector" (Ross 2003, 2). In short, historically "Nigeria has grown extraordinarily dependent on oil exports: in 2000, 99.7 percent of its export income came from oil, making it the most oil-dependent country in the world" (Ross 2003, 9).

The aforementioned tribulations have caused Nigeria to be a rentier state, that is, "a state suffering the rentier effect, a socially undesirable, economically and politically harmful situation in which governments use large revenues accruing from the sales of natural resources to pacify pressure and opposition, evade accountability and abstain from institutional reform" (Abumere 2021, 53). This is what makes it possible for the Nigerian government to distribute a large portion of its budget as patronage (Ross 2003, 4).

After all, since most of the population is poor, patronage becomes the order of the day. In 2010, the proportion of those living below the poverty line rose to 69% and has not gone lower since then. Consequently, Nigeria has the highest number of poor people in the world. In search of what will alleviate, or even totally eradicate, their poverty, the very poor population in Nigeria widely accepts a moral economy that is characterized by patron-client relations. In the next section, I will explain how this acceptance of patron-client relations has compounded the resource curse in Nigeria.

NIGERIA'S COMPOUNDED RESOURCE CURSE

On the one hand, patron-client relations are

> a special case of dyadic . . . ties involving a largely instrumental friendship in which an individual of higher socio-economic status [patron] uses his own influence and resources to provide protection or benefits or both for a person of

> lower status [client] who, for his part, reciprocates by offering general support and assistance, including personal services to the patron. (Scott 1972, 92)

On the other hand, moral economy (Thompson 1971) has to do with what is acceptable/unacceptable as reasonable/unreasonable behavior in a given economic relationship. It entails the activities persons in such relationship are expected to perform in their economic sphere. Furthermore, a "moral economic activity occurs in and helps to reproduce relationships in which the transactors have become obligated to each other because of their past transactions. This means that such activity is motivated to a significant degree by the relationship in which it occurs" (Carrier 2018, 30). For instance, politicians (patrons) provide material assistance—legally or illegally, and ethically or unethically—for electorates (clients) in certain constituencies. In return, the politicians expect that the electorates will vote for them. Alternatively, the electorates (clients) in certain constituencies vote for some politicians (patrons) and in return expect that they will get some material assistance from the politicians in the future.

Contrary to the above description of the Nigerian condition, Eric Budd (2004) classifies Nigeria as a highly (neo)patrimonial state. However, I think Budd is wrong for the following reasons. The concept of neopatrimonialism is a derivative of Max Weber's (1947 [1922]) concept of patrimony—which was first introduced by Carl Ludwig von Haller (Roth 1978)—and which does not necessarily have negative denotation and connotations. As Pitcher, Moran, and Johnston say:

> Current uses of the terms patrimonial and neopatrimonial in the context of Africa are conceptually problematical and amount to a serious misreading of Weber. His use of the term patrimonial delineated a legitimate type of authority, not a type of regime, and included notions of reciprocity and voluntary compliance between rulers and the ruled. Those reciprocities enabled subjects to check the actions of rulers, which most analyses of (neo)patrimonialism overlook. (2009, 125)

Perhaps we can talk about a certain degree of (neo)patrimonialism in Nigeria to the extent that we see what exists in Nigeria as a hybrid regime in which patrimony and rational-legal bureaucracy are intertwined (Van de Walle 2001; Erdmann and Engel 2007, 104). In this case, while the rational-legal bureaucracy expects one thing of leaders, the people expect another thing of them. On the one hand, the operating political logic of the rational-legal bureaucracy is adherence to constitutionalism, the rule of law, and due process. On the other hand, the operating political logic of the people is that their parochial interests are met by the leaders. Because what the people expect of their leaders is not what the rational-legal bureaucracy expects of the leaders, the leaders are nevertheless deemed legitimate by the people even when the leaders do not abide by the rules of the rational-legal bureaucracy.

In the case of Nigeria, to satisfy the parochial interests of the people, the leaders will need resources: the more resources the leaders have, the more they are able to satisfy the parochial interests of the people and the more the people deem the leaders legitimate. Since the resources the leaders are diverting to satisfy the interests of their people are national resources, the leaders actually become even more corrupt and rent-seeking in the quest to satisfy their people's parochial interests. In this case, leaders cannot be seen to have stolen too much and to have not shared with the right people or to have shared with the wrong people. Consequently, patronage is seen as moral and thus encouraged, and this leads people to often accept patron-client relations. No wonder in the Nigerian system, where there is already no properly functioning rational-legal bureaucracy, the more natural resources the country is able to extract, the more rent-seeking behavior increases and the more bad governance increases. Simply put, in the Nigerian system, rather than alleviating bad governance, natural resources exacerbate it.

In the current policy framework to resolve the problem of resource curse in Nigeria, transparency and accountability prevail as the remedies. Such remedies have been codified mostly as principles and requirements of the Nigerian Extractive Industries Transparency Initiative (NEITI). Nigeria joined the Extractive Industries Transparency Initiative (EITI) in 2007. "The Nigerian Extractive Industries Transparency Initiative Act 2007 mandates NEITI to promote due process and transparency in extractive revenues paid to and received by government as well ensure transparency and accountability in the application of extractive revenues" (NEITI, n.d., s.p.). In the February 27, 2019 EITI report, the EITI states that Nigeria "became the first Anglophone African country to have made satisfactory progress in implementing all the requirements of the EITI Standard. It now faces the challenge of entrenching this transparency in routine government and company systems" (EITI n.d., s.p.).

The report grades countries' progress from worst to best in the following order: no progress; adequate progress; meaningful progress; satisfactory progress; and beyond. In the report, Nigeria's scorecard shows an overall score of satisfactory in all categories. The categories include multistakeholder group oversight, licenses and contracts, monitoring production, revenue collection, revenue allocation, socioeconomic contribution, and outcomes and impact. However, the report does not amount to success because current reality contradicts the report. For instance, in the 2019 Transparency International's Corruption Perception Index, Nigeria was ranked 146th least corrupt country among 180 countries. In terms of "the perceived level of public sector corruption on a scale of 0 (highly corrupt) to 100 (very clean)," Nigeria scored 26 (Transparency International n.d., s.p.).

A major reason why the EITI/NEITI framework has not worked very well is its failure to recognize that the Nigerian population has widely accepted a moral economy of patron-client relations, which in turn compounds and exacerbates an already bad situation. This does not mean that the moral economy is wholly accepted. Nevertheless, what it means is that the moral economy has become dominant or pervasive. Consequently, any attempt to resolve the resource curse problem must take into consideration the compound nature of the problem. The EITI/NEITI framework has not worked very well because it fails to recognize that although patron-client relations are not encoded in legal rights, they are grounded in (Pitcher et al. 2009, 139), as Weber (1922 [1978]) says, "the subjects' claim to reciprocity, and this claim 'naturally' acquires social recognition as custom" (1010) (emphasis in original).

In other words, the existing legal and policy framework fails to recognize that patron-client relations are "institutionalised and grounded in *rules* that are broadly shared and understood but not, or not sufficiently, codified in law" (Pitcher et al. 2009, 139) (emphasis added). The rules are a function of poor political economy structures, institutions, and norms. Among other things, having low trust in government is one of the consequences of poor political economy structures, institutions, and norms. For instance, in Nigeria, the failure of the private sector to perform its corporate social responsibilities, and the urgency of picking up the slack and playing a leading role in development, as advocated by Africapitalism, is symptomatic of this low trust. In the next section, I will explain the problem of picking up the slack and playing a leading role in development.

THE MORAL IMPLICATIONS FOR THE PRIVATE SECTOR

The compounded resource curse problem described above has "pick up the slack" ethical implications for the private sector when Africapitalism is applied to it. One of the pick up the slack ethical implications of the compounded resource curse is the question of the role of the private sector in the development of the country, particularly whether the private sector ought to or ought not to play a leading role in development. Africapitalism (as evident in the second section) clearly thinks that the private sector ought to play a leading role in development of the country. Ceteris paribus, that is, if African governments do not abnegate their moral responsibility for economic development, then there will be no slack for the private sector to pick up. However, as we know, all things are rarely equal, and in Africa all things are not equal.

Nigeria is one of the countries where there is certainly a lot of slack to pick up. Among other factors, one chief factor for such condition is the resource curse.

In view of what Africapitalism is and in view of the stipulations of its principles, when applied to the compounded problem of resource curse in Nigeria, the economic philosophy evidently demands that the private sector should pick up the slack. This does not mean that Africapitalism encourages African governments to abnegate their role in development nor does it mean that it thinks such abnegation is morally acceptable. Moreover, Elumelu says government should only be concerned with "capacitising the private sector . . . [and] creating the right environment for a new crop of entrepreneurs to emerge" (qtd. in Edwards 2013, s.p.) because entrepreneurship is "the cornerstone to African development" (ibid.).

It is not contentious to claim that governments ought to create an enabling environment for the emergence of entrepreneurs. But it is contentious to claim that entrepreneurship is the cornerstone of African development. Whether you agree or disagree with the latter claim, and whether you think the claim is totally correct, partly correct, partly wrong, or totally wrong depends on the economic theory you subscribe to, capitalism, socialism, mixed economy, and so on.

On the one hand, if we understand Africapitalism, as Elumelu does, to be "the middle ground between business and philanthropy" (qtd. in Rosenkranz 2014, s.p.), then what the economic philosophy requires of the private sector will neither be considered to be too morally demanding nor be seen to be essentially different from corporate social responsibility. On the other hand, to claim that the private sector ought to pick up the slack when governments abnegate their moral responsibility for economic development seems too morally demanding and to be essentially different from corporate social responsibility.

Again, on the one hand, Joe Biden seems to have understood Africapitalism in the above first sense when, in support of the economic philosophy, he says, it is aimed at "creating an entire climate in which innovation and ideas flourish" (qtd. in Elumelu 2014, s.p.). On the other hand, Joel Bakan seems to have understood Africapitalism in the above second sense when, in opposition to the economic philosophy, he says, it "places profound limits on the ability to do good," it distorts "the public's relation with" the private sector "and how to deal with" the private sector "politically" (qtd. in Edwards 2013, s.p.). These opposing conceptions of the denotation and opposing perceptions of the connotations of Africapitalism are a clear indication that there is no consensus or canonical agreement on whether, when the government abnegates its moral responsibility for development, the private sector ought to or ought not to pick up the slack.

Whether we understand Africapitalism in the above first sense as Biden does or second sense as Bakan does, the economic philosophy clearly thinks that the private sector has (moral) agency and such agency ought to be exercised for the development of the African continent. As Elumelu says, "The future we all want for ourselves is one of our own making" (qtd in The Tony Elumelu Foundation 2019, s.p.).

CONCLUSION

To recapitulate the foregoing discussion, I explained that Nigeria's compounded resource curse problem has a particular moral implication for private sectors in Nigeria. To decipher what such particular moral implication is, we must remember the following. First, the two major problems associated with resource curse are the Dutch disease and rent-seeking behavior. Second, at both the micro and macro levels, there are domestic and external (international or global) actors/factors involved in the Nigerian resource curse. The Dutch disease and rent-seeking behavior and both the domestic and international or global sides of the problem must be resolved in order to have a holistic resolution to the Nigerian resource curse. Nevertheless, resolving rent-seeking behavior and the domestic side of the problem will at least alleviate the negative consequences of the problem.

Third, principles and requirements, notably transparency and accountability, of the current policy framework to resolve rent-seeking behavior and the domestic side of the problem are codified mostly in the NEITI. However, this framework has not worked very well. A major reason why the framework has not worked very well is its failure to recognize that the Nigerian population has widely accepted a moral economy of patron-client relations, which in turn compounds and exacerbates an already bad situation. This does not mean that the moral economy is wholly accepted. Nevertheless, what it means is that the moral economy has become dominant or pervasive. Consequently, any attempt to resolve the resource curse problem must take into consideration the compound nature of the problem.

So, my aim in discussing the "pick up the slack" ethical implication of Nigeria's compounded resource curse is to show what Africapitalism requires of the private sector in that situation. In other words, in view of the abnegation of responsibility by the government, should the private sector play a leading role in the development of the country? Applying Africapitalism to the ethical problem, I show that the economic philosophy answers in the affirmative. Nevertheless, there is no consensus or canonical agreement on whether the private sector ought to or ought not to play a leading role in the development of the country.

BIBLIOGRAPHY

Abumere, Frank Aragbonfoh. 2021. *Global Justice and Resource Curse: Combining Statism and Cosmopolitanism.* London: Routledge.

Auty, Richard M. 1993. *Sustaining Development in Mineral Economies: The Resource Curse Thesis.* London: Routledge.

Carrier, James G. 2018. "Moral Economy: What's in a Name?" *Anthropological Theory*, 18(1), pp. 18–35. https://doi.org/10.1177/1463499617735259.

Collier, Paul, and Anne Hoeffler. 1998. "On Economic Causes of Civil War." *Oxford Economic Papers*, 50, pp. 563–573. https://doi.org/10.1093/oep/50.4.563.

Edwards, R. 2013. "Can Africapitalism Save the Continent?" *The Guardian*, July 12.

Elumelu, Tony. 2014. "The Rise of Africapitalism." *The Economist*, November 13.

Erdmann, G., and U. Engel. 2007. "Neopatrimonialism Reconsidered: Critical Review and Elaboration of an Elusive Concept." *Commonwealth and Comparative Politics*, 45(1), pp. 95–119. https://doi.org/10.1080/14662040601135813.

Extractive Industries Transparency Initiative (EITI). Nigeria. (n.d.). https://eiti.org/nigeria#nigerias-progress-by-requirement.

Humphreys, Macartan, Jeffery D. Sachs, and Joseph E. Stiglitz. 2007. *Escaping the Resource Curse.* New York: Columbia University Press.

Kaunda, Kaunda. 1963. *Zambia Shall Be Free: An Autobiography.* New York: Frederick A. Praeger.

Lam, R., and Leonard Wantchekon. 1999. "Dictatorship as a Political Dutch Disease." Working Paper, Centre Discussion Paper 795, Economic Growth Centre, Yale University, New Haven, United States of America. http://econpapers.hhs.se/paper/wopyalegr/.

Leite, C., and J. Weidmann. 1999. "Does Mother Nature Corrupt? Natural Resources, Corruption and Economic Growth." IMF Working Paper WP/99/85, Washington DC, United States of America.

Mauro, P. 1995. "Corruption and Growth." *Quarterly Journal of Economics*, 90, pp. 681–712. https://doi.org/10.2307/2946696.

McConnell, C. R., S. L. Brue, and S. M. Flynn. 2009. *Economics: Principles, Problems, and Policies.* New York: McGraw-Hill/Irwin.

Nigerian Extractive Industries Transparency Initiative (NEITI). (n.d.) www.neiti.org.ng.

Nkrumah, Kwame. 1970. *Consciencism: Philosophy and Ideology for Decolonization and Development with Particular Reference to the African Revolution.* New York: Monthly Review Press.

Nyerere, Julius. 1968. *Ujamaa: Essays on Socialism.* Oxford: Oxford University Press.

Pitcher, Anne, M. J. Moran, and M. Johnston. 2009. "Rethinking Patrimonialism and Neopatrimonialism in Africa." *African Studies Review*, 52(1), pp. 125–156. https://doi.org/10.1353/arw.0.0163.

Rosenkranz, R. 2014. "Tony Elumelu's New Africapitalism." *Devex*, January 6. https://www.devex.com/news/tony-elumelu-s-new-africapitalism-82590.

Ross, Michael L. 2003. "Nigeria's Oil Sector and the Poor." Paper Prepared for the UK Department for International Development (DFID)'s "Nigeria: Drivers of Change" Programme. http://www.michaelross.info/papers/other/NigeriaOil.pdf.

Roth, G. 1978. "Introduction." In Max Weber (ed.), *Economy and Society: An Outline of Interpretive Sociology* (pp. xxxiii–cx). Berkeley: University of California Press.

Sachs, Jeffery D., and A. M. Warner. 1995. "Natural Resource Abundance and Economic Growth." NBER Working Paper Series, Working Paper 5398, National Bureau of Economic Research, Cambridge, MA, United States of America. https://www.nber.org/papers/w5398.

Scott, James C. 1972. "Patron-Client Politics and Political Change in Southeast Asia." *The American Political Science Review*, 66(1), pp. 91–113. https://doi.org/10.2307/1959280.

Senghor, Sedar Leopold. 1993. "Négritude: A Humanism of the Twentieth Century." In P. Williams and L. Chrisman (eds.), *Colonial Discourse and Post-Colonial Theory* (pp. 27–35). London: Longman.

The Tony Elumelu Foundation. 2019. "What Is Africapitalism." June 24. https://www.tonyelumelufoundation.org/news/what-is-africapitalism.

Thompson, E. P. 1971. "The Moral Economy of the English Crowd in the Eighteenth Century." *Past and Present*, 50(1), pp. 76–136. https://doi.org/10.1093/past/50.1.76.

Tornell, A., and P. R. Lane. 1999. "The Voracity Effect." *American Economic Review*, 89(1), pp. 22–46. https://doi.org/10.1257/aer.89.1.22.

Transparency International. (n.d.). "Our Work in Nigeria." https://www.transparency.org/en/countries/nigeria#.

Wantchekon, Leonard. 1992. "Why Do Resource Dependent Countries have Authoritarian Governments?" Working Paper, Yale University, New Haven, United States of America. www.yale.edu/leitner/pdf/1999-11.pdf.

Van de Walle, N. 2001. *African Economies and the Politics of Permanent Crisis, 1979–1999*. Cambridge: Cambridge University Press.

Weber, Max. 1947 [1922]. *The Theory of Social and Economic Organization* (A. M. Henderson, Trans. & T. Parsons, eds.). Talcott Parsons. London: The Free Press.

Weber, Max. 1978 [1922]. *Economy and Society: An Outline of Interpretive Sociology* (Vols. 1 & 2) (G. Roth & C. Wittich, eds.). Berkeley: University of California Press.

Part II

ON DEVELOPMENT

Chapter 6

Import Substitution Industrialization (ISI) as an Economic Philosophy Model for Africa

Emerson Abraham Jackson

To digress into the concept of ISI, it is necessary that an understanding is built around the philosophical doctrine of Afrocentrism, which is understandably a movement geared toward the self-empowerment of people of color and particularly in this regard, championing economic growth and prosperity in the African continent. The motivation to address policies geared toward capacitating the continent's long hope of economic growth and prosperity requires a deep understanding of the history of what makes Africa what it is, particularly in terms of its lagged state of development when compared to other thriving continents like Asia and Latin America.

Africa, for a long time in history, has been blighted by its endowed prospect for economic growth and prosperity, given the influence of Western hegemony (otherwise referred to as Eurocentricism) on the mind-set of people in the continent, which eventually resulted in the destruction of cultural identities on account of their pursued goal of mobilizing people from mainland Africa to work as slaves in the newfound land, which is now the United States of America (Warburton, 2005). As scholars of Kwame Nkrumah's movement explained, the continent was going through its style of development pathway until the arrival of the Europeans, who eventually masterminded the collapse of essential values to suit their own Westernized ways of thinking and doing things (Chawane, 2016).

Afrocentrism requires knowledge about brutality and the narcissistic destruction inflicted by the Europeans on Africans, both in Africa and the United States. As emphasized by Chitonge (2015) in his book *Economic Growth and Development in Africa: Understanding Trends and Perspectives*, the hegemonic tendencies and fabrications engineered by the voyagers in the African continent are a complete vicious ploy, involving mythical stories to derail the continent's hope of making strides in its peculiar way toward development. Notable citations of such mythical and inhumane destructions include fifteenth- and eighteenth-century fabrications that "the African continent held people with one leg, three faces, and heads of lions" (cited in Fredland, 2001: 26), and also that the continent is "inhabited by men with their mouths in their stomachs" (Chitonge, 2015: 1), respectively. With these in mind, there is certainly a need for Africans, both in the mainland continent and the diaspora, to take a stance on how best to define their identity, which would certainly serve as a way of instituting policies that make it possible for the continent to realize God's given gift of resource abundance.

With the above preface in mind on the struggles of Africans, the concept of Afrocentrism can now be defined and illustrated to make it worthwhile for knowledge acquisition to be explored widely about the continent and its people. The origin of Afrocentric philosophy cannot be proven precisely, but scholarly works have attested it to some period around 1954; this is said to be linked with a work about Marcus Garvey, who was seen as the most influential propagator for people of African descent to unify their efforts in extricating the continuous psychological torture inflicted by their colonial masters (Chawane, 2016).

The term Afrocentricity as expressly illustrated by the founding father, Molefi K. Asante (2001), is construed as an "exercise in knowledge acquisition and a new historical perspective" (Chawane, 2016: 79). Equally, Early et al. (1994) also provide an extended definition of the concept of Afrocentricity, which is construed as an "*i*ntellectual movement, a political view, and/or a historical evolution that stresses the culture and achievements of Africans." Such a movement or philosophical evolution in the area of knowledge empowerment sits well with the vision of Kwame Nkrumah (1963: 5), who was a one-time popular leader in the Gold Coast kingdom of Ghana and the continent as a whole. He worked hard at educating people in the continent about not giving in to the destruction of Eurocentric hegemony, which was intent on destroying the historical values of Africa and its cultural heritage.

A movement, which started in the Temple University School of Scholars (popularly referred to as the "*Temple Circle*") in the 1970s and continued into the 1980s by the intellectual doctrine of Asante, could be construed as a complete ethical behavior (Chawane, 2016: 78). This is also linked with the Pan-Africanist movements of "Black Power in the 1960s and Black is Beautiful in the 1970s" (Early et al., 1994). On that note, Afrocentricity can be viewed as a pioneering venture of educating African descents (both in the mainland and the diaspora) about its model of pursued intellectual methodology, theoretical and ideological approaches to unify black communities concerning their rich cultural heritage (Chukwuokolo, 2009). To dissect the aforementioned statement, the methodological venture is based on a motive of providing a firm basis for affirming the intention for a new nomenclature ascribed as Afrocentricity—this is purely rooted in the struggles of Africans under the guise of colonization. Equally, the pursued theoretical proposition is modeled on the philosophy of ethical consciousness, which affirms the need for a pursued identity of Africanism, also encapsulated in interdisciplinary teachings in universities about African history and culture.

CRITICAL VIEWPOINT OF THE AFROCENTRIC MOVEMENT

To many of its opponents, particularly nonblacks/whites, the Afrocentric approach was construed as a hostile and antithetical movement bent on destroying society's efforts. On a similar note, there is also the alluring view that such a philosophical propagation was also pursued as a means of criticizing the populist Eurocentric approach, when in fact the Afrocentric movement was based on championing resilience, with new hope for blacks to create space for championing constructive criticisms (Jackson II, 2003). Equally, there were also concerns among blacks who believed that Afrocentrism is a concept that predominated views of Afro-Americans or African Americans as it is popularly referred to by many, given that the idea originated from the United States of America. Such a claim to disregard the philosophical vision of the Afrocentric movement is thought to be left with little or no firm basis of evidence, given that the focus is intertwined on the tenet of oppression faced by Africans, both in the mainland and the newfound economy, which is the United States. The affirmation of such a unified project on which Afrocentrism rests could also be attested in the words of a popular activist by the name of Du Bois as emphasized by Asante (n/d), who spoke of himself as a son of Africa and therefore, reiterated his call for Africans from everywhere (including the United States, Ethiopia, Egypt) to connect their intellectual prowess and efforts with those in the mainland.

Critiques continued to be resounded, even from within the black community; notable of these include points about the variety of dialects that constitute the African community and power play, with allegations of politicians disguising as academics, and so on. Such critical views were treated with no ill feelings, given the fact that the Afrocentric movement is continuously engineering the means of addressing intellectual and thought-provoking views about the way forward that concern knowledge acquisition about Africa and the history of black struggles (Lefkowitz, 1997: 3, as excerpted in Chawane, 2016; Elson, 1996). The smearing campaign from Eurocentrists about Afrocentric philosophy being modeled on aggression was refuted by pro-activists, when the whole intention is to continue their propagation about black struggles under colonialism and the blighted truth that connects their origin or history with mainland Africa.

In view of allaying fears about the dismal thinking or objection of Eurocentric enchantment of Afrocentrism, the philosophical dictum of Afrocentric movement is simply based on a counterforcement of intellectual principles that is based on educating blacks and people of African descent about their history (Stikkers, 2008), which to a great extent was almost destroyed by the Europeans. On a positive note and particularly to those of its opponents, Afrocentric philosophy is not necessarily dismal of Eurocentric philosophy, despite the Europeans conceiving their practices as the best, with nothing else comparable to their rancorous campaigns. Notably, some responses, according to Chawane (2016: 97), have classified opponents of Afrocentric philosophy into three categories, namely: (i) "Capitulationists (the uncomfortable beings who considered Africans to be agents), (ii) Europeanised Loyalists (fervent believers in the view that blacks are not good at anything while being immersed in their knowledge of what is being taught by the oppressors), and (iii) Maskers (those that are afraid of being overtly Afrocentric because of being in constant fear of losing their jobs or anything that is considered alien to the oppressors)."

Based on the affirmative thinking about Afrocentric ideology by many of its followers, which seeks to empower the minds of Africans (both in the diaspora and mainland African continent), there is a need to embrace the effort of a new philosophy, which is geared to freeing up the subjected mentality of the oppressed. This notably is inclusive of anything to do with the development of knowledge in support of black empowerment—a notable highlight in this line of the non-acknowledgment of black contribution to knowledge is associated with Mathematics and Geometry, which started in ancient Egypt as confirmed by acclaimed scholars like Aristotle and many of his compatriots (Chawane, 2016). This is not necessarily a campaign to isolate blacks, more so from the rest of the world, but one that makes it possible to empower people in mainland Africa. This could also be interpreted as an opportunity to rebrand SSA's failed attempt of embracing ISI ideology (Jackson and Jabbie, 2020), which is thought to embrace the means of self-empowerment on the pathway of growth and development for those in the continent and its heritage (incorporating the inhabitants and diasporas far afield).

THE ASCRIBED NOTION OF ISI

Having addressed the concept of Afrocentrism, both in terms of its origin and critical viewpoint that pervade its philosophical movement, this section is geared toward providing a background on the notion of ISI. Based on published literatures, the concept seems to have carved its origin from the 1930s (notably, in regions around Latin America some parts of Asia and Africa) to capacitate self-empowerment of nations to address basic needs, without having to rely on external support for the sustained existence of lives (Jackson and Jabbie, forthcoming). There are a plethora of definitions that have been constructed to address the concept of ISI. In this chapter, the concept has drawn on two main definitions as cited in Jackson and Jabbie (2020):

(i) It is an industrial development program based on the protection of local infant industries through protective tariffs, import quotas, exchange rate controls, special preferential licensing for capital goods imports, subsidized loans to local infant industries, etc. (Ogujiuba et al., 2011);
(ii) It is a theory of economics doctrine typically adhered to by developing countries or emerging-market nations that seek to decrease their dependence on developed countries (Segal, 2019).

Such a doctrine can be likened to that of the Afrocentric movement, which is linked with the ethical principles of ensuring the self is capacitated in a bid to champion growth and development for the continent. This, in effect, will affirm improved self-esteem on the part of Africans to take leadership and control of productive capacity and the management of institutions. On this note, it also makes it possible for economies in the continent to embrace "*Openness*," which allows competitive advantages to be utilized by economies through trade arrangements considered to be of mutual benefit to economies. The focus of ISI was seen to be packaged under three-staged processes, namely "(i) domestic production of previously imported non-durable consumer goods; (ii) extension of production to a wide range of consumer durables and complex manufactured items and finally, (iii) exporting of manufactured goods, with the vision of diversifying to multiple ranges of items'' (Bussell, n/d). The intention as pursued in this chapter is to explore to a greater extent the notion of ISI as a form of Afrocentric philosophical movement for the future economic growth of Africa. Such an approach will take a critical standpoint on how best to invigorate self-discipline and determination into people's way of doing things on the continent. Based on the above illustration of the three-staged processes, the way forward is to ensure progress is made, which concerns industrial development in areas connected with food self-sufficiency and small-scale industries. On that note, it is the intention of this chapter to build a foundation using the *Autarky* model, which is essentially an economic system of self-sufficiency. It is assumed here that a limited level of trade will be expected to take place, with the motive of building indigenous capacity of a self-reliant economy (Yang and Borland, 1991).

There are plethora of critiques faced when dealing with the move toward capacitating an economy through ISI ideology.

In being a devil's advocate, developed economies also made moves in utilizing different versions, notably "*mercantilist policies*" around the sixteenth to the eighteenth century, with a restricted level of international trade (Bondarenko, Online). More notable in this highlight are countries like Nazi Germany (1933–1945) and that of North Korea in the name of "*Juche*" (meaning self-reliant), whose efforts are still likened with the Autarky approach (Bondarenko, Online). Equally as championed by Afrocentric philosophers, there is a need for such a move to be likened in the same spirit of ensuring the actions of merchants or colonial destruct in mainland Africa are made a public outcry and dismal failure, with the spirit of ISI championed in the direction of growth and development for the continent's good. This will ensure individual economies take control of their affairs through centralized institutional support from lead organizations such as the African Union (AU). Such an institution will serve as a moderator in facilitating best practices that support an improved level of trade, with competitive advantages managed in the best interest of the economies in the continent as a whole.

Illustratively, the initial process of Autarky for this chapter's discourse can be represented as shown in figure 6.1 (an assumed partially utopian state), where limited trade is seen to be taking place, and economies within the African continent are encouraged to negotiate better terms of trade with each other in a bid to promote competitive advantage.

Despite limitations on international trade, the Autarky model can also be linked with the principle of the Cobb-Douglas theory (Lucas, 1988); here, human capital is thought to be an independent factor of production, which, according to Zivengwa et al. (2013), is part of an endogenous growth component. The model is expressed as follows:

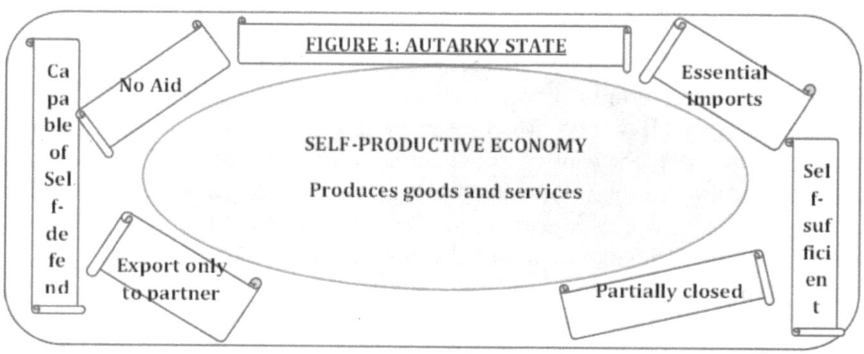

Figure 6.1 Autarky State. *Source:* Created by Emerson Abraham Jackson.

$$Y_t = A.K^{\alpha} H^{\theta} L^{(1-\alpha-\theta)} \quad \text{eq. 1}$$

where *Y* is the output, *A* is the total factor productivity or technical change, *K* is the physical capital, *H* is the human capital, and *L* is the labor.

In the spirit of expanding growth potential in the African continent, there is a need for such an effort to be supported by regional institutions, where output (*Y*) is made to increase through factors like available physical capital input (construed here as land-space utilization); a high-skilled labor (*L*) workforce, which is domestically supplied; and the enabling technological factor, which has a bigger impact on changing the dynamics of return on productivity (Jabbie and Jackson, forthcoming). There is an onus on the part of governments to avail much-needed resources, while also ensuring the political landscape is stable enough to ensure the continent can achieve its full potential of increasing productivity, while capacitating individuals to become entrepreneurs. While the effort is geared toward improving productivity through effective labor utilization and other essential production factors, collaborative effort should be made by all establishments, particularly the academia and vocational institutions, to capacitate human skills to embrace creative destruction in an emerging world of technology (Jackson, 2020c). This is considered essential in building self-sufficiency through identified channels of production, which is worthy of moving the continent in the direction of attracting (foreign) investments in technological innovation (Jackson et al., 2020).

Notwithstanding the passion of addressing the ISI doctrine, the motivation here is to build on the existing national capacity that enhances human productivity, while also creating scope for capacitating sustained levels of growth and development that are of value to both present and future generations. In the passion of building economic growth and prosperity, there is an onus to ensure the philosophy of building Africa's potential is made a national focus, where citizens are equipped to adjust with the emergent levels of skills to harness the future scope of development that may be realized from potential foreign investors. Given the stereotyping of Africa as a backward continent, ISI policy should be efficiently harnessed in the short run (as presented in figure 6.1), so that state funding in key areas of productivity is dealt with most judiciously.

Governments in respective economies should divorce themselves from the usual patronage of unequal treatment to citizens, particularly that which is built on the grounds of affiliation with a political institution. Funding should also be made available to support communities, and this should be linked with reward as opposed to the usual wastage on rent-seeking, which so far has made it impossible for Africa to experience sustained levels of growth when compared to the Asian and Latin American economies. Given the high level of structural bottlenecks prevalent in developing countries (around the SSA region, for example), seemingly associated with small markets, low per capita income, price distortion, and skills gap, it is very important that institutional capacity building is addressed as key in the process. Such an approach can be championed through the AU, in a bid to support well-balanced means of improving productivity (Ogujuiba et al., 2011).

Equally likened with Afrocentric philosophy, the focus as translated in the effort of ISI philosophy is to build capacity to expand real sector activities, which empirically have proven to be very low over the years (Aka and Guisan, 2017; Warburton, 2012). Hence, the continent's continued reliance on essential imports to sustain citizens' lives should change in the spirit of accommodating progress that is capable of addressing independent and sustained growth in mainland Africa. This will also make it possible for the continent to be very highly competitive in comparison with counterpart regions like Asia and Latin America, with its added advantages of high population size and the potential of an abundance of natural resources (renewable and nonrenewable) prevalent in many of these economies.

As evidenced in figure 6.1, policies should be set up to make sure exports of raw materials can only be used as a means for the purchase of essential resources needed to capacitate domestic institutions, for example, the purchase of capital items to invest in industrial activities (a reference to equation (1)). Where earlier intentions have been devoted to the auctioning of raw materials like precious minerals (e.g., Gold and Diamonds), relevant policies should be carved so that institutional capacity is set up to transform them into intermediate products, which eventually will provide the means for improved bargaining.

A regular review of policies initiated would be needed to make it possible to address the timely transition of the continent as a fully open and market-led environment for foreign investments. In the process that decisions are taken to open up the continent for competitive investments, effort should be focused on ensuring Africans are considered as the priority in areas relating to jobs and collaborative management of institutions (Jackson and Jackson, 2017). In this regard, governments must seek to maintain their neutrality in a bid to stimulate Public-Private Partnership by scaling down wasteful operations and reducing bureaucratic processes. The intention here is to make sure such processes are steered by independent "*quangos,*" in the spirit of promoting an ethical business environment. This will make it possible for governments to comfortably leverage the private sector when it comes to the creation and expansion of economic activities. This will thereby give governments the upper hand to build capacity for expanding social welfare facilities in a bid to support the needy during crisis times as witnessed in the recent incidence of Covid-19, and anything else that may seek to threaten livelihoods (Jackson, 2020a, 2020b).

BENEFITS OF ISI FOR AFRICA'S GROWTH AND ECONOMIC PROSPERITY

Given the above discourse regarding ISI as an economic and politically pursued ideology, there are certainly benefits to be gained, particularly with the prospect of growth and prosperity in the African continent. Despite the outcry of critics of ISI (Williams, 2015; Bahmani-Oskooee and Ratha, 2004), Africa can only be seen to pursue a venture that is suitable to its development aspirations, which eventually will help address its high level of dependence on imports, notably essentials like nonelastic goods, which is unsustainable for its citizens. This in itself is considered regressive and the option of development partners like the World Bank, which have experimented with policies like "*Structural Adjustment Programs (SAP)*," has proven to be inimical to the well-being of citizens as opposed to addressing ongoing economic crises (Segal, 2019).

A cautious approach is hereby recommended, with huge political commitments on the part of political leaders and state administrators in ministries and parastatals to exhibit prudence in their acts of planning or rebranding of ISI. Such operations are normally geared toward capacitating the real sector, considered to be the base for improving the well-being of citizens, through prospects of job creation and improved contributions to revenue base, namely "*Pay As You Earn (PAYE)*" system and corporation taxes.

Notable gains that can be seen from the effort of rebrancing ISI for Africa's new hope to promote economic growth and prosperity are to ensure cohesiveness and an equitable society are anchored as the focus of society, with resources utilized judiciously for the good of all, and inclusive of disadvantaged groups like women and the disabled (Jackson and Jackson, 2020; Jackson, 2016). Given the ill experience of past efforts made in utilizing ISI strategy, now seen to be benefiting countries like Singapore and some economies in Latin America, there should be a renewed commitment for resources to be utilized judiciously, more so in the hope of championing Africa's development. It is also hoped that this will be of immense benefit to those in the diaspora, who are also high promoters of Afrocentric philosophy, aimed at educating people about Africa's richness in resources and cultures.

CONCLUSION AND AFROCENTRIC POLICY PRESCRIPTION

Overall, the focus of a promise toward renewed venture for Africa, as promoted through philosophical thought-provoking concepts like Afrocentricity and ISI, is in themselves very welcoming to support the continent's growth and prosperity ambition. The chapter has unraveled a challenging and not so much discursive concept, which in this case is Afrocentricity, as its use is mostly attributed to building solace for African Americans based in the United States. Such negative conversations seem to have been challenged by many of its supporters, for example, Asante (n/d) and Stikkers (2008), in allaying fears about the need for a promised direction. In that same vein, the renewed effort of ISI must be championed similarly, but with collaborative efforts being devoted by people in mainland Africa and those in the diaspora that are in support of Afrocentric philosophy.

There is a high onus on the need to promote a very stable political landscape in a bid to ensure efforts channeled in the name of both Afrocentric and ISI philosophies are translated into something that will bring lasting hope for economic growth and prosperity in the continent. In that vein, the currently modeled Pan-African body of AU, also supported by scattered regional institutions such as Economic Community of West African States and others, should be proactive in the review of measures that seek to unify the continent through renewed and stable trade agreements among member countries. As ISI is geared toward building self-sufficiency in areas pertaining to basic needs such as sustained food production and the development of lite-scale industries, countries must be encouraged to take advantage of openness connected with free movement of goods and services.

In summary and as a pointer for policy recommendations, the effort of Afrocentric and ISI ventures as championed for the good of Africa and its citizens (both in mainland Africa and the diaspora) should be well planned, with the following considered as a checklist for reviewing progress:

(i) Blacks of African descent, whether in mainland Africa or somewhere in the world, must endeavor to unify in their thoughts as to how best the continent can see itself through sustained growth. Critical views are very worthwhile as a way of providing a well-balanced approach in the direction of addressing pitfalls and benefits, but such should be done with the ulterior motive of forging the continent in a new direction of growth prospect. Those in governance, be it as a country leader or in the administration of ministries or parastatals, must seek to manifest prudence in their dealings, particularly when placed in a position of trust to (ethically) act in the best interest of development objectives for the continent. In that vein, the past dealings of unproductive rent-seeking perpetrated through political patronization, which almost wrecked earlier attempts of ISI in the 1960s, must be discouraged. In this regard, accountability must be made a critical part of appraising the progress of those who are in receipt of public funding to ensure their efforts are productively transformed to make a difference, through operations connected with the creation of job opportunities for citizens. In support of the pursued philosophical truism, the determination of governments to build communities through empowerment of enterprises should also be embraced by inculcating a corporate social responsibility culture (Jackson and Jackson, 2017), where beneficiaries of public funds are committed to honoring tax dues in the spirit of supporting governments' nation building objectives.

(ii) The effort to capacitate Africa's self-sufficiency through ISI and the commitments of Afrocentric ideology must be made a timely project; initially set on a minimum of a ten-year plan, to ensure tangible gains are realized before transitioning into a fully open economy for foreign investment. This will make it possible for the continent to be seen as a good place for investment through renewed hope of structural transformation that would have been made on account of tilting efforts domestically.

BIBLIOGRAPHY

Aka, B. F., and Guisan, M. C. (2017). Cutting Poverty Rate Using Basic Income Grant and International Cooperation in Cote D'ivoire and Other Western Africa Countries. *Applied Econometrics and International Development*, 17(1), 102–116.

Asante, M. K. (n.d.). Afrocentricity and Its Critics . . . . http://science.jrank.org/pages/8216/AfrocentricityAfrocentricity-Its-Critics.html.

Bahmani-Oskooee, M., and Ratha, A. (2004). The J-Curve: A Literature Review. *Applied Economics*, 36(2004), 1377–1398.

Bondarenko, P. (Online). Autarky Economics. Encyclopaedia Britannica. https://www.britannica.com/topic/autarky info-article-history.

Bussell, J. (n.d.). Import Substitution Industrialization. https://www.britannica.com/topic/import-substitution-industrialization.

Chawane, M. (2016). The Development of Africentricity: A Historical Survey. *Yesterday & Today* (16), 78–99. http://doi.org/10.17159/2223-0386/2016/n16a5.

Chitonge, H. (2015). *Economic Growth and Development in Africa: Understanding Trends and Prospects*. New York: Routledge Publishers.

Chukwuokolo, J. C. (2009). Afrocentrism or Eurocentrism . . . . *New Journal of African Studies*, Vol. 9: 32.

Early, G., Moses, W. J., Wilson, L., and Lefkowitz, M. R. (1994). Symposium: Historical Roots of Afrocentrism. *Academic Questions*, 7(2), 44–54.

Elson, J. (1996). Attacking Afrocentrism: A Classics Scholar Sharply Challenges the Emerging Theory that Ancient Greece "Stole" Its Best Ideas from Ancient Egypt. *Time Magazine Extract*, February 19, 1996.

Fredland, R. A. (2001). *Understanding Africa: A Political Economy Perspective*. Chicago: Burnham Inc.

Jabbie, M., and Jackson, E. A. (forthcoming). Empirical Determinants of Total Factor Productivity (TFP) Growth in Sierra Leone.

Jackson, E. A. (2016). Phronesis and Resource Curse Hypothesis in Post-Independent Sierra Leone. *Ilorin Journal of Economic Policy*, 3(1), 1–10.

Jackson, E. A. (2020a). Deconstructing Sustainable Livelihood Framework (SLF) for Equitable Living in Crisis of Global Pandemic. In Leal Filho, W., Azul, A., Brandli, L., Lange Salvia, A., Ozuyar, P. G., and Wall, T. (eds.), *Reduced Inequalities: Encyclopedia of Sustainable Development Goal*. Springer Nature Publisher, pp. 822–831.

Jackson, E. A. (2020b). Emerging Innovative Thoughts on Globalization Amidst the Contagion of COVID-19. In Leal Filho, W., Azul, A., Brandli, L., Özuyar, P., and Ozuyar, P. G. (eds.), *Industry, Innovation, and Infrastructure: Encyclopedia of Sustainable Development Goal*. Springer Nature Publisher. https://doi.org/10.1007/978-3-319-71059-4_131-1.

Jackson, E. A. (2020c). Fostering Sustainable Innovation Through Creative Destruction Theory. In Leal Filho, W., Azul, A., Brandli, L., Özuyar, P., and Ozuyar, P. G. (eds.), *Industry, Innovation, and Infrastructure. Encyclopedia of the UN Sustainable Development Goals*. Cham: Springer, pp. 367–379.

Jackson, E. A., and Jabbie, M. (forthcoming). Import Substitution Industrialization (ISI): An Approach to Global Economic Sustainability. In Leal Filho, W., Azul, A., Brandli, L., Özuyar, P., and Ozuyar, P. G. (eds.), *Industry, Innovation, and Infrastructure: Encyclopedia of Sustainable Development Goal*. Springer Nature Publisher.

Jackson, E. A., Jackson, E., and Jackson, H. (2020). Nurturing Career Development for Human Resource Sustainable Development. In Leal Filho, W. et al. (eds.), *Decent Work and Economic Growth: Encyclopedia of Sustainable Development Goal*. Springer Nature Publisher. https://doi.org/10.1007/978-3-319-71058-7_2-1.

Jackson, E. A., and Jackson, H. F. (2017). The Role of Corporate Social Responsibility in Improving Firms' Business in the Directions of Sustainable Development, Accountability and Transparency. *African Journal Economic and Sustainable Development*, 6(2/3), 105–118. https://doi.org/10.1504/AJESD.2017.10010992.

Jackson, E. A., and Jackson, H. J. (2020). Global Perspectives on Gender Sensitivity and Economic Benefits. In Leal Filho, W. et al. (eds.), *Gender Equality: Encyclopedia of Sustainable Development Goal*. Springer Nature Publisher. https://doi.org/10.1007/978-3-319-70060-1_61-1.

Jackson II, R. L. (2003). Afrocentricity as Metatheory: A Dialogic Exploration of Its Principles. In Jackson, R. L. and Richardson, E. B. (eds.), *Understanding African American Rhetoric: Classical Origins to Contemporary Innovations*. New York: Routledge, pp. 115–129.

Lefkowitz, M. (1997). *Not Out of Africa: How "Afrocentricism" Became an Excuse to Teach Myth as History*. Basic Books.

Lucas, R. E. (1988). On the Mechanics of Economic Development. *Journal of Monetary Economics*, 22, 3–42.

Nkrumah, K. (1963). *Africa Must Unite*. London: Panaf.

Ogujiuba, K., Nwogwugwu, U., and Kike, E. (2011). Import Substitution Industrialization as Learning Process: Sub Saharan African Experience as Distortion of the "Good". *Business and Management Review*, 1(6), 8–21.

Segal, T. (2019). Import Substitution Industrialization. https://www.investopedia.com/terms/i/importsubstitutionindustrialization.asp.

Stikkers, K. W. (2008). An Outline of Methodological Afrocentrism, with Particular Application to the Thought of W. E. B. DuBois. *Journal of Speculative Philosophy*, 22(1), 40–49.

Verharen, C. C. (2000). Molefi Asante and an Afrocentric Curriculum. *The Western Journal of Black Studies*, 24(4), 223–238.

Warburton, C. E. S. (2005). *The Evolution of Crisis and Development in Africa*. University Press of America.

Warburton, C. E. S. (2012). ISI and New Industrial Conditions in Latin America and Africa. *Applied Econometrics and International Development*, 12(2), 19–40.

Williams, M. (2015). Development and the State. In Wright, J. D. (ed.), *International Encyclopedia of the Social and Behavioral Sciences*, 2nd edn, Vol. 6. Oxford: Elsevier, pp. 276–281. https://doi.org/10.1016/B978-0-08-097086-8.10101-1.

Yang, X., and Borland, J. (1991). A Microeconomic Mechanism for Economic Growth. *Journal of Political Economy*, 99(3), 460–482. https://doi.org/10.1086/261762.

Zivengwa, T., Hazvina, F., Ndedzu, D., and Mavesere, I. M. (2013). Investigating the Causal Relationship Between Education and Economic Growth in Zimbabwe. *Global Journal of Management and Business Research*, 12(8), 106–118.

Chapter 7

Constitutionalism and the Crisis of Development in Africa

Anthony Raphael Etuk

The importance of constitutionalism for good governance in a democracy cannot be overemphasized. Philosophers, political scientists, and jurists often regard societal development as the product of constitutionalism in any democratic society. Fundamental to the idea of constitutionalism is constitutional legitimacy, where the constitution truly represents the people's wishes and aspirations. Another is a limited government, where the government's powers are strictly subject to the rule of law. Notably, with colonialism came the introduction of the modern form of governance requiring the modern and written form of constitution adopted today in many African states. However, since constitutional governance did not matter for the colonial masters as Africa's resources, it is hardly surprising that under no colonial rule in Africa was such a principle of constitutionalism part of governance. Rather, governance was based on imposition, abuses and arbitrariness, tyranny, repression, and unrestrained exploitation.

Perhaps, what is rather surprising is the fact that several decades after the colonial rule, governance in Africa still follows the bad culture of the colonial tyrannical and repressive style. It remains painfully true that the undermining of constitutionalism, which characterized colonialism, has not only continued, but seemingly flourished in postindependence Africa. Despite their claim to democracy today, many African governments run very repressive and authoritarian regimes, administered with brute force and hatred for all democratic ideals. Over the years, this has triggered a succession of sociopolitical and economic crises, with ultimately far-reaching implications for development in the continent. This chapter examines the hindrances this has posed to development in the continent and suggests certain fundamental political adjustments in Africa as a way out.

CONSTITUTION AND CONSTITUTIONALISM

For effective discussion, it is pertinent to distinguish between constitution and constitutionalism. A constitution is a fundamental system of law by which a people in a given sovereign society are governed. It may be written or unwritten, and according to James Curry, it functions as a "power map" (qtd. in Fombad 1012), in that, it creates, states, and delineates the powers of the various organs of government as well as regulates the behaviors of the citizens, be it in relation to themselves or to the state (Olasunkanmi 272). Benedict Nchalla sees the essence of a constitution as "the distribution of power among the state and society as well as among the various branches of government" (19). For De Smith and Brazir, "the constitutions are primarily about political authority and the location of power, conferment, distribution, exercise and limitation of authority and power among agents of a state" (qtd. in Olasunkanmi 272).

It is clear from the above that a constitution is a supreme law of the land, established or accepted as a guide for governing the state. It sets up the basis for government in the state—so as to prevent anarchy—by establishing, limiting, and defining the relations of the legislative, executive, and judiciary powers of the state. It declares the sovereignty of the people and derives its authority from the will of the people. It prescribes a blueprint for representative government responsible and accountable to the people through universal suffrage at periodic elections. Governmental authority is, therefore, to be exercised only in accordance with law established pursuant to constitutional processes and consistent with constitutional prescriptions and limitations (Henkin 12). Besides, the constitution also provides for the explicit guarantee of the rights and freedoms of the people—in order to prevent tyranny in governance. The constitution also incorporates the ideological pronouncements by which the state ought to aspire as well as obligations of the citizens to the state toward these aspirations. Hence, in a democratic society, the constitution "is not just a political document but also an instrument for development" (Ihonvbere 343). Regular constitutional reforms or reviews are necessary for effective democratic processes in line with contemporary realities. However, any form of constitution reform necessarily involves the process of "constitution-making," which, according to Issa Shivji, embraces "both amending an existing constitution as well as making new constitutions" (47).

The process of constitution-making is fundamental in a democracy, since it is from the constitution that the rulers claim to derive their authority and legitimacy to operate. This legitimacy "cannot hold if the process of constitution-making did not involve the people" (Shivji 47). Hence, Nchalla maintains that "popular, inclusive, participatory and democratic are all key aspects of a successful process that bestows both legitimacy and credibility on the constitution of a country" (24). Such a process contributes to making the constitution a living document by taking it to the people so that they are in a position not just to access it, but also to understand it, claim ownership of it, respect it, and obey it. A constitution becomes devoid of legitimacy if it lacks such popular participation of the people in all the processes of making it, that is, from the social and political debates at all levels to its eventual adoption. A constitution without legitimacy is no constitution at all, and it is the foundation of the absence of constitutionalism in governance. L. Bucker says that such a constitution "is outside the law in the sense that it ought not to be respected by community against which it is applied" (671). Thus, legitimacy is a function of value for a constitution, which serves as the foundation of constitutionalism in a democratic or constitutional government.

Constitutionalism, on the other hand, implies a government subject to the constitution; a limited government, subject to the rule of law; and fractionalized authority to prevent concentration of power and danger of tyranny in governance. According to Fombad, constitutionalism "encompass the idea that a government should not only be sufficiently limited in a way that protects its citizen from arbitrary rule but also that such a government should be able to operate efficiently and in a way that it can be effectively compelled to operate within its constitutional limitations" (1013–1014). Government is for the people, but is limited by a bill of individual rights. Many constitutional systems fractionate governmental authority by some separation of powers or other checks and balances. Constitutionalism implies also that the constitution "cannot be suspended, circumvented or disregarded by political organs of government, and that it can be amended only by procedures appropriate to change of constitutional character and that give effect to the will of the people acting in a constitutional mode" (Henkin 12). In this sense, constitutionalism can be seen as a legal and political idea, based on the primacy of the constitution, which incorporates the idea of a limited government, adherence to the rule of law and the protection of human rights. It combines the idea of a limited government and an accountable government, and it implies that "public authority can legitimately be exercised only in accordance with the constitution. There can be no extra-constitutional government, no exercise of public authority by any person or institution not designated pursuant to the constitution" (Henkin 12). And there can be no continuation in office beyond the term for which officials were elected or appointed.

The fundamental idea behind constitutionalism is the need to prevent arbitrariness or tyranny in government, by ensuring that the constitution does not become an ornamental document or a sham that politicians can either ignore and violate with impunity or deploy as an instrument of oppression and repression against the people in a democratic society. Thus, in specific terms, among other things, constitutionalism denotes effective restraints upon the powers of those who govern through genuine periodic elections by universal suffrage; a guarantee of individual fundamental rights; the existence of an independent tribunal to enforce these rights; and generally, the enthronement of the rule of law, that is, the absence of any form of arbitrariness, and equality of all before the law (Friedrich 318). Constitutionalism, thus, serves as a means of evaluating the form and substance of a constitution in a democratic government. A constitution of any state will serve no useful purpose in a society without constitutionalism. A society marked by a constitution without constitutionalism is often characterized by widespread impunity, disdain for the rule of law, arbitrariness, and weak democratic institutions. Often, these provoke sociopolitical instability and economic crisis, with severe consequences for development in the society.

CONSTITUTIONALISM IN POSTCOLONIAL AFRICA

A recurrent theme in the history of postcolonial Africa has been instability due to political upheavals, ethno-religious and allied social conflicts, and economic crisis. The cause of this endemic instability has largely been the lack of constitutionalism in political governance since independence (Adewoye 136). It would be recalled that, at independence, most African countries adopted the first generation of African constitutions, crafted mainly by the departing colonial powers; for "none of the African countries under the colonial rule had the opportunity of substantial popular participation of the people in the constitution-making process" (Olasunkanmi, *Constitutionalism and the Challenges of*. . . 2). In other words, almost all independence African constitutions were more or less imposed, since the people, apart from a few elites, had not been involved in the constitution-making process (Ndulo, 101). This unfortunate trend of "imposed constitutionalism," and not allowing a substantial local participation or public involvement in the constitution-making process, has largely characterized the postcolonial African constitutional experience till date. The net result of this is the endemic constitutional crisis in the continent today.

Additionally, the colonial powers, who hastily departed the African colonies, committed into the hands of the emergent African leaders at independence states deposing enormous powers, but with little or no virile institutions to check the abuse of such powers. Such immense and almost raw powers once available to the colonial masters were now at the disposal of these African leaders, who were not loath to use them as their colonial predecessors did. Hence, under many pretexts such as the pursuit of national unity and economic development, many of the democratic principles in the independent constitutions were progressively repealed in the wave of constitutional amendments that suddenly overtook many of the postindependence African states. This rush in constitution amendments eventually produced various forms of authoritarian constitutions with high concentration of power in the executive. In most of the immediate postindependence African states, the then existing national assembly quickly transformed themselves into constituent assemblies to amend and enact new constitutions for the people. In the words of Mbondenyi and Ojienda, such undemocratic practices "watered down the essence of constitutionalism and democratic governance in the continent" (4).

With such brazen political mentality, the immediate postindependence constitutions were quickly turned into instruments of oppression and repression, and the immediate independent African states were characterized by gross violation of human rights, despite the bill of rights or constitutional provisions purported to recognize and protect human rights. The pledge of multiparty democracy eventually became a byword as opposition parties were repressed with maximum state force and the newly independent states became one-party states. They banned opposition parties and blamed multiparty system for undermining national unity. As a result, the boundaries between a party and a state structure remained blurred and "the party-state system" became the norm (Teshome 809). This kind of situation prevailed in Africa in the 1960s, 1970s, and 1980s. This repressive system of rule led to the absence of legally registered opposition parties in many African countries. In this period, the only option the opposition groups had was armed struggle to topple the incumbents by force, with dire consequences on the continent's socioeconomic and political development. It is what provoked H. Okoth-Ogendo's description of political governance in Africa as that of "constitutions without constitutionalism" (qtd. in Fombad 1013). In light of this, C. Odinakalu rightly observes that "most of the laws, institutions and repressive attitudes and violation of rights that characterized colonialism did not just survive independence, they prospered" (35).

For instance, shortly after independence in 1957, Ghana under Kwame Nkrumah became highly intolerant of opposition. In a move to destroy the opposition United Party, the government in 1958 arbitrarily abrogated all regional assemblies in the country. Later in 1964, through a whimsical constitution amendment, the government decreed Nkrumah's ruling Convention Peoples' Party as the only legal political party for the country. Kofi Quashigah adds that the amended constitution also gave the president the power to appoint and remove judges at will (118). This repressive and authoritarian political atmosphere also prevailed in Uganda, where in 1966, the then prime minister, Milton Obote, assumed absolute powers in the country through a series of autocratic actions such as the arbitrary abolition of all the kingdoms in Uganda and their constitutionally guaranteed regional statuses, as well as the institution of a unitary state (Doornbos 317). In the same autocratic and authoritarian manner, the government of Julius Nyerere crushed all oppositions and established a single party regime in Tanzania in 1967. Nyerere defended his actions and his executive presidency with enormous powers with the following words: "Our constitution differs from the American system in that it . . . enables the executive to function without being checked at every turn" (qtd. in Shivji 25).

Also, shortly after independence in 1958, the government of Guinea proclaimed the country to be "the most socialistic, radically independent, revolutionary country in sub-Saharan Africa" (Adewoye 139). It went ahead to erect a political structure that made the ruling Democratic Party of Guinea synonymous with the state and dominated practically all facets of life in the country. To heighten the force of repression in the country, then president Sekou Toure abolished and dismissed the legal profession in the country, as "a legalistic formalism which is not only useless, but also incompatible with the social realities of the young African nation" (Nwabueze 276). With the establishment of a High Court, manned by his political associates in 1961, and the reign of impunity that followed, the voices of opposition and dissent were ruthlessly suppressed together with incalculable human rights violations. By the 1970s, Guinea had emerged a full-fledged totalitarian state.

In the same line of totalitarian action, Mobutu Sese Seko of the Democratic Republic of Congo created a one-party state when he took over power in 1965. His highly centralized power allowed him the room to loot the coffers of the state with impunity, and his long reign was characterized by human rights abuses and killings of political opponents. The situation was by no means different in the Nigerian state. In Nigeria, the period from October 1, 1960, to January 14, 1966 (before the first military coup and takeover of power by the military in January 15, 1966) is generally regarded as "a dark period for democracy in Nigeria" (Sasime 154). This is because, during this period, antidemocratic forces launched a determined assault on democratic values and constitutionalism in the country. For instance, in spite of its parliamentary majority, the Northern People's Congress and the National Council of Nigeria and the Cameroons coalition federal government led by Prime Minister Abubakar Tafawa Balewa soon "showed itself unwilling to have or live with the opposition" (Ademoyega 12).

One of such steps taken by the NPC/NCNC coalition federal government to neutralize the opposition Action Group (AG) was to set up a partisan Sir Bairamian's Commission of Inquiry and Tribunals of Enquiry Act in 1961, to conduct inquiry into the affairs of the National Bank (Nwabueze 276), from which the AG was believed to receive financial support to "mount such a gargantuan country-wide campaign during the 1959 general election" (Awolowo 147). The government took several steps to undermine the judiciary when the

Supreme Court later invalidated the inquiry. Ademoyega reveals that, "within a short time, the judiciary had ceased to be a force that could stand for the rights of the people in the face of the obvious governmental high-handedness and tyranny" (10). The AG crisis of 1962, which eventually led to the arrest of Awolowo and 30 of his AG party lieutenants, and the charge of treasonable felony against them, was believed to have been hatched by the Balewa-led government, which also "afforded the federal government the opportunity to deal with the Action Group and the Western Nigerian government controlled by it" (Sasime 156).

As evident from our discussion so far, the problems were not caused by the absence of constitutions. Rather, it was the case of the African leaders' deliberate rendering of the constitutions dysfunctional by regularly undermining their provisions or by arbitrarily amending them to suit their selfish political ambitions. The general trend in the continent had been in the direction of whimsical amendment of constitutions to concentrate power on the executive and to abridge local autonomy in favor of the central government; to undermine opposition parties and establish a one-party state, using all manners of repression and suppression including detention, trial, torture, and murder. This became a recipe for the massive civil unrests, ethnic rivalry, political instability, economic decline, and the genesis of the misrule and instability in the continent that became an excuse for the military foray into politics in the 1960s, with all the negative consequences this has had on the development in the continent (Akintola 27).

With the 1963 Togolese coup d'état leading the pack, a wave of coups d'état swept across the continent with the military taking over government, purporting to clean the socioeconomic and political mess left by the civilian governments. Through their reign of suffocating impunity, suspension of constitutions, dissolution of parliament, and unreserved looting of public treasury, the military destroyed every democratic structure they encountered and further set the continent on an incredibly backward trajectory of constitutional crisis and socioeconomic and political decline. However, from the early 1990s, there was a gradual return to civil rule in many of the African states. Along with this came the third wave of constitutional reforms in the continent, "designed to introduce constitutions that promote constitutionalism and good governance" (Fombad 1007). Thus, the 1990s began with a slow and painful move toward what many optimistically hoped would usher in a new era of democratic governance and constitutionalism through the constitutional reforms. But this never happened, due to the resurgence of authoritarian rule under the guise of democracy in the continent.

In fact, from the 1990s, Africa tends to produce some of the worst dictators in world history. The reforms did not go far enough to adequately address the institutional weaknesses that made dictatorship and the concomitant repression, corruption, and economic mismanagement in the continent inevitable. Many of the new constitutions merely paid lip service to issues of separation of power and executive dominance in government and the abuses of power that go along with it. Hence, under most of these constitutions, overbearing and imperial presidents continue to reign and dominate the legislature and the judiciary. The traditional checks and balances are "either absent or too weak and ineffective" (Cranenburgh 443). By every standard, the system of governance in Africa in the post-1990s constitutional reforms has become even worse; for the so-called "democratic leaders have turned out to be more corrupt, power-drunk, manipulative and inefficient than their predecessors" (Fombad 1024).

Another issue, more troubling, is the fact that many of these constitutions were never subjected to popular debates or referenda, whereby through such avenues of open and democratic process, attention could be paid to the dreams, pains, and aspirations of the ordinary Africans in drafting the constitutions. Some of the constitutions were simply packaged by the military and imposed on the people as a condition for handing back power to civil rule. Whenever they were subjected to public debates, such debates were carefully monitored, controlled, and manipulated by the ruling elites, and the results skewed to reflect their narrow, selfish political interests. In some cases, the reports of constitutional conferences or commissions which truly reflected the desires and aspirations of the people were rejected or set aside by the state. This is why the question of legitimacy has remained an albatross around the neck of many of the post-1990s African states' constitutions.

Furthermore, the resurgence of dominant party dictatorship in the continent, which uses the "multi-partysm" provisions of the 1990s constitutional reforms as a convenient smokescreen behind which to practice dictatorship, has made a total mess of the practice of constitutionalism in Africa. Wondwosen Toshome concedes that "opposition political parties . . . are barely tolerated in the continent" (811). All that appears to have happened from the 1990s is that "the old monolithic one-party dictators . . . simply made way for multiparty 'democratic' dictators, who have maintained the inherited repressive, exploitative, and inefficient structures installed by their predecessors" (Fombad 1024). Disquiet with what most therefore perceive as "authoritarian constitutions" in their countries, coupled with general detest for the massive abuse of executive powers, have triggered not only to an unprecedented tsunami of socio-political upheavals, wars, and revolutions across the continent today. It has also led to agitations for effective constitutionalism in Africa, believed to be crucial for the continent's development.

In Nigeria, for instance, the current 1999 constitution faces a challenge of legitimacy, as it "lacks the will and consent of the people" (Chima 135). Crafted under the "shadow of the gun," during the Gen. Abdulsalami

Abubakar's military regime, the constitution was imposed on the country as a condition for the return to civil rule after over three decades of military dictatorship. Besides, the disaffection the constitution has induced in the country, due to its obvious deficiency in democratic values, fully justifiable human rights provision, and clear governmental structures that can ensure effective constitutional governance are other troubling issues surrounding the constitution (Igbuzor 22). And notwithstanding the 2010 amendments made to the 1999 constitution, it is considered highly impotent for governance for many other reasons, such as structural imbalances in the composition of the country's 36 federating states, lack of inclusiveness and accountability in governance, and devolution of powers in the federation (Igbuzor 22). This explains why nepotism, electoral frauds, institutional failure, large-scale corruption, ethnic agitations for self-determination, ethno-religious violence, banditry, and agitations for a new constitution that truly represents the wishes and aspirations of Nigerians are the order of the day in the country. Dejo Olowu's remarks poignantly describe the situation: "the best Nigeria has achieved since independence has essentially been constitution without constitutionalism, elections without democratic culture" (330).

Today, sophisticated means of rigging elections have been devised by the parties in power. Such sophisticated means of elections rigging are what sustained the life presidency ambitions of such tyrannical and dictatorial figures in Africa as Mobutu Sese Sekou of Zaire, Eyadema of Togo, Banda of Malawi, Robert Mugabe of Zimbabwe, Paul Biya of Cameroon, President Teodoro Obiang Mbasogo of Equatorial Guinea, and so on. The problem cuts across many African countries today, including Botswana—a country that has gained international reputation as the "Miracle of Africa" and "a success story on the Africa continent" (Cook and Sarkin 453). Since it achieved independence in 1966, Botswana has, undoubtedly, maintained high economic growth, sound fiscal policies, and regular elections, which have fed this image. However, this designation has been called into question, especially because of the one-party dominance in the state, with the Botswana Democratic Party as the only party in power since the country's independence in 1966. Opposition parties are widely considered to have no real chance of gaining power in the country because of the intolerant attitude of the government in power.

CONSEQUENCES FOR DEVELOPMENT IN THE CONTINENT

The foregoing simply affirms the crisis of governance in Africa arising due to "the absence of constitutionalism in governance" (Aime 163). The consequence is the gross impediments it poses to development in the continent now turned into "a faraway place, where people go hungry, bad people run government, chaos and anarchy are the norm" (Thomson 56). According to the World Bank's assessment of major impediments to Africa's development: "underlying the litany of Africa's development crisis is a crisis of good governance" (60). Of course, there can be no good governance without constitutionalism. Today, the continent as a whole is confronted with the disappearance of the basic state functions that ought to serve the fundamental needs of the people to help them live and exist as human beings. According to M. Sinjela, lack of constitutionalism in Africa has precipitated not only widespread corruption and erosion of the possibility of good governance, but also weak political institutions and economic stagnation (24–25). Fombad advanced that "the African economy has remained depressed" (1033).

It is, therefore, hardly surprising that African states frequently rank low in all indices of human development as we as occupy top positions in the Transparency International''s lists of most corrupt nations in the world. For this same reason, African countries typically fall toward the bottom of any list measuring small size economic activity such as income per capita or gross domestic product (GDP) per capita, despite the enormous resources the continent is blessed with by nature. From the statistics provided by the World Bank, for instance, the GDP of sub-Saharan Africa has continued to dwindle by the years from about 54% in 1965 to 3.2% by 2018 (qtd. in Held 6). Also in 2019, the World Bank reported that "the extreme poverty in sub-Saharan Africa translates primarily into 85% of Africans living on less than 5 US Dollar per day" (World Bank Report, 2019).

Moreover, Africa's primary commodity trade and her share of foreign direct investment, according to the World Bank Development reports of 1986 and 2000, are said to have dropped from 7% and 13% in the 1970s to less than 0.5% and 5%, respectively, in the late 1990s (qtd. in Hoogwelt 174). A recent data released by FDI Intelligence and EY Africa Attractiveness Report shows that, there has been a steady decline in the number of foreign investors and projects in the continent over the years due to socioeconomic and political instability. Moreover, in 2006, 34 of the 50 nations on the United Nations List of Least Developed Countries were in Africa (UN, LDC, 2006). In 2009, 22 of the 24 countries of the world identified by the United Nations as having "Low Human Development" were in sub-Saharan Africa (UN, HDI, 2009). And currently, 31 of the 47 countries in the United Nations 2018 List of "Least Developed Countries" are African countries (UN, LDC, 2018).

These show the close relationship between constitutionalism and quality of life in the society. It explains why, besides mass poverty and diseases ravaging African countries, a greater majority of Africans suffer from illiteracy, despite the preachments about education as the bedrock for development in the society. Joseph Omoregbe argues that "over 70% of the population of these countries are illiterate, over 80% of them live in abject poverty while corruption permeates every aspect of life" (22). There is also the escalation of armed conflicts, wars, and banditry, caused by the endemic abuse of power, disregard for the rule, and reign of impunity, which have made living in the continent today a rather dreadful experience. Mugabe graphically catalogs the sad situation thus: "Africa is now home to the world's largest number of least developed countries. The continent further boasts of the largest refugee population in the world. Furthermore, it is a theatre of endless conflicts, civil strife and gross human rights abuse" (qtd. in Igbafen, *Theories and Issues . . .* 99). This is why African countries constantly remain among the top places for ongoing conflicts and wars in the world. Currently, there are over 15 countries involved in wars, or which are experiencing postwar conflicts and tensions in Africa such as Mali, Cote d'Ivoire, Guinea, Liberia, Nigeria, Libya, Sierra Leone, Togo, Eritrea, Somalia, Sudan, and Uganda.

CONCLUSION

For Africa to experience sustainable development, there is a strong need to decisively embrace constitutionalism in political governance. For this reason, a participatory approach to constitution-making and reforms that involves the people in the entire process is strongly advocated here. Besides being essential for the legitimacy of a constitution and its binding effect on the people, this also provides the opportunity for citizens to become familiar with the nature, content, and purpose of a constitution. There is equally the need for a sustained and vigorous program of constitutional literacy and citizenship education to enable the people to defend their constitutional rights and resist the present efforts by opportunistic leaders to derail the present effort at democratization and constitutionalism. Furthermore, the government must adapt to the constitution, as a condition for peace, progress, and development in the society; while the crucial constitutional reforms that can promote constitutionalism may be considered: the recognition of the right to free and fair elections, key principles and institutions of accountability, the reduction of presidential powers, the removal of immunity clauses from the constitutions, and the incorporation of socioeconomic rights for the people in the constitutions.

BIBLIOGRAPHY

Ademoyega, Adewale. *Why We Struck: The Story of the First Nigerian Coup*. Ibadan: Evans, 1981. Print.

Adewoye, Omonyi. "Constitutionalism: A Factor in Economic Development". *Democracy, Democratization and Africa*. Ed. L. A. Thompson. Ibadan: Afrika-Link Books, 1994. 130–147. Print.

Aime, Chofor. "A Federal Constitution Devoid of Constitution: The Case of Cameroon". *Constitutionalism and Democratic Governance in Africa: Contemporary Perspectives from sub-Saharan Africa*. Eds. Morris Mbondenyi and Tom Ojienda. Pretoria: Pretoria University Law Press, 2013. 163–188. Print.

Akinola, G. "Factors in the Development of Democratic Ethos in Africa". *Democracy, Democratization and Africa*. Ed. L. A. Thompson. Ibadan: Afrika-Link Books, 1994. 16–33. Print.

Awolowo, Obafemi. *Adventures in Power: The Travails of Democracy and the Rule of Law*. Ibadan: Evans, 1987. Print.

Chima, Diala. "The Dawn of Constitutionalism in Nigeria". *Constitutionalism and Democratic Governance in Africa: Contemporary Perspectives from sub-Saharan Africa*. Eds. Morris Mbondenyi and Tom Ojienda. Pretoria: Pretoria University Law Press, 2013. 135–160. Print.

Cook, Amelia and Jeremy Sarkin. "Is Botswana the Miracle of Africa? Democracy, the Rule of Law and Human Rights Versus Economic Development". *Transnational Law and Contemporary Problems*. 19 (2010): 453–489. SSRN. Web. June 12, 2020.

Doornbos, M. "Changing Perspectives on Conflict and Integration in Uganda". *Uganda the Dilemma of Nationhood*. Ed. G. N. Uzoigwe. New York: NOK, 1982. 313–332. Print.

Fombad, Charles. "Constitutional Reforms and Constitutionalism in Africa: Reflections on Some Current Challenges and Future Prospects". *Buffalo Law Review*. 4.59 (2011): 1007–1108. Digital Commons. Web. 15 April, 2020.

———. "Constitutional Literacy in Africa: Challenges and Prospects". *Commonwealth Law Bulletin*. 44.3 (2013): 492–513. Taylor & Francis Online. Web. June 13, 2020.

Friedrich, Carl. "Constitution and Constitutionalism". *International Encyclopedia of the Social Sciences*. III. (1968): 318–325. Memoire Online. Web. March 4, 2020.

Held, David. *Democracy and the Global Order. GDP (Current) sub-Saharan Africa 2018*. MPILF. Web. June 3, 2020.

Henkin, Louis. "Elements of Constitutionalism". *The Review*. 60 (1998): 10–22. ICJ. Web. May 23, 2020.

Hoogvelt, Ankie. *Globalization and the Post-Colonial World*. Hampshire: Palgroove, 2001. Print.

Igbafen, M. *Theories and Issues in Philosophy and Development*. Ekpoma: Inno Press, 2003. Print.

———. "Existential Issues in African Philosophy". *Core Issues in African Philosophy*. Ed. Olusegun Oladipo. Ibadan: Hope, 2006. 90–101. Print.

Ihonvbere, J. "Towards a New Constitutionalism in Africa". *London Centre for Democracy and Development Occasional Papers*. 4 (2000): 343–366. Academia. Web. 5 April, 2020.

———. "A Balance Sheet of Africa's Transition to Democratic Governance". *The Transition to Democratic Governance: The Continuing Struggle*. Eds. John Mbaku and Julius Ihonvbere. London: Praeger, 2003. ABC-CLIO. Web. June 4, 2020.

Mbondenyi, Morris and Tom Ojienda. "Introduction to and Overview of Constitutionalism and Democratic Governance in Africa". *Constitutionalism and Democratic Governance in Africa: Contemporary Perspectives from sub-Saharan Africa*. Eds. Morris Mbondenyi and Tom Ojienda. Pretoria: Pretoria University Law Press, 2013: 3–11. Print.

McChesney, Allan. "The Promotion of Economic and Political Rights: Two African Approaches". *Journal of African Law*. 24.2 (1980): 170–195. SOAS. Web. May 6, 2020.

Nchalla, Benedict. "Tanzania's Experience with Constitutionalism, Constitution-Making and Constitutional Reforms". *Constitutionalism and Democratic Governance in Africa": Contemporary Perspectives from Sub-Saharan Africa*. Eds. Morris Mbondenyi and Tom Ojienda. Pretoria: Pretoria University Law Press, 2013. 15–51. Print.

Ndulo, Muna. "Constitution-Making in Africa: Assessing both the Process and the Content". *Public Administration and Development*. 21.2. (2001): 101–117. Scholarship@Cornell Law. Web. Feburary 13, 2020.

Nwabueze, B. *Judicialism in Commonwealth Africa: The Role of Courts in Government*. London: C. Hurst, 1977. Print.

Odinakalu, C. "Back to the Future". The Imperative of Prioritizing for the Protection of Human Rights in Africa. *Journal of African Law*. 1.2. (2003): 30–45. Print.

Oladipo, Olusegun. *Modernization and the Search for Community in Africa: Crisis and Conditions for Change. Remaking Africa: Challenges of the Twenty-First Century*. Ibadan: Hope, 1998. Print.

Olasunkanmi, Aborisade. "Constitutionalism and the Challenges of Development in Africa". *International Journal of Politics and Good Governance*. 5.5.4 Quarter IV (2014): 1–9. Online Research Journals. Web. June 12, 2020.

———. "Constitution Without Constitutionalism: Interrogating the African Experience". *Arts Humanities Open Access Journal*. 2.5 (2018): 272–276. AHOAJ. Web. May 23, 2020.

Olowu, Deju. "Constitutional Governance, Democratization and Military Legacy in Post-Independence Nigeria". *Constitutionalism and Democratic Governance in Africa: Contemporary Perspectives from sub-Saharan Africa*. Eds. Morris Mbondenyi and Tom Ojienda. Pretoria: Pretoria University Law Press, 2013. 315–335. Print.

Omoregbe, Joseph. *Socio-Political Philosophy and International Relations*. Lagos: Joja Educational Research and Publishers, 2007. Print.

Quashigah, Kofi. "Constitutionalism and Constitutional Reforms in Ghana". *Constitutionalism and Democratic Governance in Africa: Contemporary Perspectives from sub-Saharan Africa*. Eds. Morris Mbondenyi and Tom Ojienda. Pretoria: Pretoria University Law Press, 2013. 115–134. Print.

Sasime, Ibiba. "The Judiciary and Representative Government in Nigeria: A Study in Political Behaviour". *Democracy, Democratization and Africa*. Ed. L. A. Thompson. Ibadan: Afrika-Link Books, 1994. 149–171. Print.

Shivji, I. "Problem of Constitution-Making as Consensus Building: The Tanzanian Experience". *The State and Constitutionalism in Southern Africa*. Ed. Owen Sichone. Harare: Sapes Trust, 1998. 23–50. Print.

Sinjela, M. "Constitutionalism in Africa: Emerging Trends" *The Review*. 60 (1998): 24–35. ICJ. Web. April 4, 2020.

Teshome, Wondwosen. "Opposition Parties and the Politics of Opposition in Africa: A Critical Analysis". *World Academy of Science, Engineering and Technology*. 31 (2009): 808–822. CiteSeerx. Web. May 3, 2020.

Thomson, Alex. *In Introduction to African Politics*. London: Routledge, 2002. Print.

United Nations. "Human Development Index Report". *UN Development Programme*. Web. June 5, 2020a.

———. "Least Developed Countries 2018." UNCDP. Web. June 5, 2020b.

———. "Least Developed Countries List 2009". UNCDP. Web. June 5, 2020c.

World Bank. *From Crisis to Sustainable Growth-Sub-Saharan Africa: A Long Term Perspective Study (1989)*. World Bank. Web. July 7, 2020.

———. "GDP Per Capita (Current US$)-World Bank Open Data". World Bank. Web. June 5, 2020.

Chapter 8

Replacing Development

An Afro-communal Approach to Distributive Justice

Thaddeus Metz

Those sympathetic to Africa have often criticized development for serving nefarious functions, particularly for legitimating Western domination of Africa (Escobar 1992; Rahnema 1997; Zein-Elabdin 2011) and for expressing an attitude of superiority on the part of the West (for just one clear statement, see Ziai 2007, 8). Sometimes critics have also contended that development has failed on its own terms to alleviate poverty in Africa (Ferguson 1997; Rahnema 1997, 378–79, 391; Matthews 2004; Prah 2011; Lubieniecka 2013). I believe that while these criticisms are plausibly true of development in practice, they do not target the heart of development theory. In principle, there could be a form of development that would neither serve to facilitate Western domination of Africa, nor express Western arrogance over it, nor fail to reach its own ends. Just imagine, for example, that African governments successfully undertook development on their own. Would there still be a moral problem with *this* sort of development?

In this chapter, I defend an affirmative answer to this question. I argue that there are value judgments central to both development theory and practice that are dubious in light of a characteristically African ethic. More specifically, I focus on what a certain philosophical interpretation of the sub-Saharan value of communion entails for appraising development, drawing two major conclusions. One is that a majority of the criticisms that have been made of development by those sympathetic to African values are weak; I argue that, given the value of communion, development should not be rejected because it is essentially, say, overly materialistic and scientistic, or insufficiently spiritual and local. The second conclusion, however, is that three criticisms of development are strong from the perspective of Afro-communalism and are particularly powerful when set in that context. I argue that development theory and practice are anthropocentric, individualistic, and technocratic, and that a reading of the sub-Saharan value of communion provides a unitary foundation for rejecting these features and for grounding an alternative, more relational approach to social progress and to what justice demands from the West in relation to Africa.

WHAT IS DEVELOPMENT?

For much of the postindependence era in Africa, development had been premised on the aim of indefinite economic growth,[1] which was powerfully criticized for three major reasons, namely, for being inconsistent with ecological concerns, insufficiently related to people's quality of life, and unconcerned with the distribution of wealth, namely, toward the worst-off. However, these days, standard development theory and practice require environmental sustainability, expected improvement in people's welfare (often cashed out in terms of needs or capabilities), and a concern for who receives the benefits. Any plausible account of the nature of development should not be overly narrow for placing economic growth at its center; the latter should be understood to be merely one, unattractive form that the former once took.

Conversely, it would be a mistake to construe the concept of development too broadly, relative to my aim in this chapter, which is to target a certain Western conception of social progress. So, it will not do to think of development as merely "purposive (teleological) growth" where "the goal of development is greater human, material, technological and cultural welfare" (Tangwa 2011, 177, 178). This analysis of the concept of development does not uniquely pick out the particular sorts of practices that have been undertaken in Africa and recommended for it over the past 60 years or so.

To make headway, consider some representative examples of the way that the word "development" has been used recently in respect of sub-Saharan Africa. Quintessential instances include the World Bank, the United Nations, or a Western government enabling farmers to participate on the global market by reducing tariffs or enabling them to access seeds; offering training in macroeconomic planning and fiscal management to government employees; deploying new technologies, such as cell phone applications, to enable people to participate in the banking system; educating the police about human rights and gender issues; helping primary school teachers develop modules that will foster literacy and numeracy; and providing electronic stock management systems to medical clinics. Although development has often had a non-African agent driving it, that is not a necessary condition, as there have of course been times when African states themselves, as well as parastatals and

NGOs based in them, have done so, though typically in "partnership" with a better-resourced external body.

Using these examples as a springboard, I suggest that the following captures much of what is central to development, construed as a Western conception of progress that has often been applied to Africa and taken on board by African institutions: the quest to improve non-Western people's standard of living and to protect their human rights, as exemplified by the West, principally through changes to state policy and corporate practice that are scientifically informed and typically involve sophisticated technology, improved efficiency, and the adoption of impersonal norms.

One implication of this analysis is that the Western world, by definition cannot develop. That might in fact be welcome, since the discourse invariably distinguishes between "developed" and "undeveloped" or (more politically correct) "developing" countries. However, if the reader believes that development could take place in Europe, North America, and Australasia, then one could either remove mention of "non-Western" people as the intended beneficiaries and speak merely of "people" in general or speak of "mainly" non-Western people as the ones meant to benefit. The crucial point is that the non-Western parts of the world are supposed to "catch up" to the Western part.

I submit that the above characterization of development has the merits of avoiding being either too narrow or too broad, successfully picking out a Western approach to social progress that has been salient since the independence of sub-Saharan countries from colonial powers. The next issue to address is why one might reasonably find it objectionable. Would it not be ideal for these countries to come closer to the milk and honey conditions of the West? What in the world is wrong with projects of the sort adumbrated above?

AN INTERPRETATION OF THE AFRICAN VALUE OF COMMUNION

Although some philosophical articulations of sub-Saharan values take life-force (e.g., Magesa 1997) or the common good (e.g., Gyekye 1997) as basic, or appeal to invisible agents such as ancestors and the not-yet-born (e.g., Bujo 2005), I favor a secular and relational conception of African morality, which should be of particular interest to a global audience of philosophers, policymakers, and activists. Roughly, from this perspective, communal relationships with human persons and certain animals are what merit pursuit for their own sake. In this section, I expound this ethic, applying it only in the following sections.

My favored philosophical rendition of African values is grounded on relational ideas such as these, advanced by a variety of sub-Saharan thinkers:

> Every member is expected to consider him/herself an integral part of the whole and to play an appropriate role towards achieving the good of all. (Gbadegesin 1991, 65)
>
> (H)armony is to be achieved through close and sympathetic social relations within the group. (Mokgoro 1998, 17)
>
> The fundamental meaning of community is the sharing of an overall way of life, inspired by the notion of the common good. (Gyekye 2004, 16)
>
> (T)he purpose of our life is community-service and community-belongingness. (Iroegbu 2005, 442)
>
> If you asked *ubuntu* (the Nguni word for personhood or virtue—ed.) advocates and philosophers: What principles inform and organise your life? . . . the answers would express commitment to the good of the community in which their identities were formed, and a need to experience their lives as bound up in that of their community. (Nkondo 2007, 91)

These quotations are of interest for two reasons. One is that they suggest that a certain kind of relationship is to be pursued as an end, not merely as a means.[2] Another is that they specify the nature of this relationship, in terms of two logically distinct facets (initially reconstructed in Metz (2007)). On the one hand, there is what I call "identifying with" others, that is, considering oneself part of the whole, being close, sharing a way of life, belonging and being bound up with others, and, on the other, there is "exhibiting solidarity" with them, that is, achieving the good of all, being sympathetic, advancing the common good, serving and being committed to others' good.

I call the combination of identity and solidarity "communion" or sometimes "harmony." I abjure the word "community," in part because it is used in a variety of ways and in part because it might suggest the view that appropriate norms are determined by a group's attitudes or culture. In contrast, communion is meant to be an objective standard by which to determine whether a group's norms are appropriate, whether it has moral reason to change its culture or other practices.

Now, with whom or what should one commune? By my philosophical reconstruction,[3] beings have a full moral status (a dignity) if they are capable of being both subjects and objects of communion, that is, if they can exhibit identity and solidarity with another and another can exhibit identity and solidarity with them. Normal human persons fit this description. There is normally some moral reason to commune with such beings, at least if they have not misused their capacity to commune.

Other kinds of beings have a partial moral status, insofar as they are capable of being merely the object of communion, that is, if they cannot exhibit identity and solidarity with us but we can exhibit identity and solidarity with them. Animals "higher" than insects, arachnids, and the like can be objects of communion with us. When it comes to birds, mice, cats, dogs, giraffes, lions, elephants, and apes, we can enjoy a sense of togetherness with them, foster their ends, do what is likely to make their lives go well, and do so out of sympathy and for their own sake. There is some moral reason to commune with such beings, although less reason than with those beings that have a dignity.

The further question of precisely how to respond to the value of communion is complicated and is one I do not need to address in detail here in order to appraise development. In a nutshell, I reject a consequentialist prescription to maximize communal relationships, and instead advocate a deontological principle according to which one should respect beings insofar as they are capable of communion. Such respect will mean, in part, communing with them and helping them to commune, but it will not mean, for example, acting discordantly toward innocents even if doing so would promote the most communion in the long run.

In other work I have argued that this philosophical interpretation of the sub-Saharan value of communion easily entails and plausibly explains a variety of salient practices among indigenous sub-Saharan peoples, ones that have some intuitive moral pull even for those outside this tradition. For example, it naturally accounts for their recurrent search for consensus in decision-making; inclination toward reconciliation when responding to wrongdoing; tendency to hold land in common and to avoid great inequalities of wealth; and disposition to accord animals a partial moral standing, one lower than humans but greater than plants (for some defense of these points, see Metz 2007, 2012a, 2012b).

I lack the space to discuss further the African credentials of this principle and must focus on its prima facie plausibility as a normative ground of public policy. Whereas the utilitarian believes that institutions ought to serve the function of promoting subjective well-being, the Kantian believes they should protect and enhance people's autonomy, and the capabilities theorist believes they should ensure that people have the ability to function in objectively valuable ways, the adherent to communion contends (roughly) that institutions ought to commune and enable others to do so. The latter approach entails that conditions such as these are to be prized: a state that meets the needs of its residents, a business that is willing to forgo some profits so as to strengthen ties with stakeholders, a populace that is cohesive in the sense of enjoying a national identity and being disposed to cooperate across ethnic lines, and a household in which marriages are evenhanded and stable and in which children are reared with wisdom. From this Afro-communal perspective, roughly speaking, "immorality is the word or deed which undermines fellowship" (Kasenene 1998, 21); that is, wrongness is more or less discordant behavior that treats innocent parties as separate and inferior, subordinates them, is expected to harm them, and is done consequent to indifference or cruelty. This ethic, too, merits consideration when thinking about how to organize socioeconomic conditions.

WEAK CRITICISMS OF DEVELOPMENT

In the rest of this chapter, I take for granted the prescription to treat others with respect insofar as they are capable of being party to communal relationships. Supposing that communion is key, it follows that several of the major criticisms that have been made of development in the literature lack force for failing to capture the respects in which it genuinely undermines fellowship.

Too Little Spirituality?

Some adherents to characteristically African values have criticized the neglect by development theory and practice of "spiritual" considerations, such as the inclination to see invisible agents, say, ancestors or God, in the world. As one African scholar has put it, "(T)he alliance of progress, science and technology leads to social and spiritual bankruptcy. Having objectified nature and people, God too becomes impersonal" (Sindima 1989, 542; see also Basu 2005; Ziai 2014).

It is true that a concern to foster cell-phone banking, improve supply chain management, and facilitate trade on the world market means a neglect of what traditional sub-Saharans might consider holy. However, I do not believe that this necessarily indicates a *moral* shortcoming with development. A strict focus on the perceptible (or what Westerners would call the "physical") need not involve any failure to commune, as construed in the previous section.

There can sometimes be secular reasons for a concept of social progress to include imperceptible ("spiritual") elements. For example, if many people have exhibited identity and solidarity in a religious way over a long span of time, then considerations of communion entail that there is some moral reason not to undermine that practice (at least if it does not involve severe discord toward innocent parties). Development may indeed be faulted for running roughshod over this facet of people's lives, but the ground of the criticism is that it disregards communion, not that it neglects God.

Too Much Science?

Although some of the post-development literature, particularly with an African flavor, is critical of science for eclipsing "spiritual" ways of interpreting the world, as per the previous objection, there is the further, distinct objection that science is simply unlikely to work in a sub-Saharan context. Consider this claim:

> Attempts to achieve high productivity are often counter-productive. And usually, it is those already struggling to make ends meet who pay the price for national gambles. Science has much to answer for in Africa in this respect. Africans were encouraged to use fertilizers. Many of these fertilizers were not tested for the particular soils in which they were being used. . . . Consequently, soils got burnt with the wrong salts applied to them. (Sindima 1989, 550)

However, this sounds like the problem is bad science or not enough science, rather than too much science *simpliciter*. A good scientist would have considered whether a fertilizer that works in one kind of soil would be likely to work in another of a different chemical composition. In addition, a sensible policymaker would have run a pilot study to test the fertilizer in one, circumscribed area, before encouraging its widespread adoption.

More deeply, insofar as a communal relationship includes aid, it prescribes doing what is likely to make people's lives go better, which includes meeting their biological, psychological, and social needs. The scientific method has been humanity's most successful means by which to understand the nature of reality and should not be neglected when seeking to improve people's quality of life. Surely, it would be wrong for a government to fund any aid project intending to free up human resources in Africa by deploying zombies in the army (Mutwa 1998, 657) or to harness electricity discharged by flying witches to power African economies (Maware 2011, 98). These projects would be unjust to support because doing so would flout the communal value of solidarity, that is, would constitute a failure to do what, for all we can tell with reliable epistemic means, is likely to enable people to live well.

Too Much Materialism?

More than a few in the field suggest that standard development theory is too materialistic for addressing solely or mainly financial, technological, and consumerist interests. For instance, one finds the criticism that "development is about paving the way for the achievement of those conditions that characterize rich societies: industrialization, agricultural modernization, and urbanization" (Escobar 1992, 25) or that the key problem with development theory is that it is focused on "material affluence" and "commodities" (Ziai 2007, 8).

However, I do not believe that this objection is fair. An awful lot of contemporary development has involved seeking to improve health, education, and human rights, which are not essentially industrial or economic. This is true not merely in theory, but also in practice. Neither Amartya Sen's (1999) nor Martha Nussbaum's (2000) theoretical accounts of development, nor the programs designed to educate the police about human rights and gender issues and to help teachers impart literacy and numeracy, and, one could add, those aimed at improving the health of pregnant women and of their newborns, enhancing nutrition among children, providing emergency food assistance, fostering immunization, combating malaria, pneumonia, and HIV/AIDS, reducing instances of child marriages, making it easier to register births with the state, and creating effective asylum systems for refugees, are idiosyncratic. Although below I will argue that a drive to improve people's material standard of living has too often come at the cost of communal relationship, the present objection, that development utterly neglects noneconomic considerations, is too crude.

Too Little Locality?

Often post-development theorists strongly express "an interest in local autonomy, culture and knowledge" (Escobar 1992, 27) or urge us to move "from global thinking to local thinking" (Esteva and Prakash 1997; see also Kothari et al. 2014, 368–69; Ziai 2014, 2). Sometimes such remarks are meant to express the strong, relativist idea that the local is the source of the values and norms that are appropriate for it. One theorist remarks that "if all previous attempts at development have failed and reformist policies do not work, where does one begin? The starting point for solutions begins with cultural relativism, a rejection and total overhaul of that closed Western window" (Berg 2007, 544). Another similarly contends that the right sort of change for people is one that "could leave them free to *change the rules and the contents of change*, according to their own culturally defined ethics and aspirations" (Rahnema 1997, 385). Some indeed "bite the bullet" and reject the concept of human rights as inappropriate because of its implicit universal scope (Esteva and Prakash 1997, 282–85).

However, upon supposing a basic value of communion, there is nothing morally significant in itself about locality, construed as a source of views about social progress, and furthermore, the concept of human rights remains vital. Treating people as special in virtue of their capacity to commune means avoiding severe discordance with those who have not misused this capacity, where human rights violations are plausibly precisely that—severe forms of treating innocents as separate and inferior, subordinating them, and harming them, and doing so consequent to indifference to their good.

Another way to see the point is to consider that those who value communion would have little reason to prize localities that did not do so. For example, post-development theorists, or at least African ethicists, would generally not approve of the local as it exists in the West. They would instead tend to maintain that what is local there is undesirable (say, for undermining communion), which judgment entails that locality as such is not what truly motivates. For another example, suppose that a given non-Western culture does not allow girls to read or to be educated in certain subjects.[4] Again, what is local would not merit funding or other kinds of support, roughly for failing to commune with the girls.

Too Much Progress?

For the fifth and final objection to development sometimes made in the name of African values that I argue is weak, note that some reject development because it implies linearity or progress. Sometimes this objection is grounded on the idea that development means indefinite economic growth (Sindima 1989, 542–43; Rahnema 1997, 392, 393, 400), an association that I argued above is not necessary; in the twenty-first century, relatively few development theorists believe that it should take the form of pursuing the constant expansion of the monetary value of goods and services. However, other times the criticism is not based on this merely contingent association and appears to cut to the heart of the concept of development. Consider this claim:

> The problem is not in the lack of implementation, but rather in the concept of development as linear. . . . In indigenous knowledge, there is nothing analogous to the concept of development, often leading to a rejection of that idea. There is no concept of a linear process of life to establish a *before* and *after* state, namely underdevelopment and development, referring to the dichotomy in which people have to go through in order to achieve welfare, as in the Western world. (Kothari et al. 2014, 366, 367; see also Kuusipalo 2014)

Is It True That, for Indigenous African values, the Concept of Linearity (or Progress) Is Out of Place?

I believe not. Consider that, at the individual level, it is extremely common for indigenous Africans to invoke maxims such as "A person is a person through other persons" and "I am because we are." Although there are descriptive senses to these phrases (to the effect that one's existence and identity necessarily depend on others), there is also a prescriptive sense, namely, that one ought to become a real person or self, which one can do by prizing certain relationships with others.[5]Traditionally speaking, one should strive to become an ancestor, or at least as morally wise as one can become. Those who have utterly failed to exercise their capacity to commune and have acted in vicious ways are often labeled "non-persons" or even "animals." Now, given that the idea of *self-realization* or *self-improvement*, namely, moving away from being an animal (a before state) and toward becoming a real person (an after state), has in fact been salient in traditional sub-Saharan ethical thought, it is hardly a stretch to think in similar terms at a social level. If our aim as individuals should be to become good people, then a society's aim should plausibly be to create good institutions, ones that enable and prompt individuals to realize themselves as communal beings. If a society is failing to honor its people's special capacity to commune, then there is a reasonable sense of "progress" that it should be striving to achieve over time.

STRONG CRITICISMS OF DEVELOPMENT

Having argued that several criticisms of development theory and practice miss their mark from the perspective of an Afro-communal normative framework, I now argue that there are three criticisms that are on target. I am not the first to voice these criticisms, but I take my contribution to be showing that communion provides a unitary ground accounting for their force.

Too Anthropocentric

As noted above, standard development theory and practice now routinely integrate a concern for the environment. However, pollution is to be avoided only insofar as it would harm human beings, and sustainability is to be pursued only in the sense of using nature now in ways that are consistent with the flourishing of future generations of human beings. These approaches to the environment do not take into account what noninstrumental goodness or moral status exists beyond the human realm.

The Afro-communal ethic above entails that progress ought to be conceived as including the fulfillment of certain direct duties toward those animals that can be objects of communion with us. Recall that, by this ethic, human beings have a full moral status insofar as they can commune, and many animals have a partial moral status in that they can be communed with by us. Although our full moral status means that our urgent or most important interests should be favored when they unavoidably conflict with those of animals, their partial moral status means that our trivial interests, and perhaps some of our moderate ones, should not be satisfied at the expense of their urgent ones in (at least) being free from anxiety and physical pain.

Hence, a morally sound conception of social progress would be one that seeks to give animals their due, and does not imply that they should serve merely as a means to our ends. When evaluating a society, one ought to consider how to avoid degrading non-anthropocentric values, or, in the relational terms favored here, how to satisfy human interests while minimizing the subordination of and harm to animals capable of being party to communal relationships with us. A more stringent regulation, if not abolition, of factory farms would be a good way to start embarking on a more harmonious relationship with the most valuable parts of the natural world.

Too Individualistic

Above, I argued that development theory and practice cannot be faulted for being exclusively concerned with material, financial, or economic considerations, as they have also routinely addressed health, education, and human rights. What I do think is a fair criticism is the idea that a developmental approach to all these interests is overly *individualist*, by which I mean focused on improving goods internal to individuals and not giving enough weight to relational values.

To begin to appreciate this criticism, consider the remark, "If one defined violent crime, racism, suicide, isolation, alienation, environmental destruction and the like as major indicators of a 'bad' or 'underdeveloped' society, the industrialized countries would hardly be at the top of the 'development' scale" (Ziai 2007, 8; see also N'Dione et al. 1997, 369; Rahnema 1997, 384). Taking communion to be a basic value makes good sense of these criticisms of development. It is plausible to think of integration as a matter of people identifying with and exhibiting solidarity toward others, and to deem problems such as crime, racism, isolation, and alienation to be the undermining of these values and the manifestation of their opposites in the forms of division and ill will.

More than a few thinkers who have been inspired by Africa and criticized development have pointed out that Western economic norms tend to undermine certain relational orientations prominent in the lives of indigenous sub-Saharans. Here are some examples:

- The profit motive has often conflicted with the prestige motive, that is, the intention to give without immediate expectation of net gain or even equivalent return, common among indigenous African peoples (N'Dione et al. 1997, 371–72; Murove 2009);
- Relatedly, there has been a disposition among sub-Saharans not to accumulate wealth, but rather to spend it with the expectation of sustaining and deepening bonds, on which one could rely down the road (Busia 1962, 131; N'Dione et al. 1997, 370; Zaoual 1997, 34–36; Murove 2009, 231–32);

- Rather than deploy labor-saving technology, many indigenous Africans would employ their relatives and friends in an "economy of affection" (Zein-Elabdin 2011, 224–25);
- In contrast to a banking model, it would be natural for those inspired by indigenous African values to pool their resources and then loan them out either without seeking interest or on a profit-sharing basis (see discussion of South African *stokvels* in Louw [2001, 24–25] and of Senegalese *tontines* in Berg [2007,552]);
- Instead of those living on a plot of land being solely responsible for gathering up the produce from it, all those who had harvesting to do in many traditional sub-Saharan villages would collectively move from field to field to help one another (see discussion of the southern African practice of *letsema* in Letseka [2000, 183–84, 189–90]);
- Rather than export goods to the global market, African traders would often prefer to make goods that would benefit their compatriots; there is something prima facie wrong with a situation "where in a country with coffee crops it is impossible to drink local coffee (there is only imported instant one)" (Lubieniecka 2013,11–12);
- Instead of conceiving of poverty as bad simply because one's own needs go unmet, one should allow for the idea that "the problem with being poor is that I don't have anything to give to others" (an elderly African woman quoted in Metz [2011, 238]), which entails making allowance for some transferable goods, or at least those that can be shared by more than one agent at a time, and not merely goods that are nontransferable and indivisible;
- Rather than focusing mainly on money and commodities as what to distribute, goods or services to prioritize in the light of African values would include couples counselling, women's shelters, parenting classes, quality day care, rehabilitation programs, neighborhood parks and festivals, densification in spacious neighborhoods, job training, nonexploitive labor relations, and grassroots organizations (Metz 2011, 238–39);
- Rather than permit great inequalities of wealth, even if they were to the marginal financial benefit of the worst-off, many in the African tradition would find reason to reduce them so as to avoid envy and to foster a greater sense of togetherness (Magesa 1997, 278; Oruka 1997, 120).

The literature on African values features mainly these kinds of economic examples where development would appear to come at the cost of relationship, but it is worth noting parallel cases in the spheres of healthcare, education, and human rights. Extending the criticism in these ways would usefully clarify that an essential problem with development is not so much materialism, but rather the deeper and broader problem of individualism. So, for one example, consider the idea that one proper aim of education is to enculturate, that is, to transmit and enrich a local way of life that has been central to a people's self-conception for a long time (Goduka 2000). Such a concern to support an instance of communion contrasts with the view of education salient in the West, that its aim should be merely or mainly to enable students to rationally choose, in cosmopolitan fashion, from among a variety of global possibilities.

Too Technocratic

For a third criticism of development that I believe is incisive, consider that even those who question post-development theory tend to grant that one of its purportedly negative characterizations of development theory and practice is correct: "Development thinking is steeped in social engineering and the ambition to shape economies and societies, which makes it an interventionist and managerialist discipline" (Pieterse 2000, 182; see also Ferguson 1990; Ziai 2007, 8–9). The literature abounds with bitter criticism of development "experts" and "managers" who advise and oversee programs, occluding more democratic approaches, such as where intended beneficiaries would be involved in the construction of the programs.

As has been noted, "the importance of 'participation' has been taken on board, at least nominally, by the major international development agencies" (Devereux and McGregor 2014, 299). The question that remains is whether the logic of development theory can adequately explain why participation is morally important. The central developmental rationale for participation is one of efficiency: without input from the poor, a program intended to benefit them would be less likely to work. Generally speaking, people best know their own interests and how to realize them, a point that John Stuart Mill is famous for having invoked in his political philosophy. And, so, a development theorist might reasonably contend that consultation with intended beneficiaries is vital in order to be able to ensure that a program will indeed help them.

However, there are two problems with this rationale for participation. First, it is not *always* the case that consultation with the poor would assist in doing what is most likely to help them. *Sometimes* policymakers and activists can be in a position to know on their own what would be good for others. After all, imagine if the poor's lack of education were to get in the way and cause problems when trying to craft an effective program; in such a case, if a top-down approach would likely produce marginally better outcomes for the poor in the long run, the logic of development theory would justify it.

Second, a requirement to consult with the poor does not seem reducible to mere considerations of efficiency. There is intuitively some moral reason to include the poor that is independent of the epistemic consequences of doing so. There is something about a participative process that matters in itself when it comes to justice; there would be reason to consult with intended beneficiaries even were it the case that their lack of education would make it somewhat more difficult to help them.

Now, considerations of communion naturally give substantial moral weight to the procedure by which programs are undertaken. The way that goods or services are distributed must be done in a way that esteems relationships of identity and solidarity. It is the former element that does real work in the present context, for identifying with others is more or less a matter of enjoying a sense of togetherness and engaging in joint projects. These factors have an intrinsic significance for morally sound relationships distinct from caring (doing what is likely to meet people's needs), and they make good sense of why there is strong moral reason for programs to be participatory, beyond considerations of efficiency. Participation could range from consultation to cooperation or, as one scholar has forcefully suggested, to the provision of resources to enable the poor to undertake their own, grassroots projects (Matthews 2007).

CONCLUSION: TOWARD A RELATIONAL CONCEPT OF PROGRESS

I have argued that, even upon detaching talk of "development" from the aim of indefinite economic growth, there are three key respects in which its characteristic theory and practice remain morally questionable. Specifically, they are still overly anthropocentric, individualist, and technocratic. The African value of communion qua identity and solidarity provides a normative theoretical ground for making these three criticisms and for prescribing a different form of progress, one that includes relating to certain animals as ends, that does not invariably trade-off relational goods for non-relational ones, and that includes a participatory dimension at its core.

One major question at this point is how to speak about the direction in which a society ought to move. Some would characterize the relational values sketched in this chapter as informing an "African development" (e.g., Ajei 2011; Keita 2011; Prah 2011). However, if I am correct that for more than 60 years the word "development" has signified an anthropocentric, individualist, and technocratic approach, then such a phrase would be a contradiction in terms (supposing that "African" signified communion). Although there would be something appealing about composing a chapter that invokes the value of communion and sports the title "How the West Is Underdeveloped,"

I am more inclined to let talk of "development" go and instead to work with a different vocabulary.

Contra some in the post-development movement, I do not also eschew all talk of "progress" or the concept of linearity. Central to the African ethical tradition has been the view that people ought over time to become real persons, often construed in terms of their capacity to relate to others in certain social ways. Since it makes sub-Saharan sense to say that some immoral individuals live akin to animals and that they ought to mature, by working to manifest their genuinely human-communal features, undesirable societies seem aptly construed as those in which it is difficult for people to do so and in which key institutions instead flout the value of communion. From this perspective, a bad society is one that tends to produce bad lives, ones that are inhuman for their relationships too often being antisocial or discordant.

In sum, instead of "growth" or "development," perhaps we should try talking of "humanization." And since the West has not done a particularly good job of humanizing its institutions and relationships more generally, and since communion has not been a salient foundational value in its moral-political philosophy, the default respect in which the West ought to seek to aid Africa is by providing resources with which it could take the lead in enabling its people to become real people by communing with other people (and animals).[6]

NOTES

1. Although this is well known, one might see the trenchant analysis in Castoriadis (1984/1985).
2. I acknowledge that Gyekye is committed to denying this approach, given that he believes the common good is foundational.
3. For a fuller answer than what is given here, see Metz (2012b).
4. For a similar point, about the potential clash between infant mortality and multiculturalism, see Kiely (1999).
5. For just one exposition, in the context of a variety of sub-Saharan peoples, see Nkulu-N'sengha (2009).
6. A longer version of this paper first appeared as Thaddeus Metz, "Replacing Development," *Philosophical Papers* 46(1) (2017): 111–37 (http://dx.doi.org/10.1080/05568641.2017.1295627), and is reprinted here with permission from Taylor & Francis.

BIBLIOGRAPHY

Ajei, Martin Odei. 2011. *Africa's Development: The Imperatives of Indigenous Knowledge and Values.* Saarbrücken: Lambert Academic Publishing.

Basu, Ratan Lal. 2005. "Why the Human Development Index Does Not Measure up to Ancient Indian Standards." *Cultural Mandala* 6(2). https://epublications.bond.edu.au/cm/vol6/iss2/5.

Berg, Erik. 2007. "Post-Development Theory in Africa." *Peace Review* 19(4): 541–54.

Bujo, Bénézet. 2005. "Differentiations in African Ethics." In *The Blackwell Companion to Religious Ethics*, edited by William Schweiker, 423–37. Malden: Blackwell.

Busia, Kofi Abrefa. 1962. *The Challenge of Africa.* New York: Frederick A. Praeger, Inc.

Castoriadis, Cornelius. 1984/85. "Reflections on 'Rationality' and 'Development.'" *Thesis Eleven* 10/11: 18–36.

Devereux, Stephan and J. Allister McGregor. 2014. "Transforming Social Protection: Human Wellbeing and Social Justice." *European Journal of Development Research* 26(3): 296–310.

Escobar, Arturo. 1992. "Imagining a Post-Development Era? Critical Thought, Development and Social Movements." *Social Text* 31/32: 20–56.

Esteva, Gustavo, and Madhu Suri Prakash. 1997. "From Global Thinking to Local Thinking." In *The Post-Development Reader*, edited by Majid Rahnema and Victoria Bawtree, 277–89. London: Zed Books.

Ferguson, James. 1990. *The Anti-Politics Machine: 'Development,' Depoliticization and Bureaucratic Power in Lesotho.* Cambridge: Cambridge University Press.

Ferguson, James. 1997. "Development and Bureaucratic Power in Lesotho." In *The Post-Development Reader*, edited by Majid Rahnema and Victoria Bawtree, 223–33. London: Zed Books.

Gbadegesin, Segun. 1991. *African Philosophy: Traditional Yoruba Philosophy and Contemporary African Realities.* New York: Peter Lang.

Goduka, Ivy N. 2000. "African/Indigenous Philosophies: Legitimizing Spiritually Centered Wisdoms within the Academy." In *African Voices in Education*, edited by Philip Higgs, Ntombizolile Vakalisa, Tyobeka V. Mda, and N'Dri Thérèse Assié-Lumumba, 63–83. Lansdowne: Juta.

Gyekye, Kwame. 1997. *Tradition and Modernity: Philosophical Reflections on the African Experience.* New York: Oxford University Press.

Gyekye, Kwame. 2004. *Beyond Cultures: Perceiving a Common Humanity. Ghanaian Philosophical Studies, Volume III.* Washington, DC: Council for Research in Values and Philosophy.

Iroegbu, Pantaleon. 2005. "Beginning, Purpose and End of Life." In *Kpim of Morality Ethics*, edited by Pantaleon Iroegbu and Anthony Echekwube, 440–45. Ibadan: Heinemann Educational Books.

Kasenene, Peter. 1998. *Religious Ethics in Africa.* Kampala: Fountain Publishers.

Keita, Lansana. 2011. "Philosophy and Development: On the Problematic African Development." In *Philosophy and African Development Theory and Practice*, edited by Lansana Keita, 115–37. Dakar: CODESRIA.

Kiely, Ray. 1999. "The Last Refuge of the Noble Savage? A Critical Assessment of Post-Development Theory." *European Journal of Development Research* 11(1): 30–55.

Kothari, Ashish, Federico Demaria, and Alberto Acosta. 2014. "*Buenvivir*, Degrowth and Ecological *Swaraj*: Alternatives to Sustainable Development and the Green Economy." *Development* 57(3–4): 362–75.

Kuusipalo, Marianne. 2014. "Harmony versus Progress: Development from the Perspective of Indigenous Worldviews." *Horn of Africa Journal*. http://afrikansarvi.fi/72-Artikkeli/203-harmony-versus-progress.

Letseka, Moeketsi. 2000. "African Philosophy and Educational Discourse." In *African Voices in Education*, edited by Philip Higgs, Ntombizolile Vakalisa, Tyobeka V. Mda, and N'Dri Thérèse Assié-Lumumba, 179–93. Lansdowne: Juta.

Louw, Dirk. 2001. "*Ubuntu* and the Challenges of Multiculturalism in Post-Apartheid South Africa." *Quest* 15(1–2): 15–35.

Lubieniecka, Ewelina Róża. 2013. "Does Post-Development Theory Find Alternatives to Westernization of International Relations? An African Perspective." Paper Presented at the eighth Pan-European Conference on International Relations.

Magesa, Laurenti. 1997. *African Religion: The Moral Traditions of Abundant Life*. Maryknoll: Orbis Books.

Matthews, Sally. 2004. "Post-Development Theory and the Question of Alternatives: A View from Africa." *Third World Quarterly* 25(2): 373–84.

Matthews, Sally. 2007. "What, Then, Should We Do?" In *Exploring Post-Development*, edited by Aram Ziai, 131–44. New York: Routledge.

Mawere, Munyaradzi. 2011. "Possibilities for Cultivating African Indigenous Knowledge Systems (IKSs): Lessons from Selected Cases of Witchcraft in Zimbabwe." *Journal of Research in Peace, Gender and Development* 1(3): 91–100.

Metz, Thaddeus. 2007. "Toward an African Moral Theory." *Journal of Political Philosophy* 15(3): 321–41.

Metz, Thaddeus. 2011. "An African Theory of Dignity and a Relational Conception of Poverty." In *The Humanist Imperative in South Africa*, edited by John W. de Gruchy, 233–41. Stellenbosch: African Sun Media.

Metz, Thaddeus. 2012a. "Developing African Political Philosophy." *Philosophia Africana* 14(1): 61–83.

Metz, Thaddeus. 2012b. "An African Theory of Moral Status." *Ethical Theory and Moral Practice* 15(3): 387–402.

Mokgoro, Yvonne. 1998. "*Ubuntu* and the Law in South Africa." *Potchefstroom Electronic Law Journal* 1(1): 15–26.

Murove, Munyaradzi Felix. 2009. "The Incarnation of Max Weber's Protestant Ethic and the Spirit of Capitalism in Post-Colonial African Economic Discourse." In *African Ethics*, edited by Munyaradzi Felix Murove, 221–37. Pietermaritzburg: University of Kwazulu-Natal Press.

Mutwa, Vusamazulu Credo. 1998. *Indaba, My Children*. Edinburgh: Payback Press.

N'Dione, Emmanuel Seni, Philippe de Leener, Jean-Pierre Perier, Mamadou Ndiaye, and Pierre Jacolin. 1997. "Reinventing the Present: The Chodack Experience in Senegal." In *The Post-Development Reader*, edited by Majid Rahnema and Victoria Bawtree, 364–76. London: Zed Books.

Nkondo, Gessler Muxe. 2007. "*Ubuntu* as a Public Policy in South Africa." *International Journal of African Renaissance Studies* 2(1): 88–100.

Nkulu-N'sengha, Mutombo. 2009. "*Bumuntu*." In *Encyclopedia of African Religion*, edited by Molefe Kete Asante and Ama Mazama, 142–47. Los Angeles: Sage.

Nussbaum, Martha. 2001. *Women and Human Development*. New York: Cambridge University Press.

Oruka, Henry Odera. 1997. *Practical Philosophy*. Nairobi: East African Educational Publishers.

Pieterse, Jan. 2000. "After Post-Development." *Third World Quarterly* 21(2): 175–91.

Prah, Kwesi Kwaa. 2011. "Culture: The Missing Link in Development Planning in Africa." In *Philosophy and African Development Theory and Practice*, edited by Lansana Keita, 155–68. Dakar: CODESRIA.

Rahnema, Majid. 1997. "Towards Post-Development." In *The Post-Development Reader*, edited by Majib Rahnema and Victoria Bawtree, 377–403. London: Zed Books.

Sen, Amartya. 1999. *Development as Freedom*. New York: Alfred A. Knopf.

Sindima, Harvey. 1989. "Community of Life." *The Ecumenical Review* 41(4): 537–51.

Tangwa, Godfrey. 2011. "Philosophy, Democracy and Development." In *Philosophy and African Development Theory and Practice*, edited by Lansana Keita, 177–95. Dakar: CODESRIA.

Zaoual, Hassan. 1997. "The Economy and Symbolic Sites of Africa." In *The Post-Development Reader*, edited by Majib Rahnema and Victoria Bawtree, 30–39. London: Zed Books.

Zein-Elabdin, Eiman Osman. 2011. "Postcoloniality and Development: Development as a Colonial Discourse." In *Philosophy and African Development Theory and Practice*, edited by Lansana Keita, 215–30. Dakar: CODESRIA.

Ziai, Aram. 2007. "Development Discourse and Its Critics." In *Exploring Post-Development*, edited by Aram Ziai, 3–17. New York: Routledge.

Ziai, Aram. 2014. "Post-Development Concepts? *Buen Vivir*, *Ubuntu* and Degrowth." Paper Presented at the Degrowth Conference in Leipzig. http://www.degrowth.de/en/catalogue-entry/post-developmentconcepts-Buen-vivir-ubuntu-and-degrowth/.

Chapter 9

Black Consciousness Philosophy as Politics of Responsibility for Africa

Philip Osarobu Isanbor and George Uzoma Ukagba

The operational concerns of Black Consciousness Philosophy (BCP) are about the knowledge of the self as blacks among other racial entities. It is about the recognition of one's history by the same oneself, not to be told by the others with racial imperialistic biases. Such existential and ideological consciousness for the *Blackness of History* has been ontologically associated with the values of African Cultural Identities (ACIs). The Africans are known to be black in the existential representation and cosmological appearance (cf. Biko 1978: 13). The blackness defines their identity and personality in their quest for cultural, political, and social unity, trust, and justice. The blackness modulates their socialization and development based on the commonness of skinned particularity: a definition of common willingness rather than racial character or classification (see Isanbor 2015: 70; Isanbor 2016: 85). Though not all Africans are black-skinned, they are all Africans in mind (a commonness for cosmological trusts of relevance and purposes). They are all ontologically black in worldviews and originally situated within a communitarian mentality toward the realization of collective self-liberation and self-authenticity, which generally classifies any human person to be African (Ogbenika and Isanbor 2017: 10; Ndiovo-Gatsheni and Ndlovo 2021: 30). This is the basis of the developmental ideology of Steve Biko's BCP as a philosophy of black's politics of resistance against the operational effects of *Whiteness of History* in Africa. It has been born out of its intellectual and continental agitated consciousness from the *Negritude* as a philosophy of African sociocultural and political consciousness and recognition.

The black's politics of resistance is about the fight against the enthronements of the Politics of Antiblack Culture (PAC). For Steve Biko, *Blackness of History* appears to promote continental or racial particularity, not racial individualism, in the fight to overcome white racial oppression, suppression, and subjugation over the blacks—the effectuality and positionality of PAC in African environment. With the ethics of living, BCP has been very positive since the effects of racial assimilation can be socially and politically overruled by the existential-ontological recognition of *Blackness of History*. Racially and politically, in the conviction of Biko, "it is a sin to allow oneself to be oppressed" (Biko 1978: 45). BCP as a reorienting ideological course for decolonial existential ontology, it is the philosophy of the oppressed, imperialistically racialized Africa, and it is an articulated and expressed consciousness in order to end oppression and imperialistic subjugation of the black race (see Sithole 2016: 32; Ogbenika and Isanbor 2017: 11; Ndiovo-Gatsheni and Ndlovo 2021: 31). Without rethinking one's oppressed conditions, one necessarily and indispensably furthers the trends of future oppressions, especially through mental slavery and subjugation, and in great effects, through economic alienations and suppressions.

Like Steve Biko's decolonial meditation of BCP as an ideology of African Sustainable Development (ASD), the Africans can contemporarily recall the sociopolitical relevance of the philosophies of Julius Nyerere's *Ujamaa* (a philosophy that was predicated on the abolition of colonial English language and the adoption of Swahili as the basis of nationalism in Tanzania), Sekou Toure's *Communaucratique*, Leopold Senghor's *Negritude*, Kenneth Kaunda's *African Humanism*, and Kwame Nkrumah's *Consciencism*. They were well-referenced reformers who have seen their need for the decolonization of the African minds in order to engender holistic African liberation and development (see Falaiye 2012: 13; Isanbor 2016: 88). They remain useful tools for rallying the African people with a common ontology of reasoning and faith against a common enemy who believed that the Africans are lesser humans and they cannot be responsible in managing their affairs.

Hence, the chapter surveys the contemporary relevance of the social and developmental conceptualization of the BCP as *Politics of Responsibility* for ASD, especially through overcoming PAC seated in decolonized African minds, occasioned by the *Whiteness of History*. It recognizes that many scholars have presented and postulated many divergent and some convergent views with regard to the panacea to Africa's developmental challenges, especially in our contemporary existence. The African thinkers recognize that BCP as *Politics of Responsibility* is mainly hinged on the values, sustainability, and re-engineering of ACIs. With such philosophical engagement, thischapter calls on the Africans to value BCP as a responsive and responsible mentality in developing themselves and their societies, as against the colonized mentality that has beclouded their sense of judgment and the enthronement of inferiority complex amid their cosmological socialization of purposes and interests.

The chapter is to restate the consciousness that the Africans can govern themselves effectively if they are willing to play the *Politics of Responsibility* inherent in the *Blackness of History* as a people of common heritage and ancestry, especially instilling the principles of common good and solidarity in managing their natural and human resources (cf. Adewumi and Kolawole 2008: 12; Falaiye 2012: 14; Lukman 2018: 50). It recognizes the socioeconomic readiness of the blacks to develop Africa and Africans by the management of their resources through cooperative investments of vibrant, reliable, and sustainable business-society relationships, as currently proposed and championed in Tony Elumelu's Africapitalism. The chapter ends up by evaluating the fights of *Blackness of History* against the developmental effects of PAC in African decolonized minds as *Politics of Responsibility* in achieving ASD, and then contemporarily considering Africapitalism as the existential basis of BCP. In all, by employing an expository method, the chapter demonstrates how the BCP determined and arrived at being considered as *Politics of Responsibility*, and also evaluates to determine the credibility of arguments for BCP as a social and cultural ideology in achieving ASD.

THEORETICAL FRAMEWORK AND CONTEXTUALIZATION

According to many reflections by some thinkers on the thought of *Blackness of History*, the conceptualization of the blackness in BCP is the starting point of socio-philosophical and decolonial meditations on the ontological and cosmological recognitions of ACIs. To these thinkers, like Steve Biko, Frantz Fanon, Lewis Gordon, Aime Cesaire, Wole Soyinka, and Tendayi Sithole, such philosophy of development remains a sociocultural force predicated on the politics of "being" and claiming being from the margins of nonbeing, in overcoming the effects of white sociocultural supremacy and superiority presented in the African continent by *Whiteness of History* through the imperialistic employment of PAC (see Ogbenika and Isanbor 2017: 10; Ndiovo-Gatsheni and Ndlovo 2021: 30). Some ideological and political philosophers, especially Kwame Nkrumah and Kenneth Kaunda, with their sociopolitical indoctrination for the conscientious revamping and regenerating ACIs from the effects of slavery and colonization, the need for the return to *Blackness of History* becomes inevitable in knowing our place in the community of nations. Such a return to the pragmatic operation of BCP will help us as Africans in understanding our continental crisis and challenges through the contents of our identity and personality.

With BCP as the basis of ASD, there is a developmental need not to forget that the African political and socioeconomic environments have been long defecated, polluted, and abused by colonial interlopers, the *Whiteness of History*. By the colonial defecation, pollution, and abuse of the African political and socioeconomic environment, the African person has been culturally balkanized by PAC's "borrowed paradigm" and then has lost the values of ACIs in directing and managing African affairs and resources, and has bred crisis in the African conscience, causing a split in the self of the African person (see Ogundowole 2008: 13; Oladipo 2006: 65; Olukoshi 2004: 10). Over time, the African continent has been besieged with developmental crisis and challenges, even beyond and within various political independences of her nations. Some of her nations still blame the effects of the *Whiteness of History* for their developmental failures due to Western long political and economic interferences (cf. Adewumi and Kolawole 2008: 12; Falaiye 2012: 14; Lukman 2018: 50). Against this vision and mission of imperialistic estrangement and the economic assimilative perspectives of African economies and development by PAC occasioned by the *Whiteness of History*, the revamping socioeconomic and political mentalities of ASD associated with the pragmatic adoptions and adaptations of BCP become necessary. It behooves the need to create one's racial political and social world peculiar to one's identity and personality in relation to global commitment and development. It is about making out one's image based on one's cultural and cosmological subjectivity.

The achievable plans for the realization of ASD are beyond the dependable degrees of the advocacies for the pragmatic adaptations of BCP through the values of ACIs. In African cosmology, the individual's right to development through employment opportunities, healthcare, food, education, and the likes has everything to do with the group's agitations for the valuing of ACIs through the principles of togetherness, common good, and solidarity (Olukoshi 2014: 11; Efemini 2010: 239). With the hope for liberation and eliminating inferior complexity occasioned by the effects of the *Whiteness of History* created in the black political and social landscapes, the BCP as *Politics of Responsibility* seats purposefully to redirect the African courage and sincerity in governing their affairs (Ogundowole 2008: 30; Soludo 2006: 10). This is the politics that should be situated within the power of responsibility, and which recognizes that the African can never cease to be black, already conditioned in the mind, socialization, and development, as Tony Elumelu's ideology of Africapitalism suggests. The pragmatic ideology of Africapitalism is a contemporary ethic of authentic African living and development. It requires that Africans should work existentially and reasonably to channel the strengths of their blackness to liberate themselves from all forms of diplomatic and political limitations and inferiority complexes contemporarily presented by the *Whiteness of History*. This liberation should be done through socioeconomic investments and commitments that are based on business-society relationships in creating African wealth and capacities.

BASIS OF BCP

BCP is a pragmatic ideology for regeneration of African minds commonly championed by Steve Biko, with the mind-set of redirecting the Africans to the values of *Blackness of History* created by their very selves. For Biko, no one develops outside his or her personality and identity. One's communitarian makeups define the individual's conception and perception of development and for the valuation of commonness and solidarity (see Manganyi 1973: 20). For many African sociopolitical and ideological philosophers and thinkers, no one can deny the existence and philosophy of cultural identity that directs the people's history of their sociopolitical consciousness and development. It is a consciousness against the foundational basis of racial dehumanization of the blacks (see Ogundowole 2008: 13; Oladipo 2006: 65; Olukoshi 2004: 10). As developmentally recognized, with the operations of ACIs, we recognize that there are elements of *Blackness of History* in every African. Whether black or not, they are black in mind and worldview. Within the effects of the *Whiteness of History*, the Africans have witnessed in the past in the name of colonization, slavery and apartheid, and are still witnessing in the name of contemporary recolonization, some mental enslavement, cultural alienation, and diplomatic subjugation (see Isanbor 2015: 72; Isanbor 2016: 87). Against these trends of *Whiteness of History* in black political and sociocultural landscapes, BCP becomes *Politics of Responsibility* as it is based on the power of solidarity of cultural identity and personality.

It is in solidarity as a classification of common interests of development that BCP as *Politics of Responsibility* becomes very meaningful and reasonable, and to remain a common characteristic of African blackness. BCP must be seen by us as phenomena that are positive in themselves, and this developmental relationship means that they are desirable even outside considerations involving white domination and racialism (see Manganyi 1973: 20). Domination and racialism are elements of human and cultural alienation and subjugation. Human sense of recognition, authenticity, and intersubjectivity can reduce or eliminate racialism and domination. The society recognizes that nobody should ever have any right to tell anybody else that he or she should not be aware of himself or herself as a being of development and as a subject of lived experiences. For the sense of BCP as expressed in the present should also mean something like political continuity of black existential consciousness.

In all, for Biko, the history of our continental ideological development and consciousness will tell us that the conception of blackness of the blacks was created by the same blacks from the superiority complex they created for the whites. It was never by the whites, and seeing the whites or the so-called Westerners or Europeans in the midst created some conceptual differentiation of the selves; the black cowed themselves into nothingness but slaves and animal-human workers (cf. Adewumi and Kolawole 2008: 14; Falaiye 2012: 16; Lukman 2018: 52). Against the ethics of authentic living associated with one's existential subjectivity, the Africans inferiorly created their own image (cf. Sithole, p. 93). The blacks unmindfully created some space of superiority for the whites to dominate, owing to the strength of their skin coloration. Nevertheless, through such mimicry, without culture, no identity or personality is ontologically expressible and adequate. What is important is that BCP remains a phenomenologico-logical unmasking of the socioeconomic effects of PAC in its misguided and imperialistic quests for ASD.

BCP recognizes that African tradition has communal moral values and social structures which involve caring, humility, fraternity, and mutuality that provide the basis for social harmony. *Blackness of History* is a gift of nature to the Africans. It promotes their ontological oneness. In many instances, Biko has made it clear that, as a social and political orientation of black minds, BCP speaks to blacks in the language of their existential ontology. Tied to this is the fact that it gives much credence to the lived experience and the proximity of existential problems that afflict blacks (see Sithole, p. 32). With the fall of such historical development of blacks, we can appreciate the values or merits of traditional African communalism, when compared to the social and moral pathologies of the extreme rugged individualism of Western modernity.

BCP AS *POLITICS OF RESPONSIBILITY* FOR SUSTAINABLE AFRICAN DEVELOPMENT

Within the ethics of human duty and responsibility, morality of development is associated with human ontological culture in relation to human actions, and the Africans are no exception. The conceptualization of morality or ethics in relation to politics is centered on the understanding of political governance and public policymaking. The *Politics of Responsibility* is dependable on the moral virtues that regulate our actions and desires in our pursuits for development, and they are wisdom, patience, temperance, courage, prudence, solidarity, and sincerity and other moral qualities that make one act excellently and honorably in the society. Based on the workable recognition of democratic governance and civil societies' participation in political and economic interests for the realization of ASD, *Politics of Responsibility* demands the sociopolitical paradigmatic shift from the policies making by very few individuals that are very economically powerful to the development of commonwealth that will benefit all persons in the society (cf. Adewumi and Kolawole 2008: 12; Falaiye 2012: 14; Lukman 2018: 50). By creating enabling business investment environment and innovative opportunities, the socioeconomic thrusts for the *Politics of Responsibility* direct the African entrepreneurial giants to the building of vibrant and viable social, political, and economic institutions through the development of public affairs and resources rather than making few strong individuals capitalists to be more powerful than the governments.

According to Tendayi Sithole; "*Politics of Responsibility* for responsibility itself rests on the principle that the current existential conditions should be radically changed and there should be no compromise. It means that responsibility has to be carried out in full and its outcomes cannot be fruitful if it is compromised" (p. 37). Such consciousness of building strong institutions is hinged on having responsible citizens who are equal before the rule of law and being obedient to valuation of social contracts and principles. It is about the change in the contemporary local, national, and international systems of political and economic management of resources which has also manifested itself in terms of the shift in the rural-urban balance in favor of the rural settlements as more people in the world today live in urban areas as compared to rural areas, through investments in agriculture, mining, tourism, biotechnology, trado-medicine (see Olukoshi 2014: 11; Efemini 2010: 239). It is about being responsible with the resources at our disposal, and by recognizing the importance of those both in the rural and urban areas, and culturally managing our commonwealth through solidarity of interests and recognition. As a politics of black solidarity, we must be politically responsible to the courses of common good and social order rather than the promotion of the valleys of individualism and segregationism.

The conceptualization of the *Politics of Responsibility* as an ideology of social change and political reformation has its basis on the Platonic Politics of Human Character (Ogbenika and Isanbor 2017: 10; Ndiovo-Gatsheni and Ndlovo 2021: 30). It is a moral foundation of human character development based on the values of human actions related to public governance and policymaking (see Ogundowole 2008: 13; Oladipo 2006: 65; Olukoshi 2004: 10). It is basically grounded in natural principles (education, commendation, incentive, sanction, and constant practice of discipline) evident in human traits and not conventionally formulated. With the *ethics of living* associated with the applicability of sincerity and trust, *Politics of Responsibility* becomes that essential makeup of the people who live to express the existentiality of their authenticity and essentiality of their intersubjectivity, rather than make-belief of the individual's ability to be just, humane, and peaceable with natures and non-natures. When adopted, *Politics of Responsibility* leads every generation of mankind to come out of economics that are solidly founded on extreme individualism and work toward envisioning economics for common humanity. This is about the consciousness of establishment of common good in human society with the right disposition for the value of life through proper cultural socialization of human interests and desires. It is a situational reality that fosters the sense and workability of common goodness and reign of unification of interests.

PRAGMATIC RECOGNITION OF AFRICAPITALISM AS A BCP

The demands for ASD are based on the economic and sociopolitical operations of African self-participation and self-reliance in the fight against active effects and influences of poverty and general weight of corruption in managing African Affairs and resources by Africans themselves (see Ogundowole 2008: 30; Soludo 2006: 10). This concern prompted Tony Elumelu to propose and champion the developmental consciousness and values called Africapitalism. From many philosophical and economic observations and postulations, since the inception of *Negritude* as a pragmatic ideology for ASD, Africapitalism has been contemporarily evaluated as a vibrant and reliable developmental mentality as an offshoot of BCP. Africapitalism calls for the need for African self-reliance and self-participation on the values of ASD by the economic and social recognition of ACIs in the management of African natural and human resources. Africapitalism as a BCP is a demand for vibrant, sustainable, and reliable business investments, especially by Africans, in line with the values of ACIs in attaining rationalized, reasonable, just, and meaningful African welfare and well-being by creating job opportunities and wealth for the realization of ASD. This is by exploring, not exploiting, the African resources.

The operational objectives of Africapitalism as an ideology of ASD are centered on the blacks as a community of creative and innovative people to be readily aware of the knowledge of contemporary forces of global development that are based on business-society relationships. The knowledge of Africapitalism as a model of collective human development defines the individual as a member of a group of common survival and relevance (cf. Olatunji and Ujomu 2021: 1–2). As an organizational knowledge for the realization of ASD, Africapitalism is a technical revolutionary modeling of African socialism through the creation of business-society relationships being engineered by private business investment models in line with sustainable global economies. As a sense of *Politics of Responsibility* on which BCP is contemporarily restated for the realization of ASD, Africapitalism reminds us of Charles Soludo's Lecture: *Can Nigeria be the China of Africa*. The Soludo's lecture translated the needs of African development possibilities to be based on the socio-capitalistic values and operation of human capital investments for

African political self-reliance and economic self-identification. This development consciousness for economic self-reliance and self-identification in the midst of the effects of PAC, Elumelu is unaware of the practice of African humanistic socialism or communalism, but, with the growing nature of industrialized and technologically based economies of the Western World based on capitalistic mode of production, Elumelu proposed, designed, and championed a capitalistic conscious development based on sociocultural identities of business-society relationships.

Hence, Africapitalism as a BCP is about the creation and projection of vibrant, reliable, and sustainable business opportunities and investments being politically spirited and economically flavored by the values of ACIs. For Elumelu, the pragmatic idea of Africapitalism is based on the operations of private business developmental ventures and initiatives that should enable creative and innovative spaces of rethinking business-society relationships from an African development perspective. Though the demands of Africapitalism implore capitalism as a model of operation, its employment demands that such business consciousness should sustain the business-society relationship, where the employers and employees get satisfied and then work to sustain such establishments with the values of ACIs being defined by the *Politics of Responsibility*.

Hence, with Afroxiological epistemic conceptualization of the *Politics of Responsibility*, Africapitalism has been beyond an ideology as it is already operational and effectual based on the organizational goals and objectives of Tony Elumelu Foundation. It is the global operation of capitalism as a means of fast-growing economies in the world, but, as an indigenous and traditional principle of development, it recognizes the needs of "Africanness" or "Afroxilogical Consciousness" as a basis of *Politics of Responsibility* in the capitalist means of production, as it is a private sector's commitment to the realization of ASD. As BCP, it is a call for the Africans to develop themselves as a people and their nations by the employment of *Politics of Responsibility* based on ACIs, with a vibrant, reliable, and sustainable commitment and contribution to global commonwealth. The Africapitalistic *Politics of Responsibility* is contemporarily directing African blackness as an identity to the elimination of the culture of "borrowed paradigm" and to embracing ACIs in developing Africa integrally and sustainably through private business investments and initiatives with African socio-capitalistic flavors.

To realize ASD, Africapitalism as a pragmatic principle of common business solidarity and interests demands that the economic, political, and governmental pursuance of self-reliance be practiced at all levels of socioeconomic and resource development. It demands that such practice of self-reliance start from the level of national policy formulation and implementations based on the *Politics of Responsibility* as a condition to strengthen the relationship between the governments and the people in their involvements in the courses of African growth and advancement. Hence, Africapitalism, as BCP directs the African minds toward the need for collective self-reliance among African countries and peoples, and then directing the advancement of collective struggles and commitments against the imperialistic economic policies and programs occasioned by the *Whiteness of History*. Thereby, Africapitalism champions the ability of the Africans to do what they are already doing more humanely, efficiently, and responsibly, then adapting to the contemporary demands and values of industrialized and technological trends of development in managing their resources for their common interests of realizing ASD.

EVALUATIVE CONCLUSION

For most African minds, following the effects of the BCP, political independence has been attained, but not cultural, economic, and ideological independence, even when they are contemporarily underpinned by other sociological developmental interests associated with globalization and civilization (cf. Ayemwenre 2019: 43, Ogbenika and Isanbor 2017: 12; Ndiovo-Gatsheni and Ndlovo 2021: 33). The socioeconomic integrations of ideologies and interests for the realization of ASD demand meaningful, vibrant, and reliable implications of the sociopolitical shifts in values, from the *Blackness of History* to the mimicry and adoptions of *Whiteness of History* by the blacks. This is to be creatively and innovatively determined in decoding the enduring effects of inferiority complexes and sociopolitical subjugations presented by colonization, slavery, and political abnegation (cf. Adewumi and Kolawole 2008: 12; Falaiye 2012: 14; Lukman 2018: 50). The developmental placement of the *Politics of Responsibility* remains very inevitable and indispensable, for the sociopolitical adaptations and praxis of *Politics of Responsibility* demand the cultural reformation and regeneration of ACIs on the existential valuation of social solidarity and fraternity in the face of imposing globalized interests based on the economic waves of Western imperialistic development. This is what the African political cosmology is traditionally known for.

With Africapitalism as BCP, we can develop together as one black family by desiring peace and harmony through investments in Africa. This is the core of African humanism. The contemporary values for peace and justice in the face of globalized interests and agitations suggest that we as Africans in common political cosmology should be based on the values of ACIs. Definitely, contemporary trends require that human beings all over the globe need to reestablish stronger ties of solidarity among themselves. They need to form more purposeful-oriented communities for peace and harmony to reign rather than planning self-destructive programs when we invest and establish business empires in the same African cosmology (see Echekwube 2002: 36–37; 2005: 32). Africapitalism as a principle of ASD proposes that the operations of the principles of common good, solidarity, and peaceful coexistence are possible when Africans realize the need to advance their common ancestry through the investments in the same African cosmological socioeconomic space, as peace and harmony can reign among us if we acknowledge our common ancestry and for the respect, promotion, and protection of everyone's rights, dignity, and development.

Since it is greatly accepted by Africans that all the technical and sociopolitical theories of development, all the intellectual analyses of cultural and racial discriminations, and all ethical indoctrinations as attempts to establish the innate inferiority of *Blackness of History* by the imposing effects of *Whiteness of History*, have been contemporarily fruitless efforts of PAC, what is urgently needed is for present-day Africans to educationally and entrepreneurially decolonize their colonized mentalities toward the possibilities of ASD, and look forward to vibrant, reliable, and sustainable policies and programs in achieving it (see Kouassi 2022: 20; Isanbor 2016: 90; 2017: 85). This should be done through collective self-actualization and self-reliance of African nations and peoples contemporarily inherent in the business-society relationship principles and ideologies like Africapitalism as a sociopolitical basis of BCP.

Therefore, we need to generally understand that there have been some clashes of identities and personalities on the adoptions of development modeling and morality in our contemporary Africa, but there is a need for the Africans to politically and culturally recognize themselves through their sociopolitical and organizational capabilities and capacities in managing their human and material resources, especially through their own very actions and valued choices by the embraces of ACIs. Through *Politics of Responsibility*, the blacks should readily embrace the development modeling and morality that are in relation with the values of ACIs. Although moral and identity crises come from the fact that Africans have shifted away from their own values system and the regards of *Politics of Responsibility* and social values that go with it, it is greatly demanded that we respect who we are and face our developmental problems and challenges. With *Politics of Responsibility*, we fashion our development that will be meaningful, integral, and sustainable, based on cultural and social values, identity, and personality that promote the principles and spirits of solidarity and sincerity of purpose.

BIBLIOGRAPHY

Adewumi, S. and Kolawole, S. O. (2008). Cultural Globalization Dimension in the West African Colonial Era. *Journal of Philosophy and Related Disciplines*, 3(1&2), 7–17.

Aso, W. O. (2019). *Will Kymlicka in Nigeria: With the Scope and Morality of Liberal Multiculturalism.* Benin City: Floreat Press.

Ayemwenre, J. (2019). The Ethics of Folktales in Edo Culture. *Ekpoma Review*, 5(1), 31–44.

Biko, S. (1978). *I Write What I Like*. London: Penguin Books.

Echekwube, A. (2002). *A Metaphysical Analysis of the Concepts of Reincarnation: Towards Global Harmony and Peace*. Inaugural Lecture, Ambrose Alli University, Ekpoma.

Echekwube, A. (2005). What Is Ethics? In P. Iroegbu and A. Echekwube (eds.), *Kpim of Morality* (pp. 29–35). Ibadan: Heinemann Educational Books.

Efeemin, A. O. (2010). *Claude Ake's Philosophy of Development: Implications for Nigeria*. Port Harcourt: Paragraphies.

Falaiye, O. A. (2012). *A Philosopher Interrogates African Polis: How Can We Get It Right?* Inaugural Lecture Series, University of Lagos, Akoka, Nigeria.

Ikuenobe, P. (2016). Tradition, Modernity, and Social Development. In O. A. Oyeshile and F. Offor (eds.), *Ethics, Governance and Social Order in Africa* (pp. 43–60). Ibadan: Zenith Book House.

Isanbor, P. O. (2016). On African Cultural Humanism and its Development. *SAU Journal of Humanities*, 4(1), 81–94.

Isanbor, P. O. (2017). *The Pedagogy of African Philosophy for Integral Human Development in Scientific and Technological Culture*. Ekpoma: E-mesh Publications.

Kouassi, N. C. (2022). *Western Fallacies and the Monkeyism Theory: A Philosophical Enquiry into Why Some Men Are Not Humans.* Fourth Inaugural Lecture Series, Samuel Adegboyega University, Ogwa, Edo State, Nigeria, Thursday, July 7.

Lukman, A. D. (2018). AU and the Challenges of Democratic Governance in Africa: The Need for a Contemporary Approach. In Olayemi Akinwumi et al. (eds.), *Humanities and the Burden of Governance in Africa* (pp. 40–62). Keffi: Nasarawa State University, Nigeria.

Manganyi, C. (1973). *Being Black in the World.* Johannesburg: Sprocas/Ravan.

Ndlovo-Gatsheni, S. J. and Ndlovo, P. P. (2021). The Invention of Blackness on a World Scale. In M. Steyn and W. Mpofu (eds.), *Decolonising the Human: Reflections on Africa on Difference and Oppression* (pp. 25–45). Johannesburg: Wits University Press.

Olatunji, F. O. and Ujomo, P. O. (2021). Understanding the Impact of Knowledge in Renee Decartes' Philosophy to Development Narratives for Africa. *Albertine Journal of Philosophy*, 5, 1–10.

Ogbenika, G. E. and Isanbor, P. O. (2017). African Philosophy and the Quest for Contemporary African Development. *Nsukka Journal of the Humanities*, 25(1), 5–17.

Ogundowole, E. K. (2008). *Inexhaustibility of Self-Reliance*. Inaugural Lecture Series, University of Lagos, Akoka, Nigeria.

Oladipo, O. (2006). The Issues of African Self-Definition in the Contemporary World. In Olusegun Oladipo (ed.), *Core Issues in African Philosophy* (pp. 59–73). Ibadan: Hope Publications.

Olukoshi, A. O. (2014). *Africa: Meeting the Challenges of Leadership for a Changing World.* 2014 Convocation Lecture of the Ekiti State University, Ado-Ekiti, Nigeria.

Sithole, T. (2016). *Steve Biko: Decolonial Meditations of Black Consciousness*. London: Lexington Books.

Soludo, C. C. (2006). *Can Nigeria be the China of Africa*. Being a Lecture Delivered at the Founder's Day of University of Benin, Benin City, Nigeria, Delivered on November 23, 2006.

Part III

ON LEADERSHIP

Chapter 10

Akan Sociopolitical and Economic Thought as a Leadership Model for Africa

Alex J. Wilson

Against the backdrop of sustainability of culture for political development as stated in the culture-related documents of the sustainable development goals, the democratic system bequeathed to Africans is fraught with problems of cultural incoherence between indigenous African societies and those of Europeans. This has led to the perverse adoption of values which do not fit into indigenous African cultures and failure of African governments to meet the hopes and aspirations of their peoples. Many authors, including Ake (1996), Austin (2015), Ayittey (2005), Etekpe (2009), Gyekye (2013), Mazrui (2002), Michalopoulos and Papaioannou (2013), Muiu (2009), Obioha and Okaneme (2017), and Osabukle (2000), have attributed the failure of state policies to the systematic destruction of African states through intrusion into the social, political, and economic systems of Africa by Europeans. Taking cues from the Akan social, political, and economic systems, this chapter draws on the essence of communal values, such as unity of purpose, to examine the principal political and economic ideologies that drive indigenous Akan society and, generally, national politics in Ghana. It uses Durkheim's theory of evolution (Durkheim, 1997) to explain the social change that has affected African political and economic ideologies.

Considering the multiethnic and multicultural nature of the Ghanaian society, I avoid generalizations about Ghana and keep the discussion within reasonable anthropological bounds, though cultural diffusion and unity in diversity of culture also exist among the ethnic groups. This chapter reiterates the importance of culture in the political and economic philosophy of African states and suggests ways of developing African-centered political economies. It addresses the following themes: the justification for writing this chapter, the woes of colonialism and postindependence governments, aspects of indigenous Akan politics and political economy, and the theoretical framework. Finally, it discusses the issues raised in the literature and suggests the way forward for development of African political economies.

JUSTIFICATION

The justification for this chapter is based on the need for developing an African philosophy of political and economic ideologies within Afrocentric perspectives, considering that African philosophy and political thoughts are trapped in European thoughts and ideological categories such as liberalism, conservatism, capitalism, socialism, Marxism, fascism. These entrapments call on African scholars to construct an authentic African discourse about Africa (Coetzee, 2017; Bulhan, 2015; Mazrui, 2001; Ramose, 2003). Finally, there is the need for an African philosophy that debunks, deconstructs, and reconstructs the dehumanizing tendencies of European culture and creates social awareness for political power, political action, and the well-being of Africans (Kasanda, 2015; Rettová, 2016; Wiredu, 1996).

WOES OF COLONIALISM AND POSTINDEPENDENCE POLITICS AND THE CALLS FOR INDIGENEITY

The inadequacies of colonialism and postindependence politics in ensuring equitable distribution of public goods and resources for the well-being and survival of the masses have led to the calls for indigenous political economy. Apart from making Africans lose their right to self-government and access to viable economic resources, some aspects of colonialism stripped Africans of essential cultural values for effective participation in politics and continue to impact on the politico-economic philosophies of African countries (Martin, 2012). Colonialism was not in tandem with indigenous political and economic ideas. It was characterized by overcentralization and the concentration of power in the hands of a few people, deprivation of the masses of their rights to effective participation in government, and entrenching the claims of power by chiefs over land (Mamdani, 1996; Michalopoulos & Papaioannou, 2013).

Motivated by a strong sense of indigenous values, African nationalists led their people to fight for political independence and freedom, and laid less emphasis on economic and social development where democracy delivers socioeconomic goods. After independence, corrupted forms of philosophy of African political economy emerged and the political leaders governed the same way as the colonialists by instilling violence against the masses

(Bulhan, 2015; Fanon, 2004). Questions about effective participation in politics are rife in the contemporary democracies of African countries. In addition, African politics is bedeviled with corruption and patronage-ridden personal regimes (Biney, 2011).

In the immediate postindependence period, political opponents opposed government policies and agitated for the well-being of the people. The politicians in power felt threatened under intense political action, so they tried to maintain themselves in power by suppressing the freedom of the people. They called for governance that was in line with indigenous African politics. Paradoxically, they misappropriated the indigenous African cultures associated with communal values. They argued that indigenous African systems of politics offered examples of democracy without multiparty mechanisms by using elements of chieftaincy to justify the formation of single-party states. While trying to ensure the well-being of the masses, the leaders propagated political ideologies that were supposedly indigenous to Africa but in reality, were not. For example, Nkrumah's *Consciencism*, Nyerere's *Ujamaa*, and Kaunda's African Humanism were developed as African socialism with the aim of adopting values associated with communalism and inculcating them into the postindependence political economy.

Nkrumah, the first president of Ghana, combined the ideas of Consciencism with Pan-Africanism. He outlined four main stages of Pan-Africanism—national independence, national consolidation, transnational unity and community, and economic and social reconstruction (Biney, 2011). For him, only the first had been achieved. For the others to be achieved, he urged African leaders to unite and surrender their sovereignties to a larger Africa so that they would get rid of the inherited artificial boundaries in Africa and integrate their economies. The main idea about Nkrumah's consciencism was that African cultures have been influenced by a triple heritage made up of indigenous culture, colonialism, and Christianity on one hand, and Islam, so politics should take the changes associated with those cultures into consideration (Nkrumah, 1964).

Others like Julius Nyerere and Kenneth Kaunda had similar ideologies. Nyerere, the first president of Tanzania, emphasized the need to recognize the importance of the African family system and suggested that the values associated with it should be extended to the new independent African states and the entire humanity in his concept of *Ujamaa* (Nyerere, 1968). Kaunda, also the first president of Zambia, adopted African humanism as an ideology to reconstruct and rescue Zambia from the economic doldrums that occurred after colonialism. He perceived capitalism as exploitation, hence, he argued that it was anti-African (Kaunda, 1966). He, therefore, proposed the use of precolonial values as the basis for building Zambia, and particularly, African humanism as a moral philosophy that recognizes the intrinsic worth of humans.

From the foregoing, it is noticeable that common grounds existed among the political thoughts of these three post-independent African leaders. Their thoughts were meant to assault colonialism and racism that had denied African people of their fundamental human rights. Their responses to colonialism were purely from an economic standpoint, particularly capitalist exploitation as exists in neocolonialism and imperialism (Biney, 2011; Botwe-Asamoah, 2005; Poe, 2003). They all tried to use indigenous ideas to fight against colonialism and formulate their politico-economic thoughts (Austin & Serra, 2015; Etekpe, 2009; Gyekye, 2003; Ikambana, 2007; Mwanlimu, 2009). However, they misappropriated the indigenous African cultural ideas and values for their own personal interests as they argued that multiparty elections were alien to indigenous African societies, and indigenous African family and political systems do not encourage the ownership of private property. Also, they linked their ideologies to efforts at evenly distributing wealth among people and placed them under the ambit of African socialism. They concluded that socialism had always been part of the indigenous African values that colonialism sought to destroy (Kaunda, 1966; Nkrumah, 1961; Nyerere, 1968).

Africapitalism, an economic philosophy that embodies the private sector's commitment to the economic transformation of Africa through investments that generate both economic prosperity and social wealth, emerged in the 2010s. The proponents identified Africapitalism's potential to serve as the common discourse for collective action and a space to redress the imbalance in management research and theory on Africa. According to Elumelu (2016), the major proponent, Africapitalism is an idea that emphasizes the obligations of the private sector toward the socioeconomic development of Africa and assumes the feasibility of such an undertaking. It implies the restoration of Africanness in capitalism, reflecting the economic and social practices implicit in African culture and tradition (Amaeshi & Idemudia, 2015). Amaeshi and Idemudia noted that the international development community hinders capitalism from flourishing in Africa. To forestall this, they linked Africapitalism to the broader literature on business and society, and critically explored it as a possible management idea for business in Africa in response to the onslaught of global capitalism. They noted that Africapitalism is built on the African communitarian ethos which recognizes the interests of both the community and the individual. They argued that communalism does not proscribe self-enrichment. They perceived Africapitalism as a way of voluntary wealth distribution in which one's economic and social power is measured in the way he or she empowers others economically. They maintain that Africapitalism offers effective roles to business entities to participate in the socioeconomic development of African countries. They noted that these roles go beyond the often-limited business-case argument that underpins other concepts in the field of business and society. As an economic idea, it requires efficient economic coordination by diverse actors, such as the state, civil society, and markets.

Africapitalism is more of a business philosophy which only finds essence in political economy because it advocates business-government relations by calling on African entrepreneurs to work with their governments to achieve economic development. To realize its goals, it must bring its moral intuitions and principled commitments into alignment with modern economic practices. In addition, there is a need to delve deep into issues that bother on binaries in order to establish the suitability of the issues being raised under Africapitalism and also to avoid the scheme that if African socialism did not work for Africans, then Africapitalism will do.

Whereas African socialism and Africapitalism have common grounds, their sources of origins differ. The common platform dwells on the need to revisit indigenous African ideas, and the difference is that whereas African socialism was propounded by politicians, Africapitalism was advocated by business men. Recalling how African leaders misappropriated African cultures for their personal interests and the failures of those ideologies call for reexamination of African history, politics, and cultures in order to understand the plausibility of emerging ideologies such as Africapitalism.

ASPECTS OF INDIGENOUS AKAN POLITICS AND POLITICAL ECONOMY

Communalism drives African ways of life in the social, political, economic, and religious realms, and the Akan are no different. The Akan are a group of people who live in parts of Ghana and La Cote d'Ivoire in West Africa. In Ghana, they are the largest ethnic group, constituting about 49.1% of Ghana's population (Agyekum, 2006). About 44% of Ghanaians are nonnative speakers of Akan. There are two main groups—the Twi-speaking and the Mfantse-speaking, with diverse dialects among these major groups. The Twi-speaking group includes the Asante, Akyem, Kwahu, Akuapem, Twifu, Assin, Denkyira, and Bono, while the Mfantse-speaking ones are Nkusukum, Gomoa, Ekumfi, Enyan, and so on (Adu-Boahen, 1989; Fynn, 1987).

The Akan have a centralized system of government as laid out by the Evans-Pritchard and Meyer Fortes's classification of African political systems (Rattray, 1929; Wilks, 1993). They have complex political institutions with well-organized bureaucracies and legal institutions. Their political systems do not have political parties (Osabu-Kle, 2000). Politics emerges from social organizations, such as kinship, age sets, elder traditions, associations, guilds, and military traditions (Ajei, 2000; Busia, 1954; Etekpe, 2009; Fortes,

1974; Rattray, 1929; Wilson, 2000). The matrilineal descent system of the Akan determines a person's political and juridical status, and consequently, regulates citizenship and rights of succession (Busia, 1954; Wilson, 2007).

Indigenous Akan principles of democracy are people centered. They ensure that political leaders are accountable to the people. The people believe that power is God-given to humankind but chiefs and elders of a community hold it in trust for the people, so they have to exercise it according to custom and, more importantly, based on communal values (Busia, 1954; Rattray, 1929; Wilson, 2021). The principle espouses effective participation in politics through deliberative principles and consensus-building. Politico-economic ideas are connected to the demand for economic empowerment, better living standards, and adequate social welfare for people. Therefore, political leaders are morally obliged to appropriate a community's resources by ensuring their equitable distribution for the survival of everyone in the community.

Indigenous Akan political structure is decentralized from the state to lineages. It portrays a hierarchical order right from the lineage through to the paramountcy or kingdom. It consists of a three-tier system made up of the paramount chief, the divisional chief, and the subchief (Brobbey, 2008). The Asante, however, have a four-tier system with the *Asantehene* (King) at the top of the hierarchy. Some of the groups, like the Fantse and Akyem, have more than one paramount chief, but each of them is independent. The political structure, at each of the tiers, is made up of three levels—chiefs, elders, and the masses. At the paramountcy and divisional levels, the council of elders is made up of chiefs who are drawn from the various clans. Under the subchiefs, the various heads of clans represent their members on the council of elders. In addition, there is a bureaucracy which is built along the principles of chieftaincy; however, the bureaucracy enjoys some level of independence, which enables it to ensure some checks and balances. At each level, the council discusses issues freely until it arrives at a consensus (Osabukle, 2000; Wiredu, 1996). The will of the masses is often expressed in the council of chiefs and at public gatherings since some of the masses may only have positions in their clans but not the community.

Lineages and clans serve as the political units for participation in decision-making, allocation of power, and execution of political action. Their members occupy political positions in their clans and communities. They also constitute the economic units as they possess resources for production and distribution. They have to ensure equitable distribution. Indigenous religion plays major roles in politics as households, lineages, and communities ensure a deep sense of communion and continuity of relationship among the dead, the living, and the yet to be born.

The system also incorporates noncitizens into the existing lineages and political structure, and adopts aspects of their religion and political ideologies to build their own communities. In some situations, migrants who have similar cultures are grouped into a political organization and their leaders are given places on the chiefs' councils. This accords the groups representation and subsequently, participation in the politics of the community to which they have migrated.

Other political units are age sets (from which civil society organizations emerge), and politico-religious groups connected with rituals of installation and death of political leaders (Acquah, Amuah, & Annan, 2014; Fynn, 1987). Common among age sets are the *asafo* companies of the Fantse-speaking Akan. They have their own structures which run alongside those of chiefs. Among the Twi-speaking Akan, the youthful members of the masses constitute the *nkwankwaa* whose leader, the *nkwankwaahene*, does not participate in the meetings of council of chiefs but the council must listen to grievances coming from the youth through him (Busia, 1968). The age sets provide avenues for members of a community to present their views on issues affecting the community (Wilson, 2007). The *asafo* also executes community's orders in situations where a chief has been found guilty and has to be deposed. With these in place, their political actions have influence over the powers of chiefs. Thus, the Akan political structure has well-developed institutions with a high level of democracy and bureaucratic structures which help to devolve power and provide the means for a leadership model.

Similar structures of females exist at all levels, with queen-mothers having their own councils made up of only females. Queen-mothers also serve on councils of chiefs (only males) with more powers, including veto power for decisions taken by the council (Ajei, 2000; Arhin, 1983; Busia, 1968). Democratic principles also acknowledge the participation of women in politics. Very important advisory and administrative positions are reserved for women (Adjepong, 2015; Busia, 1968). Apart from the prerogatives of the queen-mother, women control markets and accumulate wealth (Wilson, 2011). They also influence decisions on war, as they instigate their communities to go to war or stop them from fighting (Arhin, 1983; Wilson, 2007). The *nkwankwaa* and *asafo* groups include women, who may also have leadership positions.

Akan culture upholds communalism, which Gyekye (2003) defined as the doctrine or theory that the community (or group) is the focus of activities of the individuals who live in a community and share common good by emphasizing the well-being of every member of the community, not to the detriment of any individual. The concept emanates from the idea of personhood which is premised on the belief that an individual is made up of body or blood, provided by the mother; spirit and personality provided by the father; and a soul provided by the Supreme Being. Gyekye noted that communalism places value on self-reliance and aspects of individualism by emphasizing that a group exists only as multitudes of individuals and that one should be responsible to one's self as an individual and each individual must contribute to the well-being of the community.

The concepts of personhood and communalism inform social, political, economic, and religious relationships, including moral responsibility and the proper relationships among individuals in a community. They espouse the virtues of social well-being, a sense of identity, unity of purpose, solidarity, participation in governance, and consensus-building. They amplify social justice and a strong distaste for extreme individualism, unnecessary competition, and personal enrichment. They create rules of moral expectations for individuals and members of the community from where the people hail and/or live. They influence the elements of politics and political thought, including political structure, political processes, political actions, and political power. Thus, personhood and communalism make everyone a social, political, and economic being, a value which is needed for leadership.

Inasmuch as Akan culture supports communalistic values, there is also the impression that communalism creates dependency. Nketia (1993) noted that the Akan maxim *nnipannyɛabɛdua* (no human being is a palm tree) makes dependency pervasive. He noted, however, that political dependency was resisted and that the same values for which people aver political dependency make them strive to work hard for their own economic survival. Hagan (1993) identified and accepted "interdependency," a symbiotic type of dependency where the "parasite" provides its "host" with some nourishment or a form of protection from more hostile "parasites," because of the mutual benefits that the parasite and the host derive from each other. Similarly, political leaders cannot exist without the masses and vice versa. Therefore, leaders are expected to adopt such inclusive models for mobilization, patronage, and distribution of social and economic goods for the various communities.

Indigenous Akan politics is manifested in communal values that advocate respect for social, political, economic, and religious orders, and effective decentralization of power. The values ensure a political philosophy which promotes democratic principles such as the devolution of power through effective decentralization of authority. Mazrui's (2002) typology of democracy—leadership is accountable and answerable for its actions and policies, citizens are effective participants in choosing their rulers and regulating leaders' actions, society and economy are open and transparent, and equity in governance and allocation of state resources—exists in indigenous Akan politics. Rattray noted that among the Akan, democracy involves everyone who lives in a community. It goes beyond elections as the people exert their rights and freedoms during and after the selection of a leader. Gyekye (1997) calls this participatory democracy, emphasizing the need for leaders to ensure broad consultation while the masses discuss the affairs of the state. Wiredu

(1996) noted that the minority's views become part of the final decision as the discussants arrive at consensus.

The way authority is exercised in indigenous politics ensures democracy and makes it worth adopting for contemporary politics. The indigenous Akan philosophy behind power and authority is conceived within the knowledge base and philosophies such as *tuminyinaafiri Nyame* (all power comes from the Supreme Being), *tumitesɛkosua* (power is like an egg), *neaadeɛwɔ no naodienaennyɛneaɛkɔm de nɔɔ* (power belongs to the one who has the mandate to exercise it), and *konti ne akwamu* [Konti and Akawmu (the names of two major divisions in chieftaincy)] (Wilson, 2021). *Tumi nyinaafiri Nyame* depicts the sacred nature of chieftain power. The Akan believe that the power to human beings is diffused through the divinities and ancestors. Chiefs serve as the link between the living political actors and the dead and those yet to be born (Busia, 1954). Once a person is elected a leader, rituals are performed for him or her to connect with the ancestors and, subsequently, interact with them. The symbol of office of a chief, the stool, is believed to be derived from the ancestors. It is the embodiment of unity among the lineages. The lineages of a community find their unity in the chief as he is the symbol of their identity and continuity as an ethnic group and the embodiment of their spiritual values. *Tumitesɛkosua* shows that power is delicate so it should be exercised with care. Like the egg, power breaks once a power holder holds hard unto it. Power corrupts, so it must be shared in order to eschew its abuse. If one holds firmly onto power and does not share it, it breaks. *Konti ne akwamu* communicates the regulation of power through diffusion and devolution. *Neaadeɛwɔ no naodienaennyɛneaɛkɔm de nɔɔ* communicates the exercise of authority. Though its philosophy seems to limit power to the royal lineage, considering it within the holistic political order indicates the legitimacy and diffusion of power. It enunciates legitimacy of power as opposed to usurpers who might be hungry for power, but by taking the power forcefully, a person will have no *locus standi*. The philosophy further delineates royalty and keeps its thresholds sacrosanct and devoid of contamination. With these philosophies in mind, chiefs are expected to exercise and diffuse power through division of functions. Diffusion of power provides a model of leadership which is worth emulating in contemporary politics of Ghana. People who are vested with power have to exercise it with care by following the rules of their mandate. In the case of Africa, the philosophy behind power has the potential to caution military dictators, and potential life presidents and coup makers, from usurping political power.

Once political authority is conferred on a person, he or she is also endowed with economic power. Indigenous Akan political economy examines how political authorities manage a community's resources and shape economic activities by performing rituals and putting structures in place to ensure the distribution of resources for high productivity and consumption, and the survival of individuals and families in the community (Ajei, 2000). It upholds the sacred nature of some economic spaces and resources such as markets, lands, bulk mineral deposits, and some economic trees. It indicates that chiefs hold the resources that the Supreme Being bequeathed to humanity through their ancestors in trust for the community. Chiefs conserve resources by performing rituals and ensuring their effective use. While individuals and lineages perform rituals to ensure that they are safe from injuries emanating from the use of tools and also, to ensure high yields of their produce, chiefs organize and perform rituals at the start of the planting and harvesting seasons for abundant supply of food (Busia, 1954). With the basic principle of the welfare of humanity in mind, chiefs are supposed to ensure a fair and equitable distribution of the resources. They appropriate agricultural wealth by exacting tributes from their subjects (Austin & Serra, 2015). Under the *abusa* cropping system, migrant farmers acquire lands through usufruct rights from chiefs and heads of clans, after which the proceeds are shared with the farmer getting two-thirds and the landowner getting a third of the harvest.

The political economy also examines property relations, including accounting for personal wealth, as well as those for lineages and communities. Society appreciates personal wealth which is acquired genuinely and not through fraud or any diabolic means. Rules governing inheritance and succession indicate that, as successors and heirs, they must ensure the survival of the deceased's productive ventures and also the well-being of surviving relatives of the deceased (Fortes, 1974). They must strive to increase the wealth bequeathed to them by deceased members as they use the resources of the deceased. Similarly, a chief has to increase the stock of assets which he inherited. He cannot corrupt his office by amassing personal wealth (Ajei, 2000). Any asset or liability he acquires goes to the state. A chief receives less share of a produce than everyone else, and most often, he gets them through tributes and other redistributive mechanisms. Through equitable sharing of the resources, every member of the community is expected to receive sufficient resources to meet his or her own basic needs. With the pervasive nature of corruption in many African states, the values of eschewing corruption are worthy of keeping as a model of leadership in contemporary politics.

THEORETICAL FRAMEWORK AND ITS APPLICATION

The calls for retrieval of indigenous African cultures demand the examination of Akan political institutions and structures, and assessing their suitability for contemporary politics. Recalling that the basis of indigenous politics is kinship while contemporary politics is organized around interest groups such as political parties, civil society organizations, and professional bodies, I apply Durkheim's theory of evolution to explain this effectively. The theory addresses issues of solidarity and social change. Durkheim stated that solidarity helps to maintain social equilibrium and that society must change frequently so that it can survive. He identified two types of solidarity—mechanical solidarity and organic solidarity. He noted that a society with mechanical solidarity has a strong collective conscience, where individuals share similar values so it is not easy to distinguish individual ideas from those of other members of the society. People adhere to social norms and religious practices. Durkheim likened a society with mechanical solidarity to primitive societies. He noted that in such societies, clans socialize individuals but as the population grows, the nuclear family exerts more power and does more socialization. These make individuals carve economic niches for themselves and form various social groups with different aims and objectives, resulting in a society with organic solidarity (one which is formed by a system of different organs each of which has a special role, professional backgrounds, and many more). This results in a situation where everyone brings on board his or her unique ideas and experiences and contributes to the development of the society.

There is no gainsaying that Durkheim's theory is more of social than political and has a European flavor, but the themes that it highlights are also worth drawing upon for explaining how contemporary societies have devolved from their pasts and explaining some of the good things in indigenous societies. The theory is applicable in political economy considering that indigenous African politics develops from social organization. Moreover, politics has also become complex as a result of growth in population and the dynamics of globalization. A typical example is the movement from kin-based and guild-based politico-economic structures to nonfamilial ones such as trade unions and economic chambers. Furthermore, the ideas on collective conscience and solidarity provide the bases for the concepts of personhood and communalism (Wilson, 2011), which became contemptuous in the postindependence politics and political economy. Also, the theory addresses issues of law which are used to develop politics (Wilson, 2011). Though the theory has gone through a number of critiques, the critiques are not the focus of this chapter.

For the application of the theory to this chapter, it can be noted that indigenous social, political, and economic systems fall more within societies with mechanical solidarity, as kinship serves as the basis of organization. Indigenous Akan religion cannot be delineated from the aforementioned systems, and hence, it forms a major component of the culture just as Durkheim identifies in mechanical solidarity. Recalling that contemporary politics dwells much on political parties and civil society organizations, there is a clear indication that the indigenous political system is built on mechanical solidarity while that of the contemporary period is built on organic solidarity.

The civilizing mission of colonialism brought about the needed change for indigenous African cultures to move from societies with mechanical solidarity to those of organic solidarity. The attempts by post-independent political leaders to stick to "familyhood" could best be described as a reversal into mechanical solidarity. However, they failed to realize that the dynamics of "familyhood" in African social and political systems also call for the development of nonfamilial units such as the *nkwankwaa* and *asafo* in the political structure of indigenous African societies in order to encourage dissenting views and ensure checks and balances to make a family more successful in social, political, and economic development. Colonialism and independence, with their concomitant levels of migration, did not totally usher African social, political, and economic systems into societies with organic solidarity because the indigenous family systems continue to play the role of fictive kinship among migrants. Durkheim noted that with mechanical solidarity, families had obligations, which regulated individual behavior and practices, but now society has shifted more to individualism with a weaker collective conscience. Moreover, the interests of family and kinship are now regulated by laws, conventions, and rights and duties, which make people seek redress in contemporary institutions. At the moment, though chieftaincy is still upheld as an agency for community development, much attention has shifted to elected members of district assemblies, making governance and efforts at development move from kinship-based to non-kinship-based. This does not mean that chieftaincy is totally outmoded because a modern system develops with aspects of its political traditions and hence the flaws in Durkheim's theory that there is no midway between mechanical solidarity and organic solidarity. However, it is a common knowledge in Ghana now that political parties control political activities at the district levels, though the assemblies are supposed to be nonpartisan. Also, ethnicity, which develops from the lineage system of African societies, plays major roles in contemporary politics in Ghanaian and other African societies.

THE AKAN EXPERIENCE OF DEMOCRACY AND THE PHILOSOPHY OF POLITICAL ECONOMY

This chapter establishes four basic ideas for discussion, namely democracy is cultural, so it becomes difficult to sustain it when it is crafted in the principles of other cultures; the postindependence African leaders misapplied the very foundations of the chieftaincy institution that supports the inclusion of every adult in democratic governance; personhood and communalism accommodate individualism; and African socialism has no bearing with communalism. One wonders why the postindependence African leaders were ushered into governance through elements of liberal democracies and yet they rejected the multiparty system and called for an indigenous African democratic system. Again, why did they appreciate communal values but distorted the very foundation which recognized the accumulation of wealth by individuals? The calls for indigenous systems fit into the aims of postindependence African leaders to fashion out an African-centered social, political, and economic philosophy in order to change the legacy of colonialism for the new African personality to find its highest expression. Again, they could have rekindled aspects of the indigenous cultures which had been destroyed through colonialism. However, there are concerns about the misapplication of indigenous knowledge. The foregoing discussions examine the extent to which indigenous systems of politics and economics portray democracy and ensure the well-being of individuals, how the misapplication of communalism fails to espouse African socialism and Africapitalism, and how any form of misapplication of communalism negates the possibility of adopting indigenous political and economic philosophies for Ghana's political and economic development.

Indigenous Systems of Politics and Economics for Democracy and Well-Being of Individuals

Communalism appreciates both individual and collective efforts, so it has grounds for upholding democracy in indigenous politics. However, certain aspects of the calls for unity dilute African values. For example, Nkrumah's calls for Africans to unite under the guise of Pan Africanism and surrender their sovereignties for a United States of Africa appeared quite queer. Though, Pan-Africanism is in line with African values because of the unity that it inculcates, surrendering one's sovereignty is inimical to personhood and communalism as these latter values also inculcate the strengths associated with upholding one's family and ethnic identity and, for that matter, citizenship. Among the Akan, citizenship is derived from being a member of a clan.

Issues of identity will be difficult to overlook in a typical African society since it is constructed from the micro level to a macro level. For example, an Asante is first and foremost a member of a clan in a particular community and that gives him or her an Asante citizenship. He or she shares a common language and culture with others. Indeed, indigenous religion played a major role in unifying the Asante. The sense of unity was further undergirded by the fear of suppression by the Denkyira and other stronger states, but the immediate postindependence period did not offer any serious threat to the African states, which should make any of them surrender its sovereignty to United

Africa. Again, one wonders if such unity could be achieved in the midst of Christianity, Islam, and diversity of indigenous religions and cultures. Though Nkrumah's consciencism identified the effects of multiple cultures, he underrated how these could affect the unity of African countries which he proposed. Thus, the call for unity along this line does not serve any meaningful purpose for Africa's development.

In their efforts to adopt single-party dictatorships and create life presidencies, the postindependence leaders failed to recognize that there were no political parties in indigenous African politics and also that chieftaincy was just a stratum of the indigenous political system. Whereas the postindependence leaders advocated a single-party system of government, there are no political parties for political participation in indigenous politics (Wiredu, 1996). The parties in indigenous politics (clans) do not seek power to govern as political parties do. Rather, they contribute their quota to politics for the well-being of individuals and the community. In the spirit of communalism, everyone produces their best to fulfill a common good like the provision of a good life for the members of a community.

Again, like the colonialists, the African leaders upheld chieftaincy, but not the other strata of governance such as the council of elders and the masses. They ignored the fact that deliberations and consensus-building are more manifest in the council of elders and also, the youth (mostly in the *asafo* and *nkwankwaa*) who play the role of civil society organizations. The free discussions among the youth accommodate dissent, and dissent gives room for the views of the minority to be incorporated into policymaking. The single-party system which quashed dissent is not in tandem with indigenous cultures and therefore, cannot be ideal for leadership in contemporary politics.

Communalism and Indigenous Political and Economic Philosophies

The viability of contemporary African philosophies of political economy needs to anchor on political power, the guarantee of human and civil liberties, and how economic goods are generated and distributed in society. Since African socialism was not in tandem with communalism and aspects of indigenous African economic concepts, leading to its failure, it would be expected that a new philosophy like Africapitalism will be cushioned in African culture, totally obviating the inadequacies associated with African socialism and offering the best ideas for an African political economy. It is worthy to recall that this chapter does not aim at arguing for African states to uphold capitalism or socialism.

Indeed, what existed in Akan cultures is not close to socialism as the cultures value individual wealth and personal efforts. Furthermore, the Akan uphold the principle that the wealth of a community depends on the wealth of individuals, so everyone should be supported to contribute to national wealth. With this in mind, indigenous private enterprises eschew perfect competition as it makes the survival of every individual a core value in indigenous economy. For example, in the local market, a person selling the same item as another feels alright if she entrusts her wares to her supposed competitor to sell it for her. Thus, the competitive spirit in the tenets of capitalism was negated by the essence of communalism.

The Misapplication of Communalism for African Socialism

The failure of African leaders to acknowledge the high level of individualistic tendencies with private ownership of means of production misled them to equate socialism to communalism. It will be recalled that both Nkrumah and Kaunda perceived capitalism as exploitation and anti-African (Kaunda, 1966; Nkrumah, 1964). However, Nkrumah was optimistic that socialism could coexist with private enterprise and be built with foreign investment (Nkrumah, 1964). Considering that privatization is a major component of capitalism, Nkrumah's stance can be seen as a clear case of the Akan aphorism, weakly translated as the chichi dodo bird which hates excrement but only feeds on maggots, not forgetting that maggots grow best inside the lavatory (Armah, 1968). Specifically, it refers to Nkrumah's aversion for imperialism and yet he yet accepted foreign capital which often had conditionalities that defeated the sovereignty of a country.

Nkrumah's consciencism is real, but his aversion for local capital because it gave power to chiefs and indigenous merchants was anti-African. It made his thoughts associated with neocolonialism and African unity a hoax and did not encompass all inclusiveness. Nyerere's Ujamaa and Kaunda's humanism cannot be attained in modern Africa because they fail to recognize the mega family's capacity to own private capital. Moreover, the overreliance on state capital, instead of local private capital, by the post-independent political leaders rather brought about neocolonialism, which Nkrumah and his allies averred. This was because a pool of private capital would have averted excessive borrowing from external sources.

Austin and Serra (2015) questioned the rationale behind the adaptation of African socialism as the basis for economic development when indigenous African political economy has capitalist values. They argued that the Akan encouraged free enterprise and free trade, and also economic and market transactions had profit motives. They noted that the Akan celebrated the wealth of individuals. Again, history has it that the Asante resisted attempts to repress domestic private enterprise in 1883 under *Asantehene* Mensa Bonsu, by overthrowing him.

Whereas Austin and Serra's arguments on political economy were more inclined to capitalism, arguments by Ayittey (2005), Boadi (2000), Gyekye (1997), and Wiredu (2008) were not. The latter group of authors also argued that there is no connection between communalism and socialism because historical analysis of indigenous economics does not show that communalism is the underlying principle of socialism. Furthermore, they argued that while indigenous African societies were typified by communalism, they cannot be likened to socialism because, whereas private acquisition of wealth is absent in socialism, communalism also encourages acquisition of private property which is used to support humanity; the two cannot go together. It is worth noting that Austin and Serra's argument that the Akan celebrates individual capital goes with the condition that the wealth was acquired through genuine means and that the wealthy shared their achievements with other individuals. Hence, Gyekye's argument that, while socialism is a politico-economic ideology about the production and distribution of resources, which are owned by the government, and government seeks to control every aspect of the economy, communalism is more of a socio-ethical consideration which seeks to define the sort of relationships that should exist between individuals and groups, and respond to the needs and well-being of everyone in the society, is worth considering.

The mix-up of ideas in propounding African socialism calls for a critical examination of Africapitalism from the historical and cultural bases in considering it as a politico-economic philosophy for Africa. Since the immediate postindependence African politicians and philosophers argued that African socialism was different from global socialism because it was not built around communalism, and the proponents of Africapitalism also provide similar arguments, there is also the need to delve into the validity of the arguments put up in Africapitalism.

To conclude, communalism drives African social, political, and economic systems. It is predicated on the assumption that all humans need one another, and hence everyone should support other people in the community to have access to the basic needs of life. It supports individual accumulation of wealth and does not seek to control resources in a political economy. It upholds the view that an individual's contribution to the welfare of members of his or her clan and community is important. State control of production and distribution of resources without recourse to lineages and clans does not exist among the Akan. Communalism cannot be linked to African socialism. With the collapse of the communist and socialist blocks, and the fact that the indigenous Akan political and economic systems are not in line with African socialism, it is obvious that African socialism cannot be a leadership model for leadership in Ghana, and for that matter, Africa. However, Africapitalism as a political economic idea needs to be examined within the historical and cultural context to make it viable.

(MIS)APPLICATION OF COMMUNALISM: ANY WAY FORWARD FOR AFRICAPITALISM?

It seems that Africapitalism emerged because there was the need to put words together to put Africa in the context of globalism. The proponents admitted that it was an imaginative management idea and a creative moral-linguistic artifact, which embodied a new space for appropriating capitalism in Africa (Amaeshi & Idemudia, 2015). They stated categorically that they propounded Africapitalism because of the predominance of Western epistemology in the production of knowledge in management, which tended to exclude African voices. They tried to reinstate the sense of place and belongingness in the economic globalization discourse, as a form of economic patriotism. They situated Africapitalism in a broader conversation on global capitalism and highlighted some of the salient principles that make it an aspect of global capitalism, but unique to Africa.

Africapitalism's call on the affluent to improve upon the well-being of members of their communities resonates with communalism as well as contemporary economic ideas where enterprises have corporate social responsibilities in their areas of operation. However, in the real capitalist world, enterprises perform these duties so that they reduce their taxes to enhance their profit margins.

Capitalism is associated with markets, which also generate intense competition between capitalist enterprises. The spirit of communalism exists in African markets as producers and distributors consider the survival of everyone in the economy. There is no gainsaying that the collapse of a business will affect a number of individuals and families, which will also increase the burden of the surviving business entity. Thus, Africapitalism has the potential to maintain people in business for the survival of humanity.

Though some levels of capitalism fit into indigenous Akan economic concepts, it is worth considering that the origins of capitalism are associated with individualism, profit maximization, and more importantly, exploitation. As noted, the indigenous Akan culture does not preclude individual achievements, including the accumulation of wealth. However, profit maximization to the detriment of the welfare of one's neighbors is unacceptable. Also, capitalist production depends on the exploitation of wage labor. Laborers make efforts to resist exploitation. Even in the Western world, where communalism is absent, most craft workers organized themselves into "combinations" in the eighteenth and nineteenth centuries so that they could take collective decisions to protect themselves from the attempts by capitalist employers to cheapen their labor (Fulcher, 2004). The guild system, among the indigenous Akan and other indigenous African societies, protects their bargaining powers to keep them in business.

CONCLUSION AND THE WAY FORWARD FOR AFRICAN POLITICS AND ECONOMIES

African political thought of the twentieth century did not provide useful tools for transforming the frustrations of Africans into effective political action. Africans uphold participation in politics, but for many, participation in politics should be geared toward the provision of better welfare services and survival for every individual in the community. Considering that Africa is liberalizing at a slow pace in both politics and economics, Africans have to embrace a system of democracy that inculcates their positive customs that are compatible with the new politico-economic system.

African countries should design their own approaches to democracy and make efforts at good governance by inculcating the time-tested social, political, and economic values. Wiredu's (1996) plea for a nonparty politics is worth considering. In view of the fact that political parties are the contemporary means of participating in political activities and also considering that the constitution of the Republic of Ghana debars chiefs from participating in active politics (Ghana, 1992), the best way would be to maintain the political parties as units of political organization, with more powers to the people at the grassroots of the party so that most of the membership of the party will participate in the election of their leaders instead of delegates. In that case, if people are not happy with their leaders, they can easily vote them out.

Finally, political and economic ideologies should be in line with ensuring high productivity with the masses willing to participate in production and distribution of wealth. Where necessary, the slogans attached to ideologies should be driven by indigenous cultures. Asante (2007) stated that Africa must interrogate its own past for values that might be used for renaissance. African countries must consider that their own histories have avenues for approaching modernization, integration, and revitalization. It should learn from others, but it cannot follow in the footsteps of the West as mere imitators.

BIBLIOGRAPHY

Acquah, E. O., Amuah, J. A., & Annan, J. F. (2014). The contextual and performance dimensions of Asafo music from the perspective of annual Akwambo festival. *International Journal of African Society Cultures and Traditions*, *2*(2), 50–60.

Adjepong, A. (2015). The role of women in the political development of pre-colonial Africa. In S. A. Ajayi & J. K. Ayantayo (Eds.), *Women in development yesterday and today: Essays in memory of Professor Dorcas Olubanke Akintunde* (pp. 17–40). Ibadan, Nigeria: John Archers.

Adu-Boahen, A. (1989). *African perspectives on colonialism.* London: James Currey.

Agyekum, K. (2006). Akan traditional arbitration: Its structure and language. *Journal of Multilingual and Multicultural Development, 27*(5), 359–374. https://doi.org/10.2167/jmmd428.1.

Ajei, M. O. (2000). *Indigenous knowledge systems and good governance: The traditional Akan socio-political example.* Accra, Ghana: Institute of Economic Affairs.

Ake, C. (1996). *Democracy and development in Africa.* Washington, DC: The Brookings Institution.

Amaeshi, K., & Idemudia, U. (2015). Africapitalism: A management idea for business in Africa? *Africa Journal of Management, 1*(2), 210–223. https://doi.org/10.1080/23322373.2015.1026229.

Arhin, K. (1983). The political and military roles of Akan women In C. Oppong (Ed.), *Female and male in West Africa* (pp. 91–98). London: Allen and Unwin.

Armah, A. K. (1968). *The beautyful ones are not yet born.* London: Heinemann Publishers.

Asante, M. K. (2007). The resurgence of the African world in the 21st century. In A. Mazama (Ed.), *Africa in the century toward a new future* (pp. 3–16). New York: Routledge.

Austin, G. & Serra, G. (2015). West Africa. In V. Barnett (Ed.), *The Routledge handbook of the history of global economic thought* (pp. 243–256). New York: Routledge.

Ayittey, G. B. N. (2005). *Africa unchained: The blueprint for Africa's future.* New York: Palgrave Macmillan.

Biney, A. (2011). *The political and social thought of Kwame Nkrumah.* New York: Palgrave Macmillan.

Boadi, K. (2000). The ontology of Kwame Nkrumah's Consciencism and the democratic theory and practice in Africa: A Diopian perspective. *Journal of Black Studies, 30*(4), 475–501. https://doi.org/10.1177/002193470003000401.

Botwe-Asamoah, K. (2005). *Kwame Nkrumah's politico-cultural thought and policies: An African-centered paradigm for the second phase of the African revolution.* New York & London: Routledge.

Brobbey, S. A. (2008). *The law of chieftaincy in Ghana: Incorporating customary arbitration, contempt of court, judicial reviews.* Accra, Ghana: Advanced Legal Publication.

Bulhan, H. A. (2015). Stages of colonialism in Africa: From occupation of land to occupation of being. *Journal of Social and Political Psychology (Special Thematic Section on "Decolonizing Psychological Science"), 3*(1), 239–256. https://doi.org/10.5964/jspp.v3i1.143.

Busia, K. A. (1954). The Ashanti of the gold coast. In D. Forde (Ed.), *African worlds: Studies in the cosmological and social values of African peoples* (pp. 190–209). London: Oxford University Press.

Busia, K. A. (1968). *The position of the chief in the modern political system of the Ashanti.* London: Frank Cass.

Elumelu, T. O. (2016). Africapitalism and Africa's sustainable development. *Journal of International Relations and Sustainable Development, 6*(Global South Rising: Hope of Sustainable Development), 128–135.

Etekpe, A. (2009). *African political thought and its relevance in contemporary world order*. Port Harcourt, Nigeria: Harey Publications.

Fanon, F. (2004). *The wretched of the earth*. New York: Grove Press.

Fortes, M. (1974). *The Akan family system today*, Legon Family Research Papers, No. 1. Legon, Ghana: University of Ghana.

Fulcher, J. (2004). *Capitalism: A very short introduction*. New York: Oxford University Press.

Fynn, J. K. (1987). The political system of the Fante of Ghana during the pre-colonial period. *Universitas*, *9*, 108–120. https://doi.org/10.10520/AJA00495530_9.

Ghana. (1992). *The Constitution of the Republic of Ghana*. Accra, Ghana: Assembly Press.

Gyekye, K. (1992). Person and community in Akan thought. In K. Gyekye & K. Wiredu (Eds.), *Person and community: Ghanaian philosophical studies I* (pp. 101–122). Washington, DC: The Council for Research in Values and Philosophy.

Gyekye, K. (1997). *Tradition and modernity: Philosophical reflections on the African experience*. New York & Oxford: Oxford University Press.

Gyekye, K. (2003). *African cultural values*. Accra, Ghana: Sankofa Publications.

Gyekye, K. (2013). *Philosophy, culture and vision: African perspectives*. Accra, Ghana: Sub-Saharan Publishers.

Hagan, G.P. (1993). Origins and Nature of Dependency. *Proceedings of the Ghana Academy of Arts and Sciences (The Culture of Dependency)*. 34, pp 107–119.

Ikambana, P. (2007). On governance, personal and military power in post-independent Africa. In A. Mazama (Ed.), *Africa in the 21st century* (pp. 257–262). New York: Routledge.

Kasanda, A. (2015). Analyzing African social and political philosophy: Trends and challenges. *Journal of East-West Thought*, Vol. 2(5), pp. 29–50.

Kaunda, K. D. (1966). *A humanist in Africa: Letters to Colin Morris*. London: Longmans.

Mamdani, M. (1996). *Citizen and subject: Contemporary Africa and the legacy of late colonialism*. Princeton: Princeton University Press.

Martin, G. (2012). *African political thought*. New York: Palgrave Eze,

Mazrui, A. A (2001). Ideology and African political culture. In T. Kiros (Ed.), *Explorations in African political thought* (pp. 97–132). New York and London: Routledge.

Mazrui, A. A. (2002). Who killed democracy in Africa? Clues of the past, concerns of the future. *Development Policy Management Network Bulletin*, *10*(1), 15–23.

Michalopoulos, S. & Papaioannou, E. (2013). Pre-colonial ethnic institutions and contemporary African development. *Econometrica, 81*(1), 113–152. https://doi.org/10.3982/ECTA9613.

Mwanlimu, M. R. (2009). *Found a modern nation-state on Christian values? A theological assessment of Zambia humanism*. Pietermaritzburg: University of KwaZulu-Natal.

Nketia, J. H. (1993). Breaking the code. In *The culture of dependency: Proceedings of the Ghana Academy of Arts and science*. Accra, Ghana: Ghana Academy of Arts and Science and Friedrich Ebert Stiftung.

Nkrumah, K. (1961). *I speak of freedom*. London: Heinemann.

Nkrumah, K. (1964). *Consciencism: The philosophy and ideology for decolonization and development.* London: Panaf Books.

Nyerere, J. (1968). *Ujamaa: Essays on socialism.* Dar es Salaam: Oxford University Press.

Obioha, U., & Okaneme, G. (2017). Precious, African humanism as a basis for social cohesion and human well-being in Africa. *International Journal of Humanities Social Sciences and Education (IJHSSE)*, *4*(5), 43–50. http://doi.org/10.20431/2349-0381.0405005.

Osabu-Kle, D. T. (2000). *Compatible cultural democracy: The key to development in Africa.* Peterborough: Broadview Press.

Poe, D. Z. (2003). *Kwame Nkrumah's contribution to Pan-Africanism: An Afrocentric analysis.* New York & London: Routledge.

Ramose, M. B. (2003). Discourses on Africa: The struggle for reason in Africa. In P. H. Coetzee & A. P. J. Roux (Eds.), *The African philosophy reader* (2nd ed., pp. 1–114). New York: Routledge.

Rattray, R. S. (1929). *Ashanti law and constitution.* Oxford: Clarendon Press.

Wilks, I. (1993). *Asante gold-forests of gold: Essays on the Akan and the kingdom of Asante.* Athens: Ohio University Press.

Wilson, A. J. (2000). Exploring the potential of the *asafo* for community development. MPhil. Thesis, University of Ghana.

Wilson, A. J. (2007). Women's power in the socio-political organization of the Fante of Ghana: The case of *Asafo* companies. *UMOJA*, *2*(1), 1–12.

Wilson, A. J. (2011). Mothers' wealth: Matrilineality and inheritance among the Fantse of Ghana. PhD Dissertation, Ohio University.

Wilson, A. J. (2021). Adinkra symbols and proverbs as tools for elucidating indigenous Asante political thoughts. In E. Abaka & K. Osei-Kwarteng (Eds.), *The Asante world (17–21st century)* (pp. 201–224). New York: Routledge.

Wiredu, K. (1996). *Cultural universals and particulars: An African perspective.* Bloomington: Indiana University Press.

Wiredu, K. (2008). Social philosophy in postcolonial Africa: Some preliminaries concerning communalism and communitarianism. *South African Journal of Philosophy*, *27*(4), 332–339.

Chapter 11

Ubuntu as a Social Leadership Model in Africa

Focus on Nigeria

Godwin Michael Adahada

Leadership in Africa is marred by a plethora of challenges. Nigeria is a good example for this claim. For example, Ubi (2019) clearly states that "Nigeria's fundamental challenges as a nation since independence are threefold: leadership, national unity, and economic development." Ubuntu, a social philosophy, offers good prospects and Africapitalism, an economic philosophy, complements it. Whereas several causative factors have been highlighted, the majority of scholars agree that the fundamental among them is leadership; thus, "perhaps the most oft-repeated explanation for the weaknesses of African democracy is that the continent is saddled with "poor leadership." This means that the leaders themselves constitute challenges of leadership in Africa. The challenges are deepened by their leadership approach; impoverished leadership, lack of vision and policies, and prodigal lifestyle, which plunge the masses into economic hardship and social/political unrest. In some countries, the cost of governance alone can support about 50% of the annual budget, thus making leadership a cornerstone problem itself, and hence adversely affecting the economy.

Furthermore, there are other paraphernalia problems that challenge leadership. For instance, vindictive policies, nepotism and corruption, useless and unnecessary quest for prominence are banal. The negative impact of this on the people invokes native philosophies that can offer response for both leadership and economic transformation of the continent. Therefore, Ubuntu philosophy offers remedy to leadership challenges whereas Africapitalism offers a response to economic challenges. Ubuntu underpins and crosscuts the prospective response that can transmute to a solution to the challenges of leadership in the African continent because it espouses and defends the humanism of others. This is explicit in the consciousness that "I am because they are." Though Ubuntu is African, the experience of Ubuntu is not readily present in African leadership style. The dearth of Ubuntu experience gives way to the emergence of several ills in leadership among many African leaders. On the other hand, Africapitalism, a native economic philosophy, emphasizes the role and commitment of the private sector, private individuals together with the NGOs to complement government effort in economic value. Together, since Africapitalism can only thrive in serene and enabling environments, the harmony between the two philosophies could create enabling environments for profitable economic activities. At stake in this chapter is the prescription and defense of Ubuntu and Africapitalism as the social leadership model that can respond to integral leadership challenges in Africa. Ubuntu philosophy is popularly expressed as "showing humanity to other." Its maxim emphasizes (1) acknowledgment of one's humanity and the recognition of the humanity of others, (2) hospitality and other virtues that can enhance societal cohesion, and (3) human life and welfare and prioritizes it to economic or political gains. Africapitalism, on the other hand, recaps the latter, as well as envelops the values of Ubuntu philosophy. Its principles harmonize those of Ubuntu. Besides the commitment of the private sector in creating wealth for the nation, Africapitalism translates and transfers the values of Ubuntu to economic welfare of masses, shareholders, and stakeholders. This chapter makes a case for Ubuntu and Africapitalism and argues that they are the native model philosophies for leadership for Africa; Ubuntu, a social philosophy is the flip side of Africapitalism, an economic philosophy. Since Ubuntu emphasizes humaneness, recognition of the humanity of others which is climaxed in hospitality, love, solidarity, and other values, and Africapitalism impacts its values economically. Ubuntu complements Africapitalism and is thus capable of impacting integral leadership in Africa. An integral experience of socioeconomic stability and political serenity invokes the dual native philosophies.

To present these facts, this chapter proceeds in six sections including the introduction. The second section explicates the notion of leadership, its experience and challenges in Africa. The third section explores Ubuntu ideology as a humanism toward other people, expressed by community and human-centered values like hospitality and solidarity. The fourth section exposes the notion of Africapitalism and its principles. As an economic philosophy driven by the private sector, it aims at creating wealth for the stakeholders, shareholders, and the masses. The fifth section engages Ubuntu and Africapitalism and their implication for integral leadership in Africa. It notes that the principles of progress and prosperity, sense of parity, sense of peace and harmony, and sense of place and belongingness in Africapitalism have affinity with Ubuntu principles. The sixth section concludes that in view of these uncommon but harmonious values and principles in these native philosophies, they are robust and plausible models for integral leadership in Africa.

LEADERSHIP: NOTION, NIGERIA'S EXPERIENCE, AND CHALLENGES

Leadership is one of the most embattled and contested terms in the modern world. This could partly be attributed to democracy as well as to the contemporary enlightenment. Often the very concept, "leadership" is taken for granted. It is for this reason that explanation of the notion of leadership is necessary from different perspectives. A school of thought attributes successful leadership to hereditary traits; others, to personality type and physical endowments; and still others, to intellectual acquisition, and so on. Nonetheless, no single attribute accounts for successful leadership. The following definitions shed more light on the concept. Ogbeidi (2012, p. 4) defines leadership as "a body of people who lead and direct the activities of a group towards a shared goal. It also denotes the ability to lead, direct and organize a group." This construct presents leadership as an act based on an individual's sagacity. It also harmonizes with Norman Schwarzkopf (cited in Obgeidi (2012)) as a powerful mingling of character and strategy, with character as prior and more important than strategy. Character being innate and strategy external, it implies that strategy can be acquired but not character. However, there is another broader view of leadership as a process.

Ubegbe defines leadership as "the process of creating the subordinates' identification with the group's mission and creating their desires to achieve the group's goal" (1999, p. 282). Leadership as a process implies a period for formation of the mind and acquisition of necessary tactics. Therefore, rigorous education is entailed if leadership is to achieve its objectives. In this regard, a leader must acquire leadership strategies and prowess through education. Furthermore, "*Leadership* is the art of motivating a group of people to act toward achieving a common goal. In a business setting, this can mean directing workers and colleagues with a strategy to meet the company's needs" (Ward, 2020). This view involves exhibition of charism because the leader is actively involved in inspiring and directing group's affairs in view of attaining the set-out goals. "Charism" is important in this definition since a leader must possess good character flavored by visionary and critical mind. Leadership in a political or administrative position does imply the above ideas whether in business, administration, and so on. Charism is necessary for success. It is to this end that Ward also offers an alternative definition of leadership as an "organization's management structure" (2020). Structure recalls a careful arrangement and ordering of persons and sections in an establishment to ensure effective flow of the goals of its units within the whole.

Again, Graig construes leadership as a process. In thinking the process, he associates it with social influence and absence of compulsion on the led in participating in activities that will lead to the organizational goals (2005, p. 132). The alternative definition by Ward as management and structuring indicates the complexity of the concept of leadership. This is because leadership involves a network and strata of leaders which entails a network of interactions between them and the led. As a process of social influence, leadership involves persuasion through which individuals in a group are influenced such that they follow in pursuit of the common objectives, which makes it more united and focused in accomplishing the set goals (Chemers, 2002). It follows that as a process, leadership involves a flow of relations and interactions in both directions. However, the complexity of leadership is enormous; thus, Afegbua and Adejuwon in Hackman (2006, p. 144) draw four definitional themes of leadership as follows:

> a) Leadership is about what you are: this definitional theme focuses on leader traits and attributes, and it is one of the oldest ways of conceptualizing leadership. This emphasis is identifying the characteristics that define natural or born leaders. b) Leadership is about how you act: From this perspective leadership is defined as exercise of influence or power. To identify leaders, we need to determine who is influencing whom. For instance, Hersey (1984, p. 14) defines leadership as "any attempt to influence the behavior of another individual or group." c) Leadership is about what you do: This definitional tread focuses on the role that leaders play. d) Leadership is about how you work with others: This definitional theme emphasizes collaboration. Leaders and followers establish mutual purposes and work together as partners to reach their goals. (Poulin et al., 2007, p. 302)

Traits are hereditary, not acquired. The first theme, therefore, entails that some leaders are simply born with the capacity to lead. This could imply that born leaders often have fewer challenges in managing their roles. The second theme is opposed to the first because leadership could result from exerting higher influences. Leaders of such type must exert much influence on others to remain relevant in their roles. The third theme attributes leadership to the tasks one accomplishes, which underpins achievements as the yardstick of determining success. Lastly, the fourth invokes charisma, the special endowment to carry people along and to work with them harmoniously. Charisma is prior to and enhances collaboration between leaders and followers. This chapter maintains that leadership is an act and a process through which persons or groups of persons decide, direct, and influence others to carry out certain actions toward achieving common goals. Consequently, a leader is one who pilots these affairs and must possess charisma and character, tactics, and strategy and must be able to win the confidence of his followers through his personal qualities. What follows is a brief insight into leadership experience and challenges in Nigeria as an example.

Leadership experience in Nigeria refers to administration which has been both military and democratic. After independence, military dictatorial administration interrupted the civilian rule. Nigeria's leadership has been either democratically elected or by military coup d'état. Whether elected or despotic, Ogbeidi refers to them as the ruling class and identifies their role as "the ruling class that bears the responsibility of managing the affairs and resources of a political entity by setting and influencing policy priorities affecting the territory through different decision-making structures and institutions created for orderly development of the territory" (2012, p. 4). Political leadership includes persons at the helm of affairs in the agencies and parastatals, structures elected, or appointed persons known or unknown who manage the affairs of a political entity. In Nigeria, administrative levels are in three categories: the federal, the state, and the local government. In addition, the various government machineries are valid parts of administration. Since the independence on October 1, 1960, leadership experience in Nigeria has not been smooth and laudable because the initial civilian rule was protracted by a series of military coups amid other challenges that together marred political stability, socioeconomic development, religious and human right freedom. An author has described the existence of Nigeria as a mix of military and civilian administrations characterized by excessive corruption and underdevelopment (Ogbeidi, 2012, p. 6).

The current leadership failure that has been very noticeable could be traced back to two fundamental structures, endemic corruption and tribalism/ethnicity. Corruption has been practiced since precolonial Nigeria and lingers on till date. The form of corruption has been the misuse of public funds and resources. While accountability by public officers was a fanfare, abandonment of projects was the result, and the accumulation of these incidences has resulted in the backwardness the country is plunged into today (Ogbeidi, 2012, p. 6). From the onset, Nigeria lacked credible and selfless leaders. These and other indices of corrupted practices justify the claim that the malady is endemic. Similarly, nepotism is an added-up problem. Our diversity exacerbates corruption and raises it to almost an unresolvable degree. For, ethnic divides provide and still provide shelters for corrupt politicians and other criminalities. Thus, the claim of "one Nigeria" turns out to be deceitful; and "unity in diversity," a dupe of morality. Several challenges have marred leadership in Nigeria.

First, corruption, the principal challenge of leadership in Nigeria and Africa, may hardly comprehensively defined. As a negative influence and action in the act and process of leadership, certain practices such as abuse of official powers for personal advantage, embezzlement of public funds, unaccountability, taking bribes to offer unmerited or merited favors, denial of merited favors, making false claims. "Corruption is a form of dishonesty or criminal offense undertaken by a person or organization entrusted with a position of authority, to acquire illicit benefit or abuse power for one's private gain" (Wikipedia). It is associated with bribery, money laundering, nepotism, and inflation. When leaders of any group perpetrate these ills, the consequences are obvious, namely an inability to execute projects and programs that benefit their citizenry. Lamenting this scenario, Ogbeidi notes that "the political leadership class in its quest to secure and retain power, suppress opposition, and have access to unlimited funds for personal use, have sacrificed positive leadership on the altar of corruption" (2012, p. 5). To show that corruption in Nigeria is endemic and generational and really a big challenge to leadership, he decries, "Indeed, from the first generation of political leadership class through the successive military and civilian generation of political leaders, Nigerian political leadership has grown continually in corrupt practices" (Ogbeidi, 2012, p. 5). Many African leaders have, at various eras, made the claim of fighting corruption. This lamentation acknowledges the evil of corruption. For example, the mantra of the current Buhari administration is a fight against corruption. Similarly, "in 1957, in his inaugural address as the new president of the newly independent state of Ghana, Kwame Nkrumah cited corruption as a vice that risk gravely harming millions in Africa struggling for freedom and justice" (Ntata, 2015). Corruption is a double-edged sword that is caused by poverty, but it also causes poverty. In Nigeria, corruption has transcended ordinary practices to "attitude" and "mentality." Ntata observes that "corruption has gone from a mere act of accepting bribes to a complete state of mind and way of life. It has progressed from the poor attempting to make ends meet to a sense of entitlement from anyone in a position of authority" (Ntata). This makes it a malaise in search of a cure! Therefore, it is without flaw to defend that corruption spreads its tentacles and causes other leadership crises, thus crippling any meaningful development. Corruption has a strong relationship with ethnicity (nepotism).

Second, the challenge of ethnicity is complex. Nigeria is a polyethnic and multicultural society. Despite the 1914 ceremonial amalgamation, Nigerians still identify themselves first from their ethnic origin whereas nationality becomes secondary if not tertiary. This trend has ugly implications for leadership and integral development. Commenting on the centrality and the intricacy of ethnicity in Nigeria, Ejimabo notes that "Nigeria is a multitribal system where every tribe wants to excel or suppress the other, and so they are not really on the same level playgrounds. Every person in politics is regionalized and people are capitalizing on that" (2013, p. 4). The most relevant ground of showcasing superiority of one's ethnicity is politics. Thus, political parties were invariably formed based mainly on ethnic divides and still within this arrangement they thrived in the beginning of the first republic. The negative impact of ethnicity breeds other challenges.

Third, absence of fairness that results in "rewarding friends and punishing foes" (Ntata, 2015). This attitude has been described by Nigerians in several ways, including "political witch haunting." This is an attitude of withholding fair judgment and treatment based on shared bond. Often, friends and tribesmen are favored whereas foes and people not from one's ethnicity are punished. In line with this, some Nigerians argue that some rules are promulgated to punish certain people while others are favored. For example, the recent signing of the Company and Allied Matter Act into law has generated controversies among Christians that the law aims to distract Christian churches. Similarly, the aborted Water resource bill and the promulgation of Sharia law and application of same for non-Muslims are controversial considering Nigeria as a secular state. There are similar other cases of leadership challenges. This problem is closely associated with dictatorship.

Fourth, Ntata (2015) highlights three factors that cause dictatorship in Africa including Nigeria "1) too much trust, 2) too little trust, 3) neurotic ambition." While he claims that the last factor presents no problem, he stresses the gravity of too much trust as well as too little trust in the leaders as reasons for dictatorial attitude. This is why he opines that public opinion is essential for creating public policies. Ignoring public opinion in the formulation of public policies is to risk leadership challenge.

Fifth, failure to redefine the national goals constitutes a problem. The constant evolution in politics and leadership strategy invokes dynamism in leadership strategy too and this involves redefining of the national goals. This helps in keeping pace with the contemporary times and its demands. Focusing on goals also indicates when a leader has accomplished his goals and the need to voluntarily exit the office (Ntata, 2015). Tenure elongation among African leaders could rightly be attributed to unclear visioned leadership.

Sixth, unclear vision is a problem for leadership. The consequence of blurred vision leadership is a developmental and economic setback to the nation. Rather than seeking to work for the development of the people, the attention of such leader is diverted to private affairs in defiance of the oath of office (Ntata, 2015). Lack of clear vision and achievement kindles the desire for tenure elongation, which is a problem. Thus, opposition to this triggers competition among candidates.

Lastly, "by all means" or "do or die" approach to ascending a leadership position is a problem. Those with this mentality often do not have the interest of the common good in mind. Frowning at the development, Ntata observes that this unnecessary competition, which deserves condemnation, should stop. He notes further that teamwork is productive and beneficial to national unity, development, and economic prosperity (Ntata, 2015). The concomitant cause of these challenges is the lack of a guiding leadership ideology. Thus, Ubuntu and Africapitalism philosophies propose to respond to these challenges.

UBUNTU PHILOSOPHY: NOTION AND EXPLORATION

Ubuntu philosophy is of African origin. Ubuntu is derived from the Zulu and Xhola languages and can be translated as "humanity towards others" or be interpreted as "the belief in a universal bond of sharing that connects all humanity" (Ubuntu Philosophy). Ubuntu principle recognizes and accepts the existence of other persons and as well believes not only in the welfare of human otherness but upholds the values that are vital for achieving it. It is African humanism propounded by political theorists to facilitate the transition from colonialism to indigenous government in Africa. Ubuntu stresses the essence of being human and highlights the fact that one's humanity is caught up and bound in another person's humanity. It asserts compassion and upholds the wholeness of all humanity (Inarra, 2017). Ubuntu maxims are not exclusively South African because the similarity in African values makes them African.

Zimbabwe, Rwanda, and Burundi are examples of other countries that have the concept with a similar meaning as "human generosity." Inferring from the above, Ubuntu ideology represents and emphasizes the humanity of man toward his fellow man and is expressed through hospitality in concrete actions. Ubuntu ideology is a concrete expression of the rich African values that underscore social, community, and humanistic ethics.

As a system and principle of life, Ubuntu incorporates those virtues and beliefs that enhance communal cohesion. Central among them is hospitality toward members of the society. This clarifies the axiomatic fact that sharing is an ideal and a symbol of friendship and brotherhood in African cultures. It expresses love, solidarity, unity, and concern for others. For the African people,

> Ubuntu means love, truth, peace, happiness, eternal optimism, inner goodness, etc. Ubuntu is the essence of human being, the divine spark of goodness inherent within each being. From the beginning of time the divine principles of Ubuntu has guided the African societies. How one interacts with other human beings, nature, or the Creator, Ubuntu was and is still the guiding principle. Ubuntu is extremely important in Africa and the world at large- as the world needs a common guiding principle of human values. Ubuntu is the core of human values and without Ubuntu, mankind is enveloped by greed, selfishness, immorality

and pride etc. (How Ubuntu Philosophy can have a positive impact on your business)

Ubuntu agrees with Mugumbate and Nyanguru who claim that "Ubuntu relates to bonding with others. This is in line with what the word expresses in most African languages: being self because of others. . . . I am because we are and I am human because I belong" (2013, p. 84). The meaning and implications of Ubuntu suggest a pragmatic model of leadership for Africa.

Ubuntu is acclaimed as a philosophy of Oneness. Oneness is to be understood as interconnectedness of persons, societies, and nations. As such, Ubuntu entails some implications. First, interrelationship among all human others in the community, which invariably extends to societies and nations. Second, connectedness of all lifeforms (i.e., biological and nonbiological lives—everything that the human beings interact with in the ecosphere). These implications have prospects to enrich leader's abilities and disposition to being humane.

Samkange and Samkange (1980) attempted to systematize the Ubuntu philosophy and unify it into three maxims.

1) To be human is to affirm one's humanity by recognizing the humanity of others and, on that basis establish respectful human relations with them.
2) If and when one is faced with a decisive choice between wealth and the preservation of the life of another human being, then one should opt for the preservation of life.
3) The king owes his status, including the powers associated with it, to the will of the people under him.

It is obvious that Ubuntu philosophy embodies all the virtues that can create and maintain harmony in the African society. The first maxim invokes affirmation of one's humanity and recognition of the humanity of the other. Thus, it promotes human dignity and enhances cordial relationships among people. The second affirms priority of human life as invaluable over other values. The third centers specifically on leadership and calls for collaboration with the people. Well evaluated, Ubuntu philosophy embodies the rudimentary values necessary for good leadership, human development, and societal cohesion. It is, therefore, little wonder that the former Zambian leader of government, Dr. Kenneth Kaunda, described Ubuntu as African Humanism and proposed it as a good leadership model (Mugumbate & Nyanguru, 2013, pp. 83–84).

Ubuntu has multiple tenets and nuanced coverage. Mugumbate and Nyanguru highlight some applications of the Ubuntu philosophy: (1) Ubuntu was advocated by Desmond Tutu as the core of African spirituality. He claims that the social ethic of Ubuntu is the greatest contribution of Africa to the world. For Africans, it offers resilience in difficult situations. (2) As an African political and economic ideology: African statesmen promote Ubuntu, using the philosophy to fight for liberation and to gain equality and justice. This tenet brings about egalitarianism via humanism. It was in connection to this value that Ujamaa, a community-building concept understood as family, was propounded by Julius Nyerere and central to it is a fair and equitable distribution of wealth. (3) In African management, Ubuntu informs the quality and spirit of the services rendered. Ubuntu paves the way for essentialist views and seeks homogeneity of the African people. As an ideology of common African values, Ubuntu recognizes collectivity, acceptance, and hospitality, which are essential to successful management. (4) In the code of the ethics of social work, Ubuntu embodies humanness. It emphasizes solidarity, empathy, human dignity, and recognition of the social cum communal *quiddity* of human personality. These values guide not only the work and its mission but also the personal attitude of the worker. (5) Ubuntu plays a central role in South African welfarism. This is reflected in the SA white paper that emphasizes democracy, partnership, Ubuntu, equity, and intersectoral collaboration, and so on. Ubuntu was then recognized as a principle that upholds care for the human otherness while the community is vital in recognizing the individual. (6) The Ubuntu spirit is prominent and beneficial in social work. For example, it inspires revitalization of the dysfunctional persons of the society in every facet of societal life (2013, pp. 88–97). The foregoing applications underscore the suitability of Ubuntu as Africa's leadership model.

Ubuntu philosophy is a promising socioeconomic and political leadership model. Despite this, good leadership eludes Africa. Experience shows that Africans, especially the political leaders, do not always live out the Ubuntu principle in the discharge of their official duties to the society. A recap of the challenges of leadership in Africa discussed in the previous section confirms this claim.

Despite the challenges, Ubuntu ideology is still the model ideology for building the African society. The crux of this claim is the centrality and priority of the society to the individual. The individual is first a member of the society before asserting and recognizing himself as a person. Society-centered consciousness by leaders implies the common good of all and is important for leadership. This *polis*-centric feature is natively African, and as well highlights the ontology of Ubuntu philosophy, because it shows its nature and the relations between the other people and the society. The priority of the community to the individual, arguably, represents a movement from autonomy to heteronomy. Autonomy is not a good leadership ideal because it is self-legislating, self-conscious, and egoistic and a return to the self. On the other hand, heteronomy signifies, emphasizes, and impacts a return to otherness, the larger society, thus, a good leadership attitude. Therefore, Ubuntu ideology implies rejection of egoism but coheres with what William Desmond refers to as *Agapeic services*, an expression that explains selfless services in favor of the community (2001, p. 161). Accordingly, Ubuntu ideology vouches for community-centered activities for the members as a matter of preference. It is defensible that Ubuntu is egalitarianism is disguise because it supports equal treatment and opportunities for all people regardless of any presuppositions. With these ideals, it presents a pragmatic module of leadership to Africa. Being a social leadership philosophy, a native economic philosophy could be a vital complement.

AFRICAPITALISM: NOTIONS AND PRINCIPLES

Africapitalism is a novel and indigenous African philosophy founded and developed by Tony Elumelu. It asserts and defends the belief in the sustainability of economic and development of the African continent through collaboration between the public and private sector among others. It strongly emphasizes the role of the private sector in the realization of the goal of boosting investment in the African continent. Specifically, Africapitalism "is predicated on the belief that Africa's private sector can and must play a leading role in the continent's development" (Elumelu).

Africapitalism is a new economic model within the modern African Social and Political Philosophy. It is essentially a call to action, and it upholds the thesis that the African private sector has the economic capacity to transform the economy of the African continent through long-term investments, creating both economic prosperity and social wealth. It involves the cooperative action of nongovernmental organizations, especially the private sectors, in the developmental impact of the entrepreneur on his immediate society. Africapitalism is the middle ground between business and philanthropy (Elumelu, 2014). It is an economic philosophy that embodies the commitment of private sectors of an economy to transforming the economic fortunes of African countries through investments that generate both prosperity in economic activities and social wealth (Amaeshi & Idemudia, 2015). Africapitalism promises a new model of African empowerment through active participation of the private sectors. It evaluates the index in which African economies are growing. The nature and progression of Africapitalism justify it as a median between business and philanthropy. The involvement of philanthropy serves as the nexus between the native duo of Africapitalism and Ubuntu philosophies.

Africapitalism is an action-oriented social and economic philosophy that focuses on developing people and communities. Elumelu notes that

"Africapitalism is a call to action for businesses to make decisions that will increase economic and social wealth and promote development in the communities and nations in which they operate. Such a decision will ultimately help businesses become more profitable as the communities they serve become well-off consumers, healthy and better educated employees and even entrepreneurs who go on to become suppliers and service providers" (Elumelu). Africapitalism could be understood as an anthropocentric philosophy aimed at improving the human social and economic condition and consequently, the human welfare and dignity of the African people. The people, the societies, and the countries in which this philosophy takes effect are the primary and sole focus of Africapitalism. This, therefore, defends the claim that it is anthropocentric. A further justification of this claim is evident in the principles that characterize it: (1) Long-term investment aimed at deploying capital to create economic values via extraction of resources. (2) Strategic sectors which aim at delivering financial return, social and economic welfare in the areas of agriculture, power, healthcare delivery, and financial breakthrough. (3) Development of dividends, aimed through viable business activities that deliver financial, economic, and social returns to both stakeholders and shareholders. (4) Value-added growth achieved through the exploitation of the available human and financial capital and other raw materials, thereby transforming them into higher integrated supply blocs. (5) Regional connectivity, which it aims to achieve through intra-regional commerce and trade through development of infrastructure as well as harmonization and integration of policies and their implementation. (6) Multigenerational development, aiming at strategies of sustainable investment and economic growth. (7) Shared purpose, aiming at initiating sustainable and lucrative partnerships among many variables: businesses, investors, governments, academia, civil society, philanthropists, and institutions (Elumelu). With the above principles, which could also be said to be the values which Africapitalism represents, Africapitalism is an advocacy of active business through the partnership of all for increased output of economic and social wealth. The above principles are summarized as follows: Africapitalism "is an economic philosophy that embodies the private sector's commitment to the economic transformation of Africa through investments that generate both economic prosperity and social wealth" (Amaeshi & Idemudia, 2015, p. 201). This definition presupposes that Africapitalism is an action-oriented economic philosophy that is capable of bringing about sustainable development to African countries through investment and wealth creation. Africapitalism is the key to unlocking and reviving economic and social wealth in the continent. The propensity for this assumption is the inextricable affinity between Africapitalism and Ubuntu, both being native African philosophies; Africapitalism, an economic philosophy, and Ubuntu, a social philosophy. Integration of these two philosophies, their principles, and practice will undoubtedly unleash economic and social transformation on African countries because the collaboration of the private sector, business corporations, nongovernmental organizations, and investors is surely a stronger force than any government.

The nexus between Africapitalism and transformation of Africa is the overstretched period of misery and bleak story of Africa's existence. The difficult, if not unsurmountable, challenges that militate against any meaningful development and progress in Africa is an obvious index that government alone cannot bring about the needed development. Amaeshi and Idemudia (2015) observe that "Africa has a long checkered history of colonialism, bad governance, and poverty. In addition, the continent suffers from weak institutions and distressed civil societies. Resuscitating Africa from near economic and social collapse has continued to remain a thriving business for multinational institutions, foreign governments, aid agencies, international NGOs and international donors." This observation underscores the prevalence and the potency of Africapitalism, which is founded on the private sector in alliance with other nongovernmental parastatals, together with government, to bear out the African economy and social life. It, therefore, implies that transformation of African economy and social life is possible with Africapitalism. It is from this perspective that the entailment of Africapitalism on African socioeconomic life could fully be appreciated. This, however, is the affinity that defines the duo of Africapitalism and Ubuntu as philosophies of African origin. Since government has been unable to effect the needed transformation, and since dependency on foreign governments and donors perpetually dwarfs the progress of African economy, involving the private sector is not an option. Africapitalism, therefore, proves to be the veritable key to transforming the duo of economic and social lives of the people and could meaningfully affect other sectors because a nation's economy has a robust impact on other sectors of a nation's life. Impacts of Africapitalism could be foreseen from its implication for Africa.

UBUNTU PHILOSOPHY AND AFRICAPITALISM: IMPLICATIONS FOR LEADERSHIP IN AFRICA

Ubuntu philosophy and Africapitalism are native African philosophies. Whereas Ubuntu stresses more on leadership and social life, Africapitalism is an economic philosophy. The duo have robust affinity with each other and implications to Africa. Ubuntu mirrors and provides the moral values that serve as the basis for Africapitalism. This moral basis is founded and predicated on the communitarian nature of the African culture. Moral values which the Africans cherish and prioritize are embedded in and reposed on the human person. They are anthropocentric because they serve the human person. To say this, therefore, means that the culture of the African people prioritizes and vouches for human development and flourishing. The communitarian nature is the basis for leadership which in turn impacts economy and economic development. Regarding leadership and social life, the philosophy of the Annang people of Nigeria, for example, expresses this truth in various ways, one of which is "One tree does not make a forest" (Okon, 2011, p. 397). "One tree" is a figure for autonomy, whereas "a forest," which is a collection of trees of different kinds, symbolizes heteronomy. This expression makes sense in asserting the preeminence of the society to an individual and the best leadership ideal. It is in highlighting and emphasizing the supremacy of the community or the society over the individual that this expression is valid. Furthermore, to add to the first, Okon elsewhere observes that "the king does not govern alone" (2011, p. 398). The king is an individual despite his powers. He needs others as his subjects as well as councilors, therefore, he cannot govern alone. In these expressions, one notes that in relating between the autonomy and the heteronomy, the heteronomy takes the priority position. This coheres with Samkange's third maxims of Ubuntu ideology which bothers on leadership. Regarding Africapitalism, one could observe that this value harmonizes with heteronomy and serves a veritable attempt to effect economic goods to all peoples and hence, economic development of the people. In agreement to the economic development, Amaeshi and Idemudia note that "Africapitalism is an attempt to re-imagine entrepreneurship and reunite capitalism with moral roots in Africa" (2015, p. 215). The introduction of entrepreneurship into the mainstream of the community life is to improve and enhance the economy and consequently, the life of the community. Here, Ubuntu and Africapitalism not only crosscut leadership but also impact the economic life of the people. Ubuntu in essence underscores the primordiality of the community over an individual. Translating this value to economic life entails massive transformation in the economic life of the people. The principles of Ubuntu and Africapitalism, therefore, will accomplish social and economic transformations of the entire continent and improve the welfare and well-being of the people. This returns us to the truism that the communitarian perspective of African society is a robust value in economy and leadership. For, the king despite his powers is an individual and he is a king because the people are, therefore, he is not greater or prior to the community. This agrees with Opoku who forwards that "man is man because of others, and life is when you are together, alone you are an animal" (1978, p. 92). Communality crosscuts all the facets of the societal life. Makumba observes the preeminence of the community even in religion. He notes that religiously, individuals make up the system and that no individual can be a religious community. He argues that the different stages of an individual's life, together with the accompanying ceremonies, prove that the individual recognizes himself because the community exists (2007, p. 167). This adds to the defense of the communitarian nature of the African society. Transferring this noble communal to the economic life of the people could lead to unparallel breakthroughs. In the African antiquity, being recognized as human was only within the context of the society. On this, Agulanna (2010, p. 288) concurs that "Africans believe that it is only in the community that the life of the individual acquires true meaning. It is in mutually interacting with other members of the community that the individual can ever hope to realize his social aspirations." Individuals-community bond shows the community centeredness which characterizes the nature of the African society. It is obvious that the individual-community (and vice versa) relationship was not one-sided. For, as previously noted, Ubuntu defends humanism which in ecological parlance could be rendered as symbiosis. The implication of this for leadership is that Ubuntu model being communitarian will inform leaders on people-oriented policies and leadership styles.

To clearly underscore this symbiotic relationship, Nyerere (1965, p. 166) notes "in the traditional African society we were individual within the community. We took care of the community, and the community took care of us." In thinking Africapitalism, involvement of private sectors to complement the government could parallel this view. Taking care of the society and being taken care of by the society means mutuality and the end is economic flourishing of the people. Because society—the generality of the masses—has preeminence over the individual, this offers reason why leaders should prioritize societal projects instead of their private affairs. Ubuntu philosophy further indicates the bilateral nature and entanglement of relationship in African society. It is for this reason the community spirit is the vital force of cohesion in the traditional African society that has impacted positively on individuals because individuals have accepted and lived in adherence to it and finding fulfillment in it. It also points to the place of individuals as a metaphor for private sector—the primary driver of Africapitalism. Therefore, the conclusion that Ubuntu and Africapitalism are native philosophies that interact with each other is valid.

Africans have not always lived out the principles of Ubuntu. Therefore, there is a need to reconsider Ubuntu ideals for their leadership model. This is an advocacy for the rebirth of ubuntu principles and their active experience. As highlighted previously, Ubuntu philosophy has the prospect of changing the leadership narrative in the African continent. This is because, first, as a native system, the demands for its practice are also native, thus, easy to follow. Second, as a model of leadership, the community consciousness is more reinforced in the leaders. Therefore, the values Ubuntu represents could reduce or eliminate the vices associated with the leadership challenges the continent has experienced and with Africapitalism, an upsurge in economic development. For, in almost all of the African countries, the priority of the society to the individual is degenerating and this accounts for the challenges experienced by the people. With the Ubuntu consciousness and Africapitalism, a new model of leadership and economy is dawning. The contemporary indices of corruption in government which indicate the degeneration of some of the values Ubuntu philosophy upholds will be transformed by Ubuntu values and Africapitalism and lead to a renaissance of these values. Implementing Ubuntu ideology as a leadership model will certainly and meaningfully revitalize the moral patrimony and value system of the African people and strengthen the depleted sense of community centeredness.

The Aristotelian definition of man as *zoon politikon* is based on man's relationship to the society. Man, as *Zoon politikon,* relates to *zoon logon ekhon* (a living being capable of speech) (Arendt, 1998, p. 27). The relationship between the two bothers on speech as the tool of communication in the society. In the Greek city state as well as in the ancient African societies, the community centeredness of the society was expressed in the development of the civic societies through the provision of basic infrastructures, which is one of the challenges of contemporary African leadership and this is caused by depreciating ideals of Ubuntu. It, therefore, gives reasons in defense of Ubuntu as a leadership model. Ubuntu as a leadership model will rejuvenate the African society and renew in it the human, ethical, social, political, developmental, and religious perspectives. Ubuntu principle is very expedient for African countries in the contemporary globalized world in which economic, political, social scientific, and technological powers and success constitute the variables for cooperation among the comity of nations.

Ubuntu has strong and inextricable links with Africapitalism. As a recap, Ubuntu and Africapitalism are action philosophies. Whereas Ubuntu provides moral values of the African milieu for leadership and social life, Africapitalism translates these values to concrete practical experience in the economy via investment. Amaeshi and Idemudia identify some common principles such as a sense of peace, a sense of progress, a sense of parity, and sense of place. They claim that these principles are rooted in the Ubuntu philosophy and that, in conjunction with Africapitalism, they could advance renaissance of African consciousness in capitalism because the consciousness involves translating these native values to contemporary economic practices via economic investments (2015, p. 215).

The values of Ubuntu commonly shared by Africapitalism are communal. It makes sense to assume that they are capable of effecting economic transformation of the African society via investment and formation of larger economic and trade corporations. This assumption is based on the fact that in the traditional African society, an individual identifies himself based on his creative prowess and the society not only nurtures but also shapes him. The outcomes of the societal nurture could be evident in the following cardinal values of Africapitalism:

1) *Sense of Progress and Prosperity:* Progress can be identified with prosperity and is linked to economic activities. As a political and economic system that is controlled by private sectors and individuals, profits are aimed at wealth creation. Thus, "Africapitalism is predicated on the creation of social wealth in addition to the pursuit of financial profitability" (Amaeshi & Idemudia 2015, p. 216). Economic wealth is inseparable from social wealth, and this arguably is the source and purveyor of progress and prosperity for which Africapitalism is vouched. Prosperity and progress are economic indices that entail reduction or elimination of poverty.
2) *Sense of Parity*: The experience of extreme inequality in most African societies necessitates a reduction of inequality among the peoples. Progress and prosperity could lead to a seeming egalitarian perception. This could rather be viewed as parity, which results from an equitable share of the benefits of progress and prosperity (Amaeshi & Idemudia, 2015, p. 216). Whether or not parity is achieved, a reduction in the number of extreme inequalities among the masses is a good testimony and a point of departure in the experience of the dividend of Africapitalism. The sense of progress is a value in Africapitalism, thus, a reduction in cases of inequality is an indication of progress and prosperity.
3) *Sense of Peace and Harmony*: Capitalism in the contemporary times is characterized by a strong sense of innovativeness. Since it is a free enterprise of private individuals, it involves constant contestations between the existing and upcoming businesses. For Amaeshi and Idemudia, this is a quest for creative destruction and "this quest for creative destruction is often underpinned by the logic of self-interest which creates enormous rewards for firms and entrepreneurs and has been proven to be one of the best drivers of entrepreneurial activities" (2015, p. 216). Balance, harmony, and peace is the end of investment gained through Africapitalism. Thus, contests among businesses are means to this noble end. Furthermore, free market capitalism that leads to social and environmental imbalance is injurious to human well-being. Therefore, socio-environmental harmony could be checkmated by balancing the impacts of consumption and production on the environment, society, and economy (Amaeshi and Idemudia, 2015, p. 216). Africapitalism takes into consideration the interests of stakeholders and shareholders as they create wealth both for the public and private persons. This

feature mirrors modern management philosophy that shows harmony and balance (Kramer, 1975).

4) *Sense of Place and Belonginess*: Belongingness is a primary feature in Ubuntu and Africapitalism philosophies. Belongingness implies a location and place. Place and cost are two features of capitalism that contrasts Africapitalism. In the global sense of capitalism, place is ignored but cost is given priority. The result of this is that the economic value of a place determines its position in the economic scale of preference. Thus, place is laden with economic worth in capitalism and globally, thus, a place is reduced to a space. Contrary to capitalism that ignores place but prioritizes cost, Africapitalism is place sensitive. It takes into consideration the rootedness of persons thereby showing a sense of belongingness to individual who is the subject and determiner of economic value in things (Tuan, 1977). Consideration of the place helps in making managerial decisions which is connected with the economy and self-identity of the individual person. Economic activities take place in locations and locations also define and identify persons (Amaeshi & Idemudia, 2015, p. 216). Besides identification and belongingness, consciousness of place could also express patriotism which can mean love and solidarity with one's native place. These features mark Africapitalism and distinguish it from the global sense of capitalism.

These values of Africapitalism have a robust affinity with the values of Ubuntu philosophy. The common rootedness of these two philosophies can, therefore, not be doubted when thinking African consciousness in Africapitalism as an economic philosophy, and Ubuntu as a model philosophy of social life and leadership. On the strong side, the translation of the Ubuntu values to Africapitalism without contradiction points to a transformation of the economy and hence, a rapid reduction in poverty and an uprising prosperity.

CONCLUSION: UBUNTU AND AFRICAPITALISM AS MODELS OF LEADERSHIP IN AFRICA

Ubuntu emphasizes humanism toward others. It is an African humanistic ideology. It could also serve as a model of leadership and social life. Africapitalism is a philosophy that asserts the involvement and commitment of the private sector in transforming the economy of the African states. The two philosophies have the interest, well-being/welfare, and flourishing of the society as an entity, but through the commitment of individuals and the private sector. Ubuntu is an Afro concept wherein one's sense of personhood is conceived, defined, and shaped in and by the society. It expresses the African communal lifestyle that reveals interhuman relationships at individual, communal, national, and international contexts. Two obvious perspectives of the Ubuntu principle are: First, Ubuntu philosophy is an embodiment of the humanism of others. It stresses hospitality, brotherhood, and upholds one's selfhood through the recognition of the selfhood of other people. When the above value is translated to economic investments, its social implications also bear out economic results. Since Ubuntu implies that one finds meaning and fulfillment for one's life in relation to the other people's personhood and existence, Africapitalism could also imply that one becomes economically transformed because of other's economic wealth. These philosophies offer a veritable and holistic leadership model to Africa in view of their prospect relating to leadership and economic challenges of African countries. Since Ubuntu emphasizes humane attitudes such as hospitality, love, goodness and maintains that one is because others are, a model of leadership that upholds these values will be transferred to Africapitalism and certainly ameliorates the challenges in leadership, economy, and social life. It will offer some palliatives, if not completely eradicate the socioeconomic challenges. This submission coheres with the observation that "Ubuntu is essentially about togetherness, and how all of our actions have an impact on others and on society" (Williams, 2018). For vices like corruption and bribery, nepotism and preferential treatment are opposed to Ubuntu and are inimical to leadership and followership and national cohesion. On the other hand, Africapitalism will inform commitment by private individuals and sectors to expand investments but also complement government effort.

Africapitalism concerns economy, but investments can only thrive in a stable and peaceful society. Thus, Ubuntu is a*polis*-centric and homocentric philosophy; it prioritizes the society as well as the individual and upholds values that foster societal cohesion. It therefore offers the needed rudiments for developing the society. Economically, it encourages egalitarianism and reduction of poverty among the people. Like Ubuntu, which stresses its aim as "the mission to end extreme poverty—so that everyone, everywhere, can live equally" (William, 2018), Africapitalism practically leads the way. The harmony of Ubuntu and Africapitalism will accomplish political, economic, and social transformation and societal cohesion. Unfortunately, leadership experience in most African countries is in direct opposition to the Ubuntu values and prospects, though the values of these two philosophies are capable of a renaissance of leadership values in Africa.

Ubuntu and Africapitalism, being native philosophies, embody African values. For, the African society is essentially communal. As Adahada (2020, p. 32) notes, "the life of the African man is typically characterized by strong community bond . . . . Community spirit has a formidable impact on the individual in the African society." Ubuntu and Africapitalism, as leadership philosophies, will, therefore, open leaders to giving everyone equitable opportunity necessary for reducing or ending poverty and hence, economic transformation. It will inform and empower the leaders about the provision of the basic amenities and services that are lacking in the continent. The Ubuntu leadership model would instill in all the citizens the sense of dignity and belonging necessary for patriotic actions. Ubuntu consciousness forbids amassing wealth for oneself and family, as is currently the case in most African countries, as well as tenure elongation and unwillingness to exit office voluntarily when due. If Ubuntu takes root in the African society as a leadership model, community life will become a more cherished value that creates sociopolitical impact and Africapitalism create economic well-being and transformation for all. The principles and values of Ubuntu and Africapitalism, emphasizing African humanism, are messianic because of their liberating prospect. African society is primordially Ubuntu, hence African leadership style should be an expression of Ubuntu translated to Africapitalism for integral socioeconomic and political leadership.

BIBLIOGRAPHY

Adahada, G. (2020). Re-Thinking Ethics and Morality with Haidt: Determining the Ethical Matrix for the African Society. *Journal of African Studies and Sustainable Development*, *3*(4), 25–37.

Afegbua, S., & Adejuwon, K. (2012). The Challenges of Leadership and Governance in Africa. *Harmers*, *2*(1), 141–157.

Agulanna, C. (2010). Community and Human Well-Being in an African Culture. *Trames*, *3*(14), 282–298.

Amaeshi, K., & Idemudia, U. (2015). Africapitalism: A Management Idea for Business in Africa? *Africa Journal of Management*, *1*(2), 210–223. https://doi.org/10.1080/23322373.2015.1026229.

Arendt, H. (1985). *The Human Condition, 2nd Edition*, introduction by Margret Canovan. London: The University of Chicago Press.

Chemers, M. (2002). Cognitive, Social, and Emotional Intelligence of Transformational Leadership: Efficacy and Effectiveness. In R. E. Riggio et al. (Eds.), *Multiple Intelligences and Leadership*. Mahwah, NJ: Lawrence Erlbaum Associates, pp. 139–160.

Council of Social Workers (CSW). (2012). Social Workers' Code of Ethics. Statutory Instrument 146 of 2012.

Desmond, W. (2001). *Ethics and the Between*. Albany, NY: State University of New York Press.

Ejimabo, N. (2013). *Understanding the Impact of Leadership in Nigeria: Its Reality, Challenges, and Perspectives*. Sage. https://doi.org/10.1177/2158244013490704; sgo.sagepub.com. April–June, pp. 1–14.

Elumelu, T. (2019). What Is Africapitalism? Retrieved July 25, 2022, from https://www.tonyelumelufoundation.org/africapitalism.

Friedman, S. (2019). The Problem of Leadership in Africa. Retrieved September 9, 2020, from http://democracyinafrica.org/problem-leadership-africa/.

Craig, E. (2005). *Meeting the Ethical Challenges of Leadership*. New Delhi: Sage Publications.

How Ubuntu Philosophy Can Have a Positive Impact on Your Business. Retrieved July 17, 2020, from https://www.virgin.com/virgin-unite/business-innovation/how-ubuntu-philosophy-can-have-positive-impact-your-business.

Inarra, B. (2017). Ubuntu-an African Philosophy (I am Because We Are). Retrieved July 17, 2020, from http://msolajpiced.worldpress.com2017/06/09ubuntu-an-african-philosophy-i-am-because-we-are.

Kramer, H. (1975). The Philosophical Foundation of Management Rediscovered. *Management International Review*, *15*(2–3), 47–55.

Makumba, M. (2007) *Introduction to African Philosophy*. Nairobi: Paulines Publications Africa.

Mugumbate, J., & Nyanguru, A. (2013). Exploring African Philosophy: The Value of Ubuntu in Social Work. *African Journal of Social Work*, *3*(1), 82–100.

Ntata, A. (2015). Seven Challenges of Leadership in Africa. Retrieved September 10, 2020, from https://www.linkedin.com/pulse/7-challenges-leadership-africa-z-allan-ntata.

Nyerere, J. (1965). *Freedom and Unity: A Selection from Writings and Speeches 1952–1965*. Nairobi: Oxford University Press.

Ogbeidi, M. (2012). Political Leadership and Corruption in Nigeria Since 1960: A Socio-Economic Analysis. *Journal of Nigeria Studies*, *1*(2), 1–25.

Okon, J. (2011). Imo Adeagwo (The Human Person Is Wealth): A Principle of Transcultural Neo-Humanist Philosophy of the Annang People. In E. Essien (Ed.), *Summa Philosophica*: *An Introduction to Philosophy and Logic*. Lulu Press, pp. 81–85.

Samkange, S., & Samkange, S. (1980). *Humanism or Ubuntuism: A Zimbabwe Indigenous Political Philosophy*. Harare: Graham Publishing.

South African Government. (1996). White Paper on Welfare. Government Gazette Number 16943.

Tuan, Y. (1977). *Space and Place: The Perspective of Experience*. Minneapolis, MN: University of Minnesota Press.

Ubi, E. (2019). Nigeria's Major Challenges in 59 Years of Independence. Retrieved September 15, 2020, from http://www.financialnigeria.com/nigeria-s-major-challenges-in-59-years-of-independence-blog-482.html.

Ubuntu Philosophy. Retrieved July 17, 2020, from https://www.newworldencyclopedia.org/p/index.php?title=Ubuntu_(philosophy)&oldid=1034676.

Ubuntu Philosophy-Wikipedia. Retrieved July 17, 2020, from http://en.wikipedia.org/wiki/Ubuntu_philosophy.

Udegbe, I. (1999). Leadership: Nature and Pathways to Effectiveness. In I. B. Udegbe et al. (Eds.), *Psychology: Perspectives in Human Behavior, a Publication of the Department of Psychology*. Nigeria: University of Ibadan, pp. 288–312.

Ujamaa-Wikipedia. Retrieved from http://en.wikipedia.org/wiki/Ujamaa.

Ward, S. (2020). What Is Leadership? Retrieved September 11, 2020, from https://www.thebalancesmb.com/leadership-definition-2948275.

Williams, H. (2018). What Is the Spirit of Ubuntu? How Can We Have It in Our Lives? Retrieved July 17, 2020, from https://www.globalcitizen.org/en/content/ubuntu-south-africa-together-nelson-mandela/.

Chapter 12

Managing Diversity and Protecting Racial and Ethnic Minorities in Africa

The Limitations of the Quota System

Frank Aragbonfoh Abumere

It is not contentious to assert that the failure to manage diversity has been an intractable problem in many African states, nor is it contentious to assert that racial and ethnic crises have been intractable problems in many African states. However, it is contentious to assert that, generally, leaders in Africa have not attempted to manage diversity, or specifically to manage racial and ethnic differences. But what is less contentious to assert is that many of the devices or mechanisms through which the leaders have attempted to manage diversity, including racial and ethnic differences, have failed. Therefore, their attempts have been a project in futility. One of such devices or mechanisms is the quota system. There are two ways to discuss the problem of the quota system. One way is to discuss the quota system sui generis. The other way is to discuss the quota system as applied. I am opting for the second, rather than the first way. This is because the merits and demerits of the quota system can only be properly assessed when the quota system is applied rather than when it is sui generis. Sui generis quota system is neither advantageous nor disadvantageous, it is just neutral. But when applied, the quota system ceases to be neutral, it becomes advantageous or disadvantageous. Hence, I will deal with the quota system as applied in African states rather than as sui generis. The quota system can be applied to different cases whose list might be inexhaustible. But I shall only focus on the cases of race and ethnicity. This focus is due to the fact that race and ethnicity have been, and still are, some of the most complex and problematic cases in Africa—and the rest of the world. We only need to look at the historical and current situations of countries such as South Africa, Zimbabwe, Zambia, Kenya, Nigeria, Rwanda, Burundi, Cameroon,

Sierra Leone, Liberia, Democratic Republic of Congo—outside Africa we can look at the United States of America, Israel, and Palestine, and so on—to see what complex problems either race or ethnicity have been.

Quota system is very attractive to its proponents. It is at once popular with some people and unpopular with others. So while it is tempting to adopt racial and ethnic quotas as the solutions to racial and ethnic differences in Africa, they are not ready-made solutions. I contend that racial and ethnic quotas are not the answers to differences in racial and ethnic demographics. My contention is based on the following reasons. First, racial and ethnic demographics are just some facets of the multifaceted demographics of societies. Second, other things equal, racial and ethnic demographics do not warrant being given any precedence over other demographics. Third, racial and ethnic demographics are only problems if they are exploited as sources of injustice and unfairness or if they are directly or indirectly linked with injustice and unfairness. Finally, quota system should only be adopted if and only if it is the best possible way to remedy injustice and unfairness. In order to argue for my position, I present a hypothetical scenario in which racial and ethnic identities are not more important than other identities in a state called Azania. Then I tease out whether racial and ethnic differences are necessary and/or sufficient conditions for injustice and unfairness. Furthermore, I show why racial and ethnic quotas are not "the answers" but just "an answer" to racial and ethnic disparities. Many countries are currently experiencing disparities in demography. Such disparities often pose difficult problems to policymakers in that it is always difficult to make and implement robust public policies that can adequately respond to such disparities. Among the various demographic disparities in different countries, racial and ethnic disparities are some of the major disparities.

Depending on how disparities in racial and ethnic demographics are dealt with by policymakers, there can either be an erosion of social and political cohesion and economic downturn or an enhancement of social and political cohesion and improved economic growth. In this regard, the marginalization of racial and ethnic minorities is more likely to disrupt social and political cohesion. And the racially and ethnically marginalized are less likely to contribute, at their full capacity, to social and political cohesion and economic growth since their human resources, social, political, and economic capital may not be fully employed, appropriately deployed, and well channeled into social and political cohesion and economic development. The question I will be wrestling with in this discussion is whether racial and ethnic quotas are the answer to disparities in racial and ethnic demography. In other words, I am concerned with whether racial and ethnic quotas can be appropriate public policy responses to racial and ethnic disparities pertaining to the demography of various countries.

THE CASE OF AZANIA (A HYPOTHETICAL AFRICAN STATE)

Imagine a country called Azania with a population of 10 million. The population of the youth is nine million, as opposed to people of other ages. The population of blacks is nine million as opposed to other races. Zulu blacks make up eight million of the black population, while Xhosa, Bapedi (North Sotho), Basotho (South Sotho), Batswana, (South) Ndebele, Venda, Tsonga, and Swazi blacks make up the remaining one million. The population of believers is nine million as opposed to nonbelievers who are one million. Christians make up eight million of the nine million and Catholics make up seven million of the Christian population. Western-educated persons make up nine million of the population as opposed to one million non-Western-educated persons. The affluent make up nine million as opposed to the middle and lower classes who make up one million. The nonphysically challenged make up nine million, while the physically challenged make up one million. Males make up nine million while females make up one million of the population. We can go on and on. Because of the demographic asymmetries, Azania opted for a quota system. What singular criterion should the policymakers use to determine the quota system: gender, race, religion, education, economic class, health, and so on? No citizen has a singular demographic identity; rather, citizens have multifaceted demographic identities. For instance, no citizens are males and males only or females and females only. They also belong to other categories.

They are also believers or nonbelievers or at least agnostics. If they are believers, some are Christians, some Muslims, and others might practice other religions. Among the Christians, some are Catholics, Protestants, Pentecostals, Evangelicals, and so on. Some Catholics are youths and others are not. Some youths are white, some black, and so on. Some whites are Afrikaans, others are not. Some Afrikaan whites are educated, others are not. Some educated persons are affluent; others are not. So on and so forth. In Azania, we see that apart from racial and ethnic disparities, there are other disparities. Notably, these disparities in identities are not only multiple but are also complex. Isolating racial and ethnic identities amid these multiple and complex identities is merely unnecessarily problematizing racial and ethnic identities, because such isolation makes racial and ethnic identities the paramount identities when other identities may even be more relevant.

For instance, the Occupy Wall Street movement in 2011 had economic inequality as an issue rather than racial or ethnic demographics. Consequently, the sources of real or perceived injustice were not racial or ethnic demographics but class demographics. So, if the United States of America were to adopt any quota system, it would be based on class rather than race or ethnicity. But, surely, a quota system was not going to be the answer, and it is not the answer, to the grievances of the protesters. Also, in many Islamic states, religion and gender are the "relevant" demographics rather than race and ethnicity when it comes to the sources of injustice and unfairness. Consequently, if there were to be quota system in such states, it would be based on religion and gender rather than race or ethnicity in spite of disparities in racial and ethnic demographics.

RACIAL AND ETHNIC DISPARITIES AND THE PROBLEM OF MARGINALIZATION

My subject matter, whether racial and ethnic quotas are appropriate public policy responses to disparities in racial and ethnic demography, has three parts. The first part is "racial and ethnic quotas," the second part is "appropriate public policy response," while the third part is "disparities in racial and ethnic demography." Although the second part serves as the conjunctive between the first and third parts, it is the second part that is the crux of our discussion. Nevertheless, a helpful way to deal with our subject matter is to take the third part sui generis and ask if disparities in racial and ethnic demographics|| in particular or disparities in demographics in general can be sources of injustice and unfairness against some or certain racial and ethnic groups. Discussing racial and ethnic quotas as the answers to racial and ethnic disparities as an intellectual plausibility will be at best a thought experiment, and proposing it as a practical possibility will be at best a project in futility unless we can ascertain whether racial and ethnic disparities cause injustice or unfairness to some or certain racial and ethnic groups.

If some or certain persons, as collectives or individuals, are treated unjustly and unfairly because of their race or ethnicity, it is easily ascertainable that their race or ethnicity is being exploited as a source of injustice and unfairness against them. If the state, the government, or the basic structure of society has institutionalized the exploitation or marginalization of some or certain racial or ethnic groups, whether de jure or de facto, then it is crystal clear that such racial or ethnic groups, simply because of their race or ethnicity, are categorically treated unjustly and unfairly.

In the above case, it is safe to say, without probing further, that racial or ethnic disparities are at once necessary and sufficient conditions for the injustice and unfairness such racial or ethnic groups are suffering. Consequently, we can argue that racial or ethnic disparities are at once a necessary and sufficient condition for racial or ethnic quotas, albeit if and only if racial or ethnic quotas will remedy the injustice and unfairness. However, there are individual exploitative actions by persons from some racial or ethnic groups against other persons from other racial or ethnic groups which, if looked at as individual actions, will be non-consequential but are very consequential when looked at as collective actions. Let us assume that these actions were done because of racial and ethnic disparities and some or certain racial or ethnic groups were targeted simply because of their race or ethnicity. But let us also assume that these actions were done by individuals independently. It is only when we look at the individual actions as a collective that they constitute a "normalized" marginalization of some or certain racial or ethnic groups, which in turn can be seen as an institutionalization of the marginalization of some or certain racial or ethnic groups. But we have to note that if isolated as individual actions, these actions are neither necessary nor sufficient conditions for the institutionalization of the marginalization of such racial or ethnic groups.

Also, we have to note that many times there are actions that are not intended to cause the institutionalization of the marginalization of some or certain racial or ethnic groups, although the actions inadvertently cause it. So, in racial and ethnic marginalization, although some individual actors do not have the intention to cause the institutionalization of racial and ethnic marginalization, their actions, which are propelled by other motives, result in it and perhaps a host of other negative consequences. What the above discussion shows is that disparities in racial and ethnic demographics first, can, but may not, be both a necessary and sufficient condition for racial and ethnic marginalization; second, can, but may not, be a necessary condition for racial and ethnic marginalization; and third, can, but may not, be a sufficient condition for racial and ethnic marginalization. Therefore, we can reasonably conclude that disparities in racial and ethnic demographics are subject to probability in terms of causing or not causing, whether directly or indirectly, the marginalization of some or certain racial and ethnic groups. Consequently, disparities in racial and ethnic demographics do not always trigger the marginalization of some or certain racial and ethnic groups.

In order to reduce the probability of disparities in racial and ethnic demographics causing the marginalization of some or certain racial and ethnic groups, the state must have background institutions whose nature is just and fair. In his conception of the state as a social cooperative machine or entity, the American political philosopher, John Rawls, asserts that the state has a basic structure which is "the way in which the major social institutions fit together into one system and how they assign fundamental rights and duties and shape the division of advantages that arises through social cooperation" (Rawls 1993, 258). The basic structure is necessary to ensure fair cooperation: on the one hand, among citizens; and on the other hand, between citizens and the state. Because, as Rawls says: each person possesses an inviolability founded on justice that even the welfare of society as a whole cannot override. For this reason, justice denies that the loss of freedom for some is made right by a greater good shared by others. It does not allow that the sacrifices imposed on a few are outweighed by the larger sum of advantages enjoyed by many. Therefore, in a just society, the liberties of equal citizenship are taken as settled; the rights secured by justice are not subject to political bargaining or to the calculus of social interests (Rawls 1999a, 1).

In view of Rawls's‘ assertions, quota system can be adopted as the answer to disparities in racial and ethnic demography based on at least one of two conditions. First, it must be ascertained that the basic structure, in its allocation of duties and rights, and in its allocation of advantages and disadvantages, discriminates against some racial and ethnic groups. Second, it must be ascertained that due to their racial or ethnic identity, some persons have been marginalized. So if racial and ethnic groups are justly and fairly treated, we do not need to have recourse to racial and ethnic quotas even in spite of disparities in racial and ethnic demography. Even if persons of certain racial and ethnic groups are treated unjustly or unfairly, and they are treated as such not because of their race or ethnicity but due to other reasons, such as their religion, age, or education, we do not need a quota system based on racial or ethnic demography in spite of disparities in racial and ethnic demography.

RACIAL AND ETHNIC QUOTAS

Here, I shall be arguing that racial and ethnic quotas are not the answers, but rather some of the answers to disparities in racial and ethnic demography. Generally, there are eight possible reasons we may argue that racial and ethnic quotas are the answer to disparities in racial and ethnic demography. I termed these arguments the-only-answers argument, the intellectual plausibility argument, the practical possibility argument, the legality argument, the customary argument, the efficiency argument, the moral reasonableness argument, and the synthetic argument.

First, in the-only-answers argument, we may argue that racial and ethnic quotas are the only answers that there are; there are no other available answers. However, there are various solutions that can be proffered to the problems of disparities in racial and ethnic demography; so this first reason is not cogent.

Second, in the intellectual plausibility argument, note that arguments of sufficiency (meeting everyone's basic individual or societal needs is enough), equality (everyone is treated equally), and related arguments are subsumed in this intellectual plausibility argument. In the intellectual plausibility argument, we may argue that although other answers are more practical, moral, and so on than racial and ethnic quotas, racial and ethnic quotas are the most intellectually plausible, and intellectual plausibility is to be preferred to practical possibility, moral reasonableness, and so on. However, unless we demonstrate that racial and ethnic quotas are actually the most intellectually plausible answers and intellectual plausibility is to be preferred to practical possibility, moral reasonableness, and so on, we might just jettison this second argument.

Third, in the practical possibility argument, we may argue that although they are not the most intellectually plausible, morally reasonable, and so on, racial and ethnic quotas are the most practically possible answers and practical possibility is to be preferred to intellectual plausibility, moral reasonableness, and so on. Again, unless we can prove that racial and ethnic quotas are actually the most practically possible answers and that practical possibility is to be preferred to intellectual plausibility, moral reasonableness, and so on, we might just as well jettison this third argument like the second one.

Fourth, in the legality argument, we can argue that given the legal framework, laws, or constitution of the state—that is, given that the laws of the state require or support or permit racial and ethnic quotas—racial and ethnic quotas should be adopted. However, the problem is that, as we know, that which is legal is not always necessarily morally right, and that which is morally right is not always necessarily legal. For instance, in legal parlance, when that which is legal, say a judgment, is not morally right, it is said to be procedural justice and not substantive justice. During the holocaust in Nazi-ruled Germany, it was legal for Nazis to kill Jews but immoral. Also, apartheid in South Africa, racial segregation in the United States of America, and so on, were legal but today are widely accepted as immoral. While it was legal to own slaves and sell slaves, and even abuse slaves—after all, slavery itself is an abuse, the very nature of slavery is inherently dehumanizing in many ways and in many cases—today it is widely accepted that slavery is immoral. Furthermore, in view of many negative externalities and deplorable practices in extractive industries, the main problem concerning oil extraction and trade is not illegality but immorality. Many condemnable practices and activities in the extraction and trade are very legal but are very deplorable too. The adoption of the legality argument will rather help justify such practices.

Fifth, in the customary argument, note that my construal of customs is broad rather than narrow. By customs, I mean cultural, religious, sociological, and other related practices of a people. In the customary argument, we can argue that racial and ethnic quotas are entrenched in the customs of a people or the state, that is, racial and ethnic quotas are required, supported, or permitted by the customs of a people or state. Hence, it is customarily correct to adopt racial and ethnic quotas. However, the customariness of a practice does not necessarily make it the most intellectually plausible, practically possible, morally reasonable, and so on practice. So, we will have to prove that customariness is the standard for appropriate public policy, or we will have to prove that beyond customariness, that intellectually plausibility, practical possibility, moral reasonableness, and so on do not matter.

Sixth, in the efficiency argument, we may argue that racial and ethnic quotas are the policies that are most likely to enhance social cohesion, political cohesion, and economic growth, and the least likely to disrupt social cohesion, political cohesion, and economic growth. In other words, racial and ethnic quotas maximize positive effects and minimize negative effects. Hence, it is efficient to adopt racial and ethnic quotas. Nevertheless, we will still have to prove that efficiency trumps, say, moral reasonableness, customariness, and so on, in order for this argument to succeed.

Seventh, in the moral reasonableness argument, we can argue that the standard for any appropriate public policy is moral reasonableness. No matter how intellectually plausible, practically possible, legal, customary, and efficient a public policy is, unless it is moral it should not be adopted. In fact, as long as a public policy is moral, irrespective of intellectual plausibility, practical possibility, legality, customariness, and efficiency, such public policy should be adopted. So, if racial and ethnic quotas are morally reasonable, they ought to be adopted. However, given the usual gap in society between "what is" and "what ought to be," it is difficult to immediately move from "what is" to "what ought to be" in a manner that is fiat-like. So, the argument of moral reasonableness which argues for the (immediate) transition from the status quo (which is deemed immoral) to racial and ethnic quotas (which are deemed moral) should not discount intellectual plausibility, practical possibility, legality, customariness, and efficiency. This brings us to the synthetic argument.

Finally, in the synthetic argument, we may argue that considering intellectual plausibility, practical possibility, legality, customariness, efficiency, and moral reasonableness, although there are other answers, racial and ethnic quotas are the best answers that there are. Nevertheless, unless it is proven that racial and ethnic quotas are actually the best answers that there are, this final argument should not be accepted prima facie. To show that racial and ethnic quotas are not "the answers" but "some answers" to racial and ethnic disparities, I shall employ the ideal theory and nonideal theory approaches. These two approaches are, arguably, the hub around which theories of justice revolve. Hence, if I can employ them to show that racial and ethnic quotas are not "the answers" but "some answers" to racial and ethnic disparities, then my assertion will not only be sound and valid, but also morally right.

In his first and influential book *A Theory of Justice*, and later in his last book *The Law of Peoples*, John Rawls (1999a, 1999b) argues that we can approach the subject of justice in two different ways. We can either approach the subject of justice through the ideal theory or through the nonideal theory. The ideal theory presupposes perfect compliance and propounds the principles that guide well-ordered societies. Furthermore, the ideal theory stipulates or recommends an ideal society that we should strive to achieve. In addition, it is based on this ideal society that our current institutions should be assessed. Complementing the ideal theory, but unlike the ideal theory, the purpose of the nonideal theory is to arrive at or actualize the conception of a just society which has already been stipulated or recommended by the ideal theory. Therefore, the nonideal theory tells us how this long-term goal might be achieved, or worked toward, usually in gradual steps. It looks for courses of action that are morally permissible and politically possible as well as likely to be effective. So conceived, nonideal theory presupposes that ideal theory is already on hand. For until the ideal is identified, at least in outline—and that is all we should expect—nonideal theory lacks an objective, an aim, by reference to which its queries can be answered (Rawls 1999b, 89–90).

Now let us apply the ideal and nonideal theories to our subject matter. In spite of, or given, disparities in racial and ethnic demography, one of two possible conditions will hold. First, we may still live in ideal, just, and fair societies in which there are no racial and ethnic marginalization and other societal, institutional, and structural injustices. If this is the case, then we do not need racial and ethnic quotas. Therefore, racial and ethnic quotas will not be the answer to disparities in racial and ethnic demography because racial and ethnic disparities will not be a problem.

Second, we may have a structurally unjust society in which disparities in racial and ethnic demography have been exploited negatively to marginalize some or certain racial and ethnic groups. Consequently, we will have to formulate principles, make laws and policies, or take other measures to eradicate or at least alleviate the injustices. We might legislate that any act of marginalization is punishable by imprisonment. We might make laws that ban people from holding public offices or any strategic public or private position if they have been found guilty of racial or ethnic marginalization. The laws and policies might work extremely well or they might not even work at all. We might deem it fit that the way to go is to adopt racial and ethnic quotas. In principle or theory, a quota system is a plausible answer to marginalization. In practice, like other laws and policies, it may work extremely well or it may not even work at all. So, we do not have grounds to prefer racial and ethnic quotas to other policies or laws.

On the one hand, the ideal theory does not specify which particular law or policy we should make. It only tells us what a just and fair society should look like and what just and fair institutions, structures, laws, and policies should look like. So, a quota system is not the answer prescribed by the ideal theory. On the other hand, the nonideal theory tells us the laws and policies to make in certain places to deal with particular issues. But there is no reason to say that in the cases of disparities in racial and ethnic demography, racial and ethnic quotas should be the answers. As already mentioned, a quota system—just like other laws and policies—might or might not work.

Racial and ethnic quotas ensure that there will be a fixed number of persons from some or certain racial or ethnic groups, for instance in every sector and division, office or position; this will reduce the number of persons from such groups who are marginalized. By definition, quota is a fixed number; hence, not every marginalized person from such groups will benefit from racial and ethnic quotas. In order to solve a problem of real or perceived injustice, a quota system is adopted. But a quota system ensures that a fixed number is "necessary" but the rest is "unnecessary." To think that catering for the well-being of a part is sufficient despite the plight of the whole is morally arbitrary. Given this limitation of a quota system, to think that a quota system is capable of resolving complex issues is tantamount to fetishizing it. In other words, a quota system is attributed the capability it apparently does not possess.

However, one can argue that even if some persons from such groups do not benefit from racial and ethnic quotas, such groups as a collective benefit from racial and ethnic quotas. But as Robert Nozick (1974) says, "there is no social entity with a good that undergoes some sacrifice for its own good. There are only individual people, different individual people, with their own individual lives. Using one of these people for the benefit of others uses him and benefits the others. Nothing more" (32). If this Nozickean assertion sounds extreme and libertarian, then perhaps we should turn to a moderate and liberal view.

The moral arbitrariness in our example remains whether we see our example through the eyes of extreme Nozickean libertarianism or moderate Rawlsian liberalism. As Rawls says, and as quoted earlier: each person possesses an inviolability founded on justice that even the welfare of society as a whole cannot override. For this reason, justice denies that the loss of freedom for some is made right by a greater good shared by others. It does not allow that the sacrifices imposed on a few are outweighed by the larger sum of advantages enjoyed by many. Therefore, in a just society, the liberties of equal citizenship are taken as settled; the rights secured by justice are not subject to political bargaining or to the calculus of social interests (Rawls 1999a, 1).

CONCLUSION

In view of the foregoing discussion, we can conclude that this chapter helps us to reach the following realizations. First, we have realized that the quota system has apparent limitations and the failure to understand this is the reason why the quota system is fetishized. In other words, this chapter makes us realize that we only attribute the quota system the capacity it does not possess when we fail to consider the apparent limitations of the quota system. Second, in view of the disparities in the multiple and complex identities persons share in societies, we realized that isolating racial and ethnic identities is merely unnecessarily problematizing such race and ethnicity. As shown in the course of this chapter, race and ethnicity are not necessarily problematic. Third, ultimately we realized that if we do not fetishize quota system and if we do not problematize race and ethnicity unnecessarily, then we will be able to understand that the quota system is not the go-to solution to the disparities in racial and ethnic demography.

BIBLIOGRAPHY

Nozick, Robert. 1974. *Anarchy, State and Utopia*. New York: Basic Books.
Rawls, John. 1993. *Political Liberalism*. New York: Columbia University Press.
Rawls, John. 1999a. *A Theory of Justice*. Rev. ed. Cambridge: Harvard University Press.
Rawls, John. 1999b. *The Law of Peoples*. Cambridge: Harvard University Press.

Chapter 13

Power in African Politics

What It Is and How It Ought to be Used

Frank Aragbonfoh Abumere

In dealing with crises and conflicts, African political leaders often commit one of the following four errors of strategy: (i) the failure to use hard power when and where it is required, (ii) the failure to use soft power when and where it is required, (iii) the use of hard power when and where a combination of hard and soft powers (smart power) is required, and (iv) the use of soft power when and where smart power should be used. These errors of strategy have sometimes had grave and disastrous consequences. In this chapter, I aim to prove that in order to successfully prevent, resolve, manage, or deal with crises and conflicts, African political leaders need to acknowledge that some situations require hard power, some require soft power, while others require both hard and soft powers (smart power). To contextualize the above hypothesis, I shall address the antebellum period of the Nigerian Civil War. In the end, I will show that the above-mentioned four errors of strategy led to war. If hard, soft, and smart powers had been used whenever and wherever they were required, the war could have been avoided.

I divided the chapter into five sections. The first and fifth sections are the introduction and conclusion, respectively. In the second section, I will clarify the key concepts. It is very important to do so because they are the hinge around which the discussion revolves. In the third section, I will narrate a brief history of the antebellum period of the Nigerian Civil War. Then, in the fourth section, I will explain the erroneous strategies that led to the war. I chose this crisis/conflict precisely because many people believe that the war was unavoidable. General Yakubu Gowon, the Nigerian head of state at the time of this war, refers to it as "an unfortunate and unpleasant, yet unavoidable, occurrence in the history of Nigeria" (Gowon 2007, 10). While I totally agree with Gowon that the war was unfortunate and unpleasant, I totally disagree with him that it was unavoidable. As I will show below, the war was avoidable. It is a combination of the already mentioned four errors of strategy that led to it.

POLITICAL CONCEPTION OF POWER

Outlining the conceptual and theoretical framework is much more the staple of lengthy research papers than a chapter like this one. Nevertheless, I need to offer some important clarifications regarding the key concepts that I will use and the sort of analysis I will undertake. These key concepts have various connotations; hence, it is vital to make clear their meanings. To understand what the power concepts of hard power, soft power, and smart power are, let us begin by explaining what power is. Power is "the ability to affect others to get the things you want. You can do that in three ways: you can use coercion, sticks; you can use payments, carrots; or you can use attraction and persuasion" (Nye 2011a, 46). Joseph Nye, in *The Future of Power*, introduced the distinction between hard power, soft power, and smart power. For Nye, hard power has to do with "coercion and payment," while soft power with "persuasion and attraction" (Nye 2011b, xiii). In hard power, "coercion" is largely seen as a military force, while "payment" as economic resources. Hence, there are two kinds of hard power: military hard power and economic hard power. The first may be used as a threat of violence or, in actual violence, defensively or offensively, while the second in the form of sanction or of an offer of favorable economic conditions or resources.

Soft power as attraction entails the other people in valuing or cherishing what you are, what you have, or what you represent, making them want to imitate you, join you, share in, or benefit from what you are, what you have, or what you represent. By doing so, they become amenable to you, so you can affect them to get what you want. Soft power as persuasion entails successfully convincing others without using threat or payment, which is a better way to make them accept your arguments or advice. While "smart power is the combination of the hard power of coercion and payment with the soft power of persuasion and attraction" (Nye 2011b, xiii), it also refers to "the ability to combine hard and soft power into . . . strategies in varying contexts" (Nye 2011b, xiv). "A strategy relates means to ends, and that requires clarity about goals (preferred outcomes), resources, and tactics for their use" (Nye 2011b, 208). Hence, a smart power strategy "must be able to handle very different distributions of power in different domains and understand the trade-offs among them" (Nye 2011b, 213). Although there are military hard power and economic hard power, in this chapter I employ the term "hard power" only as military hard power, and I treat economic hard power as soft power. Furthermore, the concepts of hard power, soft power, and smart power are used in reference to foreign policy and security policies of states, in particular, and global politics, in general. I will use the concepts in reference to domestic policy, domestic politics, internal security policies, and local strategies.

Regarding the Nigerian Civil War, my focus is not on the war itself; rather, it is on the causal factors of it. Of course, conflicts are manmade phenomena; they are caused by human activities. I am dwelling on the identification of different human activities that caused the war. There is no doubt that, in order to resolve or manage particular conflicts, it is imperative to know the causal factors and the multifaceted nature of the activities that caused them. The Nigerian Civil War can be divided into three historical periods: ante-bellum, bellum, and postbellum. For the purpose of my analysis, by the bellum period I mean July 6, 1967, to January 15, 1970. The postbellum period starts from January 15, when the war ended. Although it shows the impact that the war had and continues to have in Nigeria, I will not focus on it. I am more preoccupied with how this war could have been avoided, rather than how it was fought. In other words, my main concern is prevention, rather than combat.

The antebellum period ended on January 15, when the war started. The beginning can be set as far back as 1914, when Nigeria came into being or might be limited to October 1, 1960, when Nigeria gained its independence. For the purpose of my analysis, I will consider its beginning on January 15, 1966, when the so-called five-majors-coup took place. I am settling on this date because this event was the most prominent of all possible causes of the war. Since I am concerned with how the war could have been avoided, it is proper that I focus on the antebellum period, and for the purpose of my analysis, I will consider the antebellum period as starting on January 15, 1966, and ending on July 6, 1967—a period of one year, five months, and three weeks.

For analytic, practical, and moral reasons, I consider the war as a "bad thing" that ought to be avoided if it were possible. But I am not interested in how the war should have been avoided; rather, I am interested in how it could have been avoided. Furthermore, for analytic and moral reasons, I consider secession as a neutral, rather than a good or bad thing. For me, secession is what you make of it; it is bad when you make it bad, and good when you make it good. This does not mean that I am encouraging secession or saying that it might be good or bad, but that secession in itself is morally neutral. For instance, if a people decides to secede in order to expropriate others from the collective national investment, wealth, and development, which the entire country labored to produce, this is a bad thing. In the case of Biafra, it will be implausible to say that the secession was based on this ground. However, if a people have to secede in order to avoid pogrom, massacre, carnage, and so on, surely this sort of secession must be a good thing. On this ground, we can say that the Biafran secession was morally justified.

THE ANTEBELLUM PERIOD OF THE NIGERIAN CIVIL WAR

From the beginning to the end of the antebellum period, the geopolitical structure of Nigeria was as follows. From January 15, 1966, to May 27, 1967, there was the Northern Region (dominated by the Hausa/Fulani), the Eastern Region (dominated by the Igbo), the Western Region (dominated by the Yoruba), the Mid-West Region (a combination of minority ethnicities), and the Federal Territory of Lagos. On May 27, 1967, the Northern Region was divided into North-Eastern State, North-Western State, North Central State, Benue-Plateau State, Kano State, and Kwara State. The Eastern Region was divided into East-Central State, South-Eastern State and Rivers State. The Western Region (except the Colony Province) became the Western State. The Colony Province of the Western Region and the Federal Territory of Lagos became Lagos State, while the Mid-West Region was renamed Mid-West State. On May 30, 1967, East-Central State, South-Eastern State and Rivers State—that is, the dissolved Eastern Region—seceded from Nigeria and were renamed the Republic of Biafra. This was the final event that led to the civil war.

In the postindependence history of Nigeria (since October 1, 1960), the civil war was the greatest catastrophe that has befallen it. The war, which started on July 6, 1967, and effectively ended on January 12, 1970, but officially ended on January 15, 1970, had both remote and immediate multi-faceted causes. Many scholars and analysts often reduce its causal factors to ethnicity. This is tantamount to reductionism because, although ethnicity was the principal causal factor, there were other factors too. Almost as important as ethnicity was the regional affiliation. Clearly, the Igbo were the main target in the Eastern Region, and they were its champions. But while the Eastern Region was predominantly Igbo, there were other ethnic groups in that region too. Moreover, during the antebellum period, the Northern Region, unlike the Eastern Region, did not present a particular ethnic group as the champion of the Northern Region, and hence no particular ethnic group was the main target in this region. Conversely, no particular ethnic group was the target in the Northern Region, hence the region did not present any particular ethnic group as its champion. Regional, rather than ethnicity, was the main affiliation there.

Some scholars and analysts erroneously give religion a prominent role in the causation of the war. But a proper analysis of the causes and fighting will show that religion had no consideration in this war. Although the Eastern Region was predominantly Christian and the Northern Region was predominantly Muslim, the principal actors on both sides were Christian: both Chukwuemeka Odumegwu Ojukwu and Yakubu Gowon were Christians.

Furthermore, many key players on the Nigerian side were Christians: Benjamin Adekunle, Olusegun Obasanjo, Godwin Alabi-Isama, Theophilus Danjuma, Obafemi Awolowo, and so on.

Alongside ethnic and regional factors, the economic factor also played a crucial role. Since the war, petroleum has remained a factor in Nigerian conflicts. Oil played a strategic role in the fighting of the war. Although Chukwuemeka Odumegwu Ojukwu—the leader of Biafra—was primarily fighting for the Igbo, he annexed the South Eastern State (non-Igbo) and Rivers States (Igbo and non-Igbo). One reason for this annexation might be because of the Igbo in Rivers State; but if so, then he would have also annexed Mid-West State because of the Igbo there. Another reason for the annexation was that South-Eastern State and Rivers State were part of the dissolved Eastern Region. Yet, a more plausible reason is that of strategy. Strategically, he needed to annex the two states for military and economic reasons. Militarily, first, he would have had more people to fight for him in these places, while the federal government would consequently have had less, and, second, these places would have been a buffer between the core Igbo state and Nigeria. It was for the same reasons that he forced the Mid-West State to be neutral in the early days of the war and even forced them to declare independence, which lasted one day.

The economic strategy for the annexation was simply because these states had oil; at least this is the most plausible economic reason. In order to thwart the military and economic strategies mentioned above, when the strongest command of the Nigerian Army during the war (the Third Marine Commando commanded by Benjamin Adekunle, who was later replaced by Olusegun Obasanjo) invaded Biafra, the first task of the commandoes was to recapture these states for Nigeria. With the recapturing of the states, Nigeria not only reduced the military and political strength of Biafra but also, because of the oil, Nigeria could fund the war, while Biafra could no longer fund it. This, to a large extent, contributed to Nigeria winning the war and Biafra losing it.

Nevertheless, among the remote and immediate multifaceted causes of the war, the most important factors are the January 1966 coup; the July 1966 countercoup; the pogrom before, during, and after the counter-coup; the failure of the Aburi Accord; and, finally, the secession of the Eastern Region, which was renamed the Republic of Biafra. The October 1, 1960, independence theoretically set Nigeria on a journey to greatness. Having been freed from the clutches of British colonialists, Nigerians felt they had "their destiny" in their own hands and could go on to achieve greatness. But these beliefs and hopes of the average Nigerian were dashed by the political class, which was characterized by corruption, violence, electoral malpractices, and regionalist favoritism. Having been disenchanted with politicians, middle-ranked military officers attempted to overthrow the government on January 15, 1966, in a failed coup d'état.

On the one hand, most of the prominent leaders of the January 15, 1966, coup were Igbo. Among them were Majors Emmanuel Ifeajuna, Chukwuma Kaduna Nzeogwu, Timothy Onwuatuegwu, Christian Anuforo, Humphrey Chukwuka, Don Okafor, Captains Ben Gbulie, Emmanuel Nwobosi, and Ogbu Oji. Moreover, many of the prominent persons who were killed during the coup were northerners. Among them were Abubakar Tafawa Balewa (prime minister), Ahmadu Bello (premier of the Northern Region), Brigadier Zakar-iya Maimalari (brigade commander, 2nd Brigade), Col. Kur Mohammed (chief of staff, Army), Lt. Col. Abogo Lagerma (commanding officer, 4th Battalion), Lt. Col. James Pam (adjutant-general, Army Headquarters), and so on. When a northerner-prime minister, Tafawa Balewa, was killed, he was succeeded by an Igbo head of state, Major General J. T. U. Aguiyi-Ironsi. Due to the above facts, northerners saw the coup as an Igbo coup against the north. Consequently, northern military officers launched the July 29, 1966, countercoup, primarily against the Igbo. Aguiyi-Ironsi was assassinated together with many Igbo officers. Although a northerner, Lt. Col. Yakubu Gowon, succeeded Aguiyi-Ironsi as the head of state, the northern vengeance against the Igbo did not stop after the countercoup. Northern military officers engaged in massacring Igbo military officers, but also many non-Igbos from the Eastern Region. This escalated the pogrom against the Igbo, a pogrom which already started in the north before the countercoup. When thousands of Igbo and other easterners continued to lose their lives, the rest of them had to seek refuge in their region, for they could no longer feel safe anywhere else. To curb the pogrom, soldiers were asked to return to their regions of origin. Furthermore, the governor of the predominantly Igbo region—Eastern Region—Lt. Col. Chukwuemeka Odumegwu Ojukwu (an Igbo)—called on easterners to leave other parts of Nigeria and return to the Eastern Region, while he ordered non-easterners to leave the Eastern Region.

On January 1967, in order to resolve the crisis, the delegates of the Eastern Region, led by Ojukwu, and those of the federal government, led by Gowon, met in Aburi, Ghana. At the end of the meeting, Ojuwku and Gowon signed the Aburi Accord. However, among the clauses of this accord, two of them turned out to be problematic. The first stated that federal legislative and executive powers should continue to reside in the Supreme Military Council, which was saddled with the responsibility of making decisions on all national matters. This clause had a provision which stated that when it is impossible for the Supreme Military Council to meet and decide on national matters, such matters should be decided by the regional military governors. The other problematic clause stated that the country should revert to the Republican Constitution that existed before January 15, 1966, by repealing the decrees passed since January 15, 1966. In other words, the semiautonomous status of the regions should be restored, and power should be decentralized.

Despite the Aburi Accord, the enmity between the two sides of the conflict continued. Gowon feared that Ojukwu was leading the Eastern Region to secession. In order to avoid the feared secession, Gowon declared, on May 27, 1967, a state of emergency, dissolved the existing four regions, and created, in their stead, 12 states. The Eastern Region was split into three states, namely East-Central State, South-Eastern State and Rivers State. Notably, the Igbo were separated from the minority ethnic groups in the former Eastern Region. The new home of the Igbo became the East-Central State. While there were some Igbo in Rivers State and Mid-West State, they were by no means dominant there. It was only the East-Central State that the majority of Igbo could properly call home.

In the struggle between Gowon and Ojukwu, Gowon's dissolution of regions and the creation of states gave him three advantages, which were, in turn, Ojukwu's disadvantages. First, the Igbo lost the support of the minority groups that used to be part of the dissolved Eastern Region. Second, the petroleum resources that belonged to the dissolved Eastern Region became the property of South-Eastern State and Rivers State, where the Igbo did not have control. Third, Ojukwu's reign as governor of Eastern Region had come to an end since there was no more Eastern Region; hence, Ojukwu was to lose his political power. Regarding the strategic dissolution of the existing four regions and the creation of 12 states, Gowon said:

> Even Decree No. 81 or Confederation or Loose Association will never survive if a section of the country is in the position to hold the others to ransom. This is why the item in the political and administrative programme adopted by the Supreme Military Council last month is the creation of states as a basis for stability. This must be done first so as to remove the fear of domination. (Vanguard 2010)

After realizing his disadvantages and how the new development had breached the clauses of the Aburi Accord, Ojukwu stated the well-known phrase: "On Aburi we stand." On May 30, 1967, he declared the secession of the entire former Eastern Region, which was renamed the Republic of Biafra. Three reasons for this secession can be plausibly deduced from the antebellum period. The main one—the protection of lives of the Igbo, in particular, and the lives of the people of the Eastern Region, in general. The second, closely related to the first, is the promotion of the interests of the Igbo, in particular, and the interests of the people from the Eastern Region, in general. The third reason, which is closely related to the second, is that given the petroleum resources in the Eastern Region, secession would mean that this resource would belong to the Eastern Region alone, rather than the entire Nigeria;

hence Biafrans would have been better-off economically if they were to secede. Declaring the Republic of Biafra, Ojukwu said:

> You, the people of Eastern Nigeria . . . aware that you can no longer be protected in your lives and in your property by any Government based outside eastern Nigeria; believing that you are born free and have certain inalienable rights which can best be preserved by yourselves; unwilling to be unfree partners in any association of a political or economic nature; rejecting the authority of any person or persons other than the Military Government of Eastern Nigeria to make any imposition of whatever kind or nature upon you; determined to dissolve all political and other ties between you and the former Federal Republic of Nigeria; . . . having mandated me to proclaim, on your behalf and in your name, that Eastern Nigeria be a sovereign independent Republic. Now therefore I . . . do hereby solemnly proclaim that the territory and region known as and called Eastern Nigeria together with her continental shelf and territorial waters shall henceforth be an independent sovereign state of the name and title of The Republic of Biafra. And I do declare that all political ties between us and the Federal Republic of Nigeria are hereby totally dissolved. (Siollun 2008a)

In reaction to the secession, the federal government immediately imposed economic blockades on Biafra in order to weaken its ability to successfully secede. A month and a week later, on July 6, 1967, the Nigerian Civil War officially started with the advancement of federal troops into Biafra. The Biafran soldiers surrendered on January 12, 1967, and the war officially ended on January 15, 1970. An estimated one million civilians and one hundred thousand soldiers lost their lives. There are many reasons why we can say that the federal government did not acquiesce to the Eastern Region's secession bid. These include the geographical reason, namely territorial integrity. In order to explain why he rejects the Eastern Region's "insistence on its separate existence as a sovereign unit," Gowon said: "the citizens of this country [Nigeria] have not given the Military Regime any mandate to divide up the country into sovereign states and to plunge them into bloody disaster" (Vanguard 2010).

The problem with allowing a particular section of a country to secede is the fear of the domino effect, in which other parts might follow the model. Moreover, the domino effect might go beyond its borders. Here is a good proof of this:

> Britain was a key arms supplier to the federal government, enabling it to crush the rebellion because it believed that Biafran secession would create regional instability. The British . . . Foreign Secretary, Michael Stewart, agonised over this policy. "It would have been quite easy for me to say: this is going to be difficult—let's cut off all connexion with the Nigerian Government," he says, now "If I'd done that, I should have known that I was encouraging in Africa the

> principle of tribal secession—with all the misery that could bring to Africa in the future." (Barnaby 2000)

Moreover, in one of his speeches during the war, Ojukwu said that the Nigerian leaders "have also attempted to confuse the Africans and indeed world opinion by propagating the despicable falsehood that our independence would be a precedent for separation in other African states" (Ojukwu's Speech 2010).

Another reason for not acquiescing to secession is the fraternity. Since the amalgamation of the Southern and Northern Protectorates in 1914, Nigeria has been a "fraternal unit." Although the easterners wanted to secede, the federal government felt that the fraternal unity was priceless. According to Gowon:

> Whilst it was commonplace for the media reports to refer to the crisis as a "Civil War," we preferred to call it a rebellion, and to therefore term the action taken to deal with it as "Police Action/Military Action," not war. These terms were deliberately used because I believed that the term "war" promoted the image of a battle between two hostile enemies. I did not consider the Eastern Region and the Igbos an enemy, but rather a misled area. Furthermore, the war would have entailed the excessive use of force and justify unethical behaviour and action that, in my opinion, was unacceptable. (Gowon 2007, 13)

Gowon's sense of fraternity and unity was reflected, at the end of the war, in the ideas of "no victor, no vanquished" and "no medals for the federal soldiers" in order to foster reconciliation and reintegration. In the official declaration at the end of the war, Gowon said:

> On our side, we fought the war with great caution, not in anger or hatred, but always in the hope that common sense would prevail. Many times we sought a negotiated settlement, not out of weakness, but in order to minimize the problems of reintegration, reconciliation and reconstruction. We knew that however the war ended, in the battlefield, or in the conference room, our brothers fighting under other colours must rejoin us and that we must together rebuild the nation anew. (Siollun 2008b)

Other reasons for not acquiescing to secession are economic and political. On the economic side, the vast petroleum resources in the Eastern Region would have made Nigeria a more viable economy. On the political side, a balkanized Nigeria is a weaker Nigeria, while a non-balkanized Nigeria is a stronger one. In this regard, Gowon said:

> The world knows how hard we strove to avoid the civil war. Our objectives in fighting the war to crush Ojukwu's rebellion were always clear. We desired to

> preserve the territorial integrity and unity of Nigeria. For, as one country, we would be able to maintain lasting peace amongst our various communities; achieve rapid economic development to improve a lot of our people; guarantee a dignified future and respect in the world for our prosperity and contribute to African unity and modernization. On the other hand, the small successor states in a disintegrated Nigeria would be victims of perpetual war and misery and neo-colonialism. (Siollun 2008b)

THE FAILURE OF POWER

The war failed to be avoided because of a combination of strategy errors made by the principal actors during the antebellum period. First, hard power was used when and where soft power was required. Second, soft power was used when and where hard power was required. Third, hard power alone was used when and where a combination of hard power and soft power (smart power) was required. Finally, soft power alone was used when and where a combination of soft power and hard power (smart power) was required. In considering these errors of strategy, I will focus on the principal actors of the antebellum period, since their actions and omissions were of utmost importance. I am not necessarily isolating the principal actors as individuals; I see them both as individuals and representatives of the various collaborators with whom they acted or failed to act, and the various constituencies they represented. The various errors of strategy are as follows.

The leaders of the coup from January 1966 believed that they could bring the revolution they wanted only through hard power. According to Major Chukwuma Kaduna Nzeogwu, "the aim of the Revolutionary Council is to establish a strong united and prosperous nation, free from corruption and internal strife. Our method of achieving this is strictly military" (Siollun 2008c). This extreme reliance on military hard power did not result only in the July 1966 countercoup and the subsequent crisis, which culminated in secession and civil war. It also produced a domino effect that established a coup culture and military rule in Nigeria until May 29, 1999.

The leaders of July 1966 countercoup believed that the only way in which they could get the "justice" they wanted for the slain northern political and military leaders, the change of leadership of the country, and the secession of the northern region was through hard power. Aguiyi-Ironsi's failure to "adequately" punish the January 1966 coup leaders and Gowon's total failure to punish the July 1966 countercoup leaders can be considered to be grave strategic failures of relying on soft power when hard power should have been relied on. Aguiyi-Ironsi was seen as being too "soft," rather than "hard," by the January 1966 coup leaders. This fact contributed to northern military officers' quest for "justice" or vengeance, which resulted in the July 1966 countercoup. To what extent Aguiyi-Ironsi should have used hard power to adequately punish the coup leaders is difficult to tell. But he already used hard power to successfully check the coup leaders and arrest most of them, prosecuting and adequately punishing them. On his part, Gowon's placating and pacifying the July 1966 countercoup leaders rather than punishing them contributed to the Igbo (in particular) and the easterners (in general) deciding they were no longer safe anywhere in the country except in their own region. It was this grounded feeling of insecurity that, one year later, led to secession and, subsequently, to war.

Aguiyi-Ironsi did not use military power to stop northerners from massacring the Igbo, in particular, and killing easterners, in general. Here, Aguiyi-Ironsi needed to act urgently; he should have immediately used hard power to stop the massacre, and then employ soft power to pacify, reconcile, and reintegrate both sides of the conflict. Gowon too did not use hard power to stop the northern soldiers who were massacring Igbo soldiers, in particular, and killing soldiers from the eastern region, in general. Furthermore, Gowon did not use military force to stop northern civilians from massacring Igbo civilians, in particular, and killing eastern civilians, in general. Like Aguiyi-Ironsi, Gowon erroneously relied on soft power alone and failed to use hard power when and where he should have.

Aguiyi-Ironsi opted for extreme pacifism and persuasion to the extent that although the country was very volatile, he failed to employ military power to quell the ongoing unrest and prevent the imminent violence that was almost certain to happen. He only relied on "soft" consultations and persuasions. He went on a nationwide tour to seek the support of leaders in the different regions (especially traditional rulers) in pacifying and persuading their people to shelve violence. It was on that tour that he too was assassinated. While engaging in pacifism and persuasion, Aguiyi-Ironsi should have at least put the security threat level on "red," and hence put his hard power on alert since he knew the country was facing a severe security risk.

Like Aguiyi-Ironsi, Gowon relied extremely relied on soft power and failed to use hard power when he should have used it to prevent an imminent civil war. In essence, he failed to combine hard power with soft power; in other words, he failed to use smart power when it was required. Dissolving the existing four regions and creating 12 states in order to avoid secession, Gowon said:

> Nigeria has been immersed in an extremely grave crisis for almost eighteen months. We have now reached a most critical phase where what is at stake is the very survival of Nigeria as one political and economic unit. . . . The whole world is witness to the continued defiance of federal authority by the Government of the Eastern Region. . . . The consequence of these illegal sets has been the increasing deterioration of the Nigerian economy. It has also produced

> uncertainty and insecurity and pushed the country with increasing tempo towards total disintegration and possible civil war and bloodshed on a massive scale. In the face of all these, I have shown great restraint, hoping that through peaceful negotiations a solution acceptable to all sections of the country can be found. Unfortunately, the hopes of myself and my other colleagues on the Supreme Military Council have been disappointed. (Vanguard 2010)

While engaging in pacifism and persuasion, Gowon should have at least put the security threat level on "red," and hence put his hard power on alert since he knew the country was facing severe security risks. Gowon believed that persuasion would work; hence the Aburi meeting which led to the Aburi Accord. Gowon would later agree that persuasion failed. Referring to the failure of persuasion, Gowon said:

> but what has been the response of the Eastern Region Government? Complete rejection of Decree No. 8 and insistence on its separate existence as a sovereign unit. . . . The response of the east has been completely negative and they have continued their propaganda and stage-managed demonstrations for "independence." . . . Even Decree No. 8 or Confederation or Loose Association will never survive if any one section of the country is in a position to hold the others to ransom. (Vanguard 2010)

Gowon believed that the "appeasement" of Ojukwu and the eastern region could work. He said:

> I have spared no effort to conciliate the East in recognition of their understandable grievances and fears since the tragic incidents of 1966. To this end, I agreed with my other colleagues on the Supreme Military Council to the promulgation of the Decree No. 8 which completely decentralized the government of this country and even went further than the Republican Constitution as it existed before 15th January 1966. (Vanguard 2010)

But Gowon later agreed that the appeasement failed. Referring to the failure of the appeasement of Ojukwu, he said:

> Lt. Col. Ojukwu has continuously increased his demands as soon as some are met in order to perpetuate the crisis and lead the Eastern Region out of Nigeria. We know very well the tragic consequences of such a misguided step. Not only will the regions themselves disintegrate further, but before then, pushed by foreign powers and mercenaries who will interfere, this dear country will be turned into a bloody stage for chaotic and wasteful civil war. (Vanguard 2010)

Even when he used hard power, Gowon was extremely cautious to the extent that rather than using military action to prevent the secession, he opted for, and attempted to use, police action. It was only when his first and preferred option failed that he opted to use military action. He said: "a breakup of the country was imminent and needed to be prevented. Police Action was taken but the defiance escalated and was insufficient to stop the drift towards secession. [Then] a full military action was ordered" (Gowon 2007, 12). Nevertheless, to his credit, Gowon was conscious of the fact that in trying to prevent a civil war like the Nigerian one, the problem with using excessive hard power is that even if it succeeds in preventing the war, it will still be counterproductive later on. Using too much hard power, even if it succeeds in preventing the secession, may make the Igbo resentful of Nigeria. If the Igbo's resentment of Nigeria is a continuous one, then this raises questions of domination and legitimacy. Continuously forcing a people to be under you against their will can be argued to be tantamount to domination and hence the question of legitimacy will becloud the achieved "forced unity."

During the January 1966 coup, Ojukwu relied on hard power to contribute to stopping the coup leaders from taking over the country. After the coup, during the subsequent crisis that ensued, Ojukwu initially relied on soft power—as evidenced by the Aburi meeting. But he later resorted to hard power to get the secession of the Eastern Region. First, when he needed to use hard power, during the January 1966 coup, he did. Second, when he needed to use soft power during the subsequent crisis which ensued after the coup, he did. However, third, when he totally jettisoned soft power and absolutely relied on hard power in order to guarantee the secession of the Eastern Region, he fell into an error of strategy. During the Aburi meeting, he wanted a clause to be included in the accord, which was to allow regions to secede if they wished to do so. But the clause was rejected by the representatives of the federal government. Nevertheless, the war became inevitable the moment he decided to totally jettison soft power and absolutely rely on hard power. Ojukwu over-relied on hard power and then got his strategy wrong. Perhaps it was Gowon's reputation for overreliance on soft power that led Ojukwu to wrongly believe that he could use hard power to intimidate the former. As Gowon says:

> During the crisis, my colleague and brother, Emeka Ojukwu, said: "We know Gen. Gowon, he is a Christian and he would not like to fight. Do you know the first thing he puts in his suitcase? His Bible; and that will make him not to engage in a fight." I think, unfortunately, he was proved wrong. As a Christian soldier, it was my duty to keep my country together. (Punch 2015)

In short, it is not that Ojukwu, the January 1966 coup leaders, and the July 1966 countercoup leaders should have totally rejected hard power and absolutely opted for soft power. Also, it is not that Aguiyi-Ironsi and Gowon should have totally rejected soft power and absolutely opted for hard power.

Soft power, as well as hard power, might work extremely well or might not work at all. Some contexts require soft power just as some others require hard power. But, there are situations that require smart power. Given that smart power contains the resources of both soft and hard powers, it has the best chance of success and, hence, it is the best possible option. In an economic analogy, soft power and hard power can be seen as mono-product economies, while smart power as a diversified economy. Just as a diversified economy, rather than a mono-product economy—or an almost mono-product economy—is a safer way to produce economic growth, in particular, and economic development, in general, so smart power is preferable to soft power on the one hand, and hard power on the other. Nevertheless, there are contexts that require only hard power or soft power, just as there are contexts that require smart power.

The problem is not that Ojukwu, the January 1966 coup leaders, and the July 1966 countercoup leaders relied on hard power, nor that Aguiyi-Ironsi and Gowon relied on soft power. Rather, it is that the January 1966 leaders and the July 1966 coup leaders exclusively relied on hard power to the extent that they totally rejected or, at least, had no consideration for soft power in their strategy. Similarly, the problem is that Aguiyi-Ironsi and Gowon over-relied on soft power and neglected hard power to the detriment of their strategies. Also, in the end, Ojukwu over-relied on hard power and jettisoned soft power. Ironically, the January 1966 coup leaders, especially Nzeogwu—the most popular of them—used the soft power of ideology to recruit soldiers for the coup. But they totally abandoned soft power when they planned and executed their revolution. Similarly, it was the soft power of regional affiliation that united northerners, and it was based on this regional affiliation that the northern coup leaders of the July 1966 countercoup sought to seek "justice" for fellow northerners. But they threw soft power out of the window when they embarked on their mission to seek "justice." Also, ironically, it was hard power that Aguiyi-Ironsi used to successfully check the January 1966 coup. But after this, he jettisoned hard power, just as it was soft power that took Ojukwu to Aburi.

CONCLUSION

The foregoing discussion shows that the Nigerian Civil War failed to be avoided because of four errors of strategy. In other words, if hard power, soft power, and smart power were used whenever and wherever they were required, the war could have been avoided. To resolve, manage, or deal with cases such as the antebellum period of the Nigerian Civil War, we need strategies that are at once balanced and flexible. On the one hand, by balanced strategy, I mean a strategy that neither only considers hard power and discounts soft power nor only considers soft power and discounts hard power. Rather, it contains both—smart power. On the other hand, by flexible strategy, I mean a strategy that is not only suitable for crises and conflicts that require hard power or soft power but is at once suitable for crises and conflicts that require hard power, soft power, or smart power (Abumere 2015, 7–8). As Nye says, "an approach too rigid to strategy can be counterproductive" (Nye 2011b, 212). The three merits of a balanced and flexible strategy are: it has hard power to deal with crises and conflicts when and where hard power is required; it has soft power to deal with crises and conflicts when and where soft power is required; and it has smart power—that is, it can combine both hard power and soft power in order to deal with crises and conflicts (Abumere 2015, 7–8). Hence, it eliminates, or at least reduces, the frequency of occurrence of these three errors of strategy.

Nye aptly asserts that "power always depends on context" (Nye 2011b, xiv). In view of the above assertion, using hard power in a context that requires soft power will be counterproductive or, at least, will lead to failure; and using soft power in a context that requires hard power will have the same negative result (Abumere 2015, 7–8). In other words, hard power is useless in a context that requires soft power, and soft power is useless in a context that requires hard power. "In the relationship between strategy and crisis or conflict, the nature of the crisis or conflict should determine the nature of the strategy that is formulated and implemented to deal with them" (Abumere 2015, 7–8). In order to know when and where to use hard power, soft power, or smart power, we should ask the following questions: (i) "what goals or outcomes are preferred?"; (ii) "what resources are available and in which contexts"; (iii) "what the positions and preferences of the targets of influence attempts are?"; (iv) "which forms of power behaviour are most likely to succeed?"; (v) "what the probability of success is?" (Nye 2011b, 208–209). Depending on the answers to these five questions, we will know whether we should rely on only hard power, only soft power, or we should use smart power.

BIBLIOGRAPHY

Abumere, Frank Aragbonfoh. 2015. "Development-Related Conflicts: A Policy Framework for Sub-Saharan African Countries." *Researchers World*, *6*(4), 1–9.

Barnaby, Phillips. 2000. "Biafra: Thirty Years on." *BBC News*, 13 January. Available at http://news.bbc.co.uk/2/hi/africa/596712.stm. Accessed July 30, 2015.

Gowon, Yakubu. 2007. "Governance Challenges in Crisis and Post-Conflict Countries." General Yakubu Gowon, Plenary Speaker, UN 7th Global Forum, June 27, Vienna, Austria.

Nye, Joseph S. 2011a. "The Future of Power." *Bulletin of the American Academy*, 64(3), 46–52.

Nye, Joseph S. 2011b. *The Future of Power*. New York: Public Affairs.

Ojukwu, Chukwuemeka Odumegwu. 1969. *Biafra: Selected Speeches and Random Thoughts of C. Odumegwu Ojukwu*. New York: Harper and Row.

Punch. 2015. "Ojukwu Never Imagined I'd go to War – Gowon." *Punch*, May 15.

Siollun, Max. 2008a. "Declaration of Biafra by Chukwuemeka Odumegwu Ojukwu on 30 May, 1967. Nigeria's Great Speeches." Max Siollun's Website: The Home of Nigerian History and Contemporary Affairs. Available at https://maxsiollun.wordpress.com/great-speeches-in-nigerias-history/. Accessed July 30, 2015.

Siollun, Max. 2008b. "The Dawn of National Reconciliation, Gowon's Civil War Victory Message to the Nation, January 15, 1970. Nigeria's Great Speeches." Max Siollun's Website: The Home of Nigerian History and Contemporary Affairs. Available at https://maxsiollun.wordpress.com/great-speeches-in-nigeriashistory/. Accessed July 30, 2015.

Siollun, Max. 2008c. "Radio Broadcast by Major Chukwuma Kaduna Nzeogwu – Announcing Nigeria's First Military Coup on Radio Nigeria, Kaduna on 15 January, 1966. Nigeria's Great Speeches." Max Siollun's Website: The Home of Nigerian History and Contemporary Affairs. Available at https://maxsiollun.wordpress.com/great-speeches-in-nigerias-history/. Accessed July 30, 2015.

"The Biafrans During the Nigerian-Biafran War." Ojukwu's Speech, Part 2, March 2, 2010. Available at https://www.youtube.com/watch?v=UrfUrJO-E0A. Accessed July 30, 2015.

Vanguard. 2010. "Speech by Major General Yakubu Gowon Declaring a Twelve-State Structure for Nigeria - May 1967." *Vanguard*, September 30.

Conclusion

A Recapitulation of African Political and Economic Philosophy

Ephraim-Stephen Essien and
Frank Aragbonfoh Abumere

The African experience has been a repudiation of anything black or African in the eyes of Europe, America, and currently China. Trade in human persons has resurfaced. The struggle and partition of Africa by European powers in the nineteenth century has reemerged; but this time, by China and America and the dominant European nation over Africa, France. There is an ongoing struggle and partition of Africa by Sino-American powers. On June 1, President Paul Kagame had to expel 18 Chinese from Rwanda and sent them back to China for mistreating Rwandan workers and grabbing lands for farming from them, warning that Africans do not want to be slaves again (www.thevoicenews.net). While China is busy trying to occupy all of black Africa and pretending generosity in giving gargantuan loans, America is stationing military bases all over Africa and acting the big brother in defending Christians in Nigeria against fundamentalist attacks. With the emergence of the Covid-19 pandemic and its apocalypse of the emptiness of nations and peoples, Africa must rise to prove herself a strong force to reckon with. This can begin from our mental theorizing on how best we can have a legally organized public life through government. This, then, becomes the role of African political and economic philosophy.

To play our part in the aforementioned role, we dealt with Africapitalism, development, and leadership in this book. To deal with Africapitalism, we turned to Essien (who explored "African Political and Economic Philosophy with Africapitalism"), Sharomi (who explored "A Moralist Interrogation of Africapitalism as an African Economic Philosophy"), Arodovwe (who explored "E. K. Ogundowole's Self-reliancism and Tony

Elumelu's Africapitalism: Complementary Economic Ideologies for Sustainable Development in Africa"), Amoateng (who explored "International Political Economy of Africapitalism"), and Abumere (who explored "Africapitalism and the Moral Implications of African Governments' Abnegation of Responsibilities"). Relying on Jackson, Etuk, Metz, Isanbor, and Ukagba, we explored various topics on, and issues in, development such as (i) Import Substitution Industrialization as an Economic Philosophy Model for Africa, (ii) Constitutionalism and the Crisis of Development in Africa, (iii) Replacing Development: An Afro-communal Approach to Distributive Justice, and (iv) Black Consciousness Philosophy as Politics of Responsibility for Sustainable African Development. So, too, relying on Wilson, Adahada, and Abumere, we explored various topics on, and issues in, leadership, such as (i) Akan Sociopolitical and Economic Thoughts as a Leadership Model for Africa, (ii) Ubuntu as a Social Leadership Model in Africa: Focus on Nigeria, (iii) Managing Diversity and Protecting Racial and Ethnic Minorities in Africa: The Limitations of the Quota System, and (iv) Power in African Politics: What It Is and How It Ought to Be Used.

Index

About the Contributors

Frank Aragbonfoh Abumere is a visiting fellow at the University of Religions and Denominations, Qom, Iran.

Godwin Michael Adahada is a researcher of philosophy at Hoger Instituut voor Filosofie, Katholieke Universiteit, Leuven, Belgium.

Nana Kwasi Amoateng is a research fellow at the University of Ghana and the Kofi Annan International Peacekeeping Training Centre, Accra, Ghana.

Emmanuel Ogheneochuko Arodovwe is a philosopher at the Department of Philosophy, University of Lagos.

Ephraim-Stephen Essien is a professor of philosophy at the Ahmadu Bello University, Zaria, Nigeria.

Anthony Raphael Etuk is a philosopher at the Department of Philosophy, University of Uyo, Nigeria.

Philip Osarobu Isanbor is a philosopher at the Department of Philosophy, St. Albert Institute, Kaduna State, Nigeria.

Emerson Abraham Jackson is a PhD researcher at the Centre of West African Studies, University of Birmingham, UK, and a Research Economist, Senior Manager and Head of Model Building and Analysis Section at the Research Department, Bank of Sierra Leone.

Thaddeus Metz is a professor of philosophy at the Department of Philosophy, University of Pretoria, South Africa.

Abayomi Sharomi is a visiting researcher at the Department of Philosophy, University of Lagos, Nigeria.

George Uzoma Ukagba is a philosopher at the Department of Philosophy, University of Benin, Nigeria.

Alex J. Wilson is the director of the Centre for African and International Studies, University of Cape Coast, Ghana.